故園畫憶

庚寅中秋
韓馨遠題

《故园画忆系列》编委会

名誉主任： 韩启德

主　　任： 邵　鸿

委　　员：（按姓氏笔画为序）

万　捷	王秋桂	方李莉	叶培贵
刘魁立	况　晗	严绍璗	吴为山
范贻光	范　芳	孟　白	邵　鸿
岳庆平	郑培凯	唐晓峰	曹兵武

故园画忆系列
Memory of the Old
Home in Sketches

老北京民居宅院
Old Beijing's Courtyard Houses

郑希成　绘画　撰文
Sketches & Notes by Zheng Xicheng

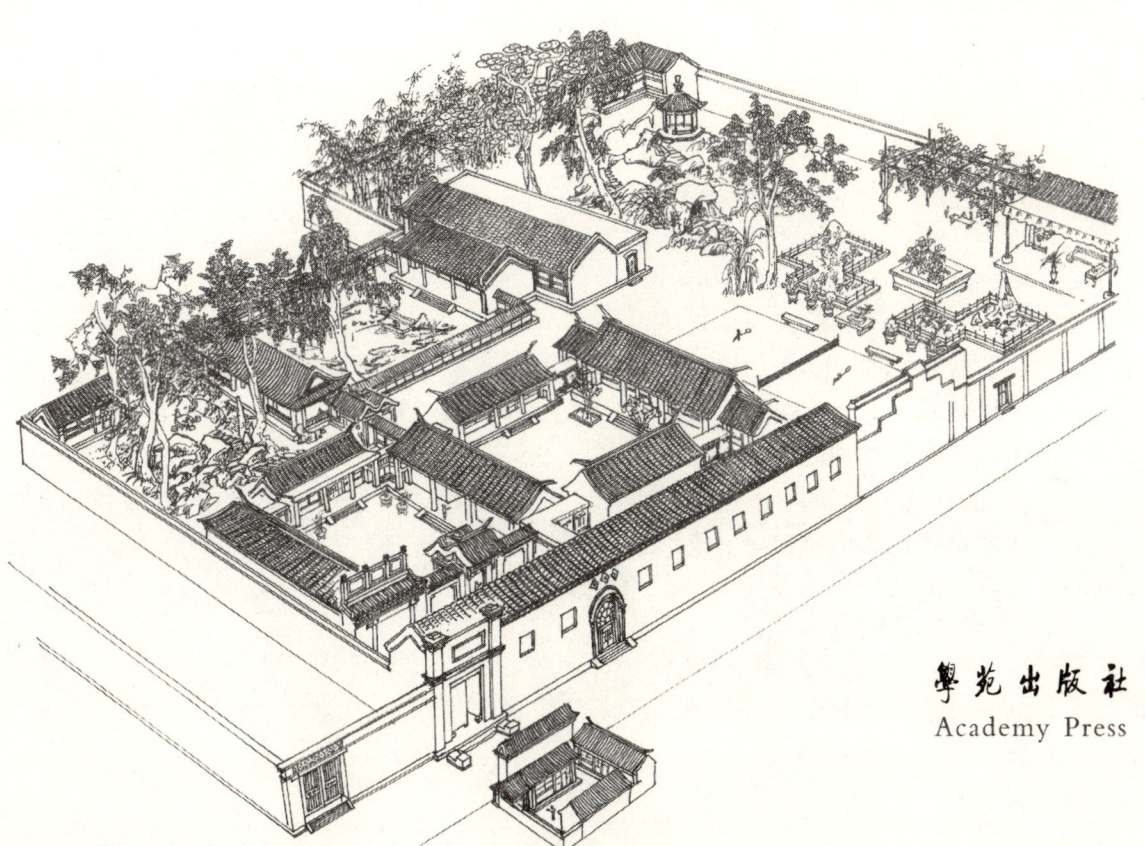

学苑出版社
ACADEMY PRESS

图书在版编目（CIP）数据

老北京民居宅院 / 郑希成绘画、撰文. —北京：学苑出版社，2012.2
（故园画忆系列）

ISBN 978-7-5077-3973-2

Ⅰ．①老… Ⅱ．①郑… Ⅲ．①民居－北京市－图集
Ⅳ．① TU241.5-64

中国版本图书馆 CIP 数据核字（2012）第 021510 号

出 版 人：	孟　白
出版发行：	学苑出版社
社　　址：	北京市丰台区南方庄2号院1号楼
邮政编码：	100079
网　　址：	www.book001.com
电子信箱：	xueyuanpress@163.com
销售电话：	010-67601101（营销部）、67603091（总编室）
经　　销：	全国新华书店
印 刷 厂：	三河市灵山红旗印刷厂
开本尺寸：	889×1194　1/24
印　　张：	9.5
字　　数：	20千字
版　　次：	2012年2月北京第1版
印　　次：	2016年3月北京第3次印刷
定　　价：	68.00元

留住城市記憶

己丑正月
謝辰生題
時年八十又八

北京尚存王府和旧四合院经郑老希成先生规季绘制留存极为珍贵特此致贺

古建筑学界第十代传人

马旭初书

目 录

松竹剧社忆童年…………2
前店后厂义盛号…………4
晋陕风格"奴欺主"………6
裕德粮店有磨房…………8
恒兴木厂大门洞…………10
地界不利墙找方…………12
民俗遗韵泰山石…………14
宅地凹陷墙遮眼…………16
二门筑廊开双道…………18
正房前后勾连搭…………20
紫气东来经营巧…………22
皮之不存毛焉附…………24
少堵多隔成四合…………26
鸡窝廊子拐子罩…………28
北方园林好庭院…………30
半坡巧用显广宅…………32
切割亦留整体美…………34
完颜府里三垂花…………36
完颜新宅静安居…………38
临街经商铺面房…………40
世代祖居进士第…………42
祁家行医睦邻里…………44

小门小户亦欢颜…………46
格扇二门独此家…………48
八月十五云遮月…………50
正月十五雪打灯…………52
廊墙围绕作何用…………54
知是风水详不解…………56
标准外院求严谨…………58
宽敞外院有豪情…………60
倒座房上风水墙…………62
马家致富购三宅…………64
深藏不露小住宅…………66
西藏活佛自家院…………68
多设屏门遮欠缺…………70
祈福遇福共赏福…………72
符合标准有厨卫…………74
标准二进四合院…………76
兄弟三宅院连院…………78
山东叔侄一家亲…………80
四周更道保平安…………82
田家祖宅名人住…………84
陡山门外观景楼…………86
御使衙门院深深…………88

传统外衣现代囊…………90
春松小院南北居…………92
中西结合小巧院…………94
庙之西界不开门…………96
亲睹先辈扩宅院…………98
房顶烟道烧暖炕…………100
清洁地炉古有之…………102
宅基不正分割巧…………104
高耸商铺留国魂…………106
倒座北屋是正房…………108
香河中医置京产…………110
小巧玲珑寸土金…………112
魏忠贤宅伴冰窖…………114
影壁横挡外客院…………116
影壁还能做更房…………118
慈禧赏赐重建宅…………120
不吉门位巧安门…………122
品位不高乱安置…………124
喜静避客精巧院…………126
新宅院里庆周岁…………128
新宅院里庆周岁…………129
严谨舒畅三合院…………130

1

增设三门军客多……………132	李万春武圣故居……………184
垂花门退待高宾……………134	东四四条绵宜宅……………186
休闲听戏自家乐……………136	河沟交错三转桥……………188
花卉满院为谁开……………138	厂甸遗路房应保……………190
和睦兄弟廊相联……………140	可园保护需整体……………192
孝悌楷模今尚在……………142	通州大寺庙……………………194
明亮南屋南有窗……………144	文化大家冯公度……………196
东直门街此宅高……………146	九爷府………………………198
丁家大院多层次……………148	
二门后退前庭宽……………150	后　记………………………200
冬雪春风度闲日……………152	
夏雨秋霜美景寒……………154	
统一规划居易里……………156	
夹缝小门做二门……………158	
通州漕运积仓廪……………160	
羊市口街羊肉铺……………162	
二条口外铺面楼……………164	
京城"水会"忙灭火…………166	
正对二条风水楼……………168	
东四四条美阳台……………170	
临街筒瓦何讲究……………172	
孝和艺辉敬真主……………174	
马连良大师故居……………176	
风水不吉连遭难……………178	
胡同之神我辈存……………180	
通州贡院小而全……………182	

Contents

A Childhood Memory ········2
Yishenghao with Shop and
　Residence all in one ······4
Servant Trumps Master ······6
Grain Shop with Mill ·········8
Hengxing Timber Yard with
　Wide Gate ················10
Regular Yard on Irregular
　Plot ·······················12
Taishan Stone to Ward off
　Evil ·······················14
A Wall to Hide a Sunken
　Yard ······················16
Two Gates Set in a Corridor
　Between the Courtyards ···18
Two Buildings Back-to-back
　···························20
Purple Haze from the East
　···························22
When the House Is Gone, Can
　Plaques Live on? ·········24
Block and partition to Make It
　Square ···················26
A Porch Was Cover ·········28
A Northern Garden Set with
　Stately Courtyards ········30
A Single-Slope Roof Gives
　Illusion of Space ·········32

Beauty Remains Despite its
　Breakup ··················34
Triple Chuihua Gate of the
　Wanyan Mansion ·········36
A Quiet New Dwelling for the
　Wanyan ···················38
A Shop Front Dwelling ······40
Ancestral Home of Jinshi ···42
Doctors of the Qi Family Served
　the Neighborhood ·········44
A Happy Family Behind a Low Gate
　and Small Doorway·········46
An Inner Gate with Unique Screen
　Door ·····················48
The Moon Obscured by Clouds on
　Moon Festival ············50
Lunar January fifteen a light
　snow ·····················52
Why the Cloister? ···········54
Mysterious Objects to Contend
　with Fengshui ············56
Conventional Outer Courtyard leaves
　more to be Desired ········58
A Wide Forecourt Offers Breadth
　of Feeling ················60
A Fengshui Ridge atop the Front
　···························62
The Wealthy Ma Family Buy

Three Courtyards ·········64
A Gem, Tucked away Inconspicu-
　ously ····················66
A Tibetan Living Buddha's
　Residence ···············68
Extra Screens to Cover up
　Inadequacies ············70
Seek, Encounter and Enjoy Good
　Fortune ··················72
All Modern Conveniences ···74
A Standard Double Courtyard
　···························76
Three Brothers in Three Adjoining
　Courtyards ···············78
A Northwest Gate-Most Unusual!
　···························80
Watchman's Passage all Around to
　Guard the Peace ··········82
The Tian Family's Ancestral
　Courtyard ················84
A Two Story Building with a View
　···························86
An Imperial Magistrates Court
　···························88
Traditional Exterior - Modern
　Interior···················90
North and South Wings ······92
East-West Fusion ············94

- No Gates to Face a Temple from the West ·················· 96
- Witness to Courtyard Expansion ·················· 98
- Flues in the Roof Bring Heat from the Kang ·················· 100
- Floor Heating from Below ··· 102
- An Irregular Plot Cleverly Used ·················· 104
- A Scholar Tree behind the Tall Shop ·················· 106
- Street-side Wing as the Main Wing ·················· 108
- A Country Doctor's Beijing Mansion ·················· 110
- Where Land is the Price of Gold ·················· 112
- A Eunuch's House near an Ice House ·················· 114
- A Screen to Hide the Guest Courtyard ·················· 116
- Spirit Screen Doubles as Guard Room Wall ·················· 118
- A House Rebuilt with Money from the Empress Dowager Cixi ··· 120
- Clever Placing of an Auspicious Gate ·················· 122
- A Messed up Layout due to Lack of Refinement ·················· 124
- A Serene Inner Courtyard to Hide from Guests ·················· 126
- A Birth Celebrated in a New Courtyard ·················· 128
- A Precise Three-wing Courtyard ·················· 130
- A General's House Needs much Privacy ·················· 132
- The Chuihua Gate Set Back to Leave More Space for Guests ·················· 134
- Leisure listen their music ··· 136
- A Flower Garden in the Rear Courtyard ·················· 138
- Two Brothers Live together in Harmony ·················· 140
- A Model Filial Family ·················· 142
- A Bright Southern Wing with Big Windows ·················· 144
- Front and Back Entrances Span the Block ·················· 146
- Ding Family Compound with Multiple Courtyards ·················· 148
- A Gift Turned into a Hospital 150
- A House Purchased with Bolts of Cloth ·················· 152
- A Battle to Preserve an Old Courtyard ·················· 154
- A Li Courtyard Group ·················· 156
- A House with Murals ·················· 158
- Store Houses for Grain Shipped up the Canal ·················· 160
- A Mutton Shop on Mutton Lane ·················· 162
- A Shop Near Dongsi ·················· 164
- Fire-fighting in the Late Qing Dynasty (1644-1911) ··· 166
- Chinese-Western Fusion Roof ·················· 168
- A Weranda above a Festoon Gate ·················· 170
- Roof Styles of Shops ·················· 172
- A Devout Muslim Artist's Home ·················· 174
- The Home of an Opera Master ·················· 176
- An Unpropitious Gate ·················· 178
- Neighborhood of Old School Mates ·················· 180
- Tongzhou Examination Halls ·················· 182
- Opera Master and Opera Troupe ·················· 184
- Home of a Vice Minister of Census ·················· 187
- Where Old Canals Used to Run ·················· 189
- The Protected Courtyards at Changdian Region ·················· 191
- Keyuan Garden, Dongcheng District ·················· 192
- Tongzhou Great Temple ·················· 194
- Top Scholar's Home with a Family Shrine ·················· 196
- Ninth Prince's Palace ·················· 198
- Later on ·················· 200

说　明

2010年7月1日，经国务院批准，北京市宣布撤销原宣武区、崇文区，分别并入西城区与东城区。

现在沿着北京古老的中轴线的东西两侧分属，东城区与崇文区合并成立新的东城区，西城区与宣武区合并成立新的西城区。

老北京旧城的核心地带（东城、西城、宣武、崇文）四大城区，勾勒出明清北京城"凸"字形城廓。本书所收画作大多于并区之前完成，且为介绍老北京老旧胡同，故沿用旧的东城、西城、宣武、崇文四区名称规列，特此说明。

Introduction

On July 1,2010, with the approval of the state Council, the Municipal Government of Beijing abolished the administrative Districts of Xuanwu and Chongwen, wthich were meiged with Xicheng and Dongcheng respectively.

The central axis of the city is ancient and grand, going from Yongdingmen Gate, along the Qianmendajie Street, across Zhengyangmen Gate and Tian'anmen Gate, through the golden glazed tiles of the Forbidden City, and finally out the Deshengmen Gate. Now the eastern and western sides along the central axis have been adjusted, with Dongcheng District and Chongwen District merged as the new Dongcheng District, Xicheng District and Xuanwu District as the new Xicheng District.

The core area of old downtown Beijing (Dongcheng, Xicheng, Xuanwu, Chongwen) formerly known as the four districts, is convex-shaped, an outline of the Beijing city in Qing Dynasty and Ming Dynasty times. This book mainly focuses on the dated Hutong (lanes) in Beijing. So in the book, all the names of the former four districts, the core area of old downtown Beijing, remain according to the historical convention, for the convenience of the readers.

Glossary-common types of gate

Ruiyi Gate (如意门): a small double door is set at the front of the gate house.

Manzi "Barbarians" Gate(蛮子门): a wide double door is set at the front part of the gate house.

Jinzhe Gate(金柱门): a wide double door is set in the center of the gate house.

Guangliang Gate(广亮门): a wide double door is set at the back of the gate house.

Chuihuamen / Festoon Gate(垂花门): usually the door linking the forecourt wiht the main courtyard, this kind of gate has two bits of wood sticking down in front, carved and painted like flower buds.

序

郑希成先生画北京民居宅院是从2001年开始的。当时他被北京旧城内整片拆毁民居四合院的行动震惊了，折毁的规模之大、速度之快是空前的。北京虽然在1983年被政府公布为第一批历史文化名城，但对北京旧城如何保护，却争论了半个世纪，陆陆续续的拆毁一直未停。也就在公布为历史文化名城之后，事情起了变化，北京旧城改造工程引进了房地产开发商，政府划拨土地，开发商出资拆迁重建。在巨额利润的驱使下，拆迁疯狂地进行着。郑先生就是在这种背景下，开始与推土机争时间，抢画北京民居宅院。

郑先生做这件事时已年近七旬。他自幼有足疾，行动不变，冒着酷暑严寒，骑着自行车，奔波于街巷胡同之间，以超人的毅力画了百多幅即将消失的北京民居宅院素描图。他生于北京，长于北京，对北京有着深厚的感情，其中包括家庭宅院之情、邻里之情，弥漫在胡同中的淳朴民风，则是令人难忘的乡情，都在他的画稿和说明中体现出来。

郑先生是画家、是雕刻艺术家，他不是以建筑师的眼光来作画的，所以，这些画不是建筑实测图；同时，他也不是从文物保护的角度来记录院落保存的实况的，所以，画中没有画出四合院中私搭乱建不堪入目的景象。他通过实地调查，根据历史照片或图像，尽量恢复院落和建筑物的原来风貌，有的就是在他记忆中很熟悉的北京四合院的固有风貌，把最美的东西奉献给了读者。郑先生曾亲眼目睹过野蛮拆迁的惨况，他不会忘记这些历史场面，但他却理智地采取怨而不愠的方式，在画稿中主要表现北京历史风貌之美。这正是本书精华所在的永恒主题。

这本画册特别注意了院落主人或居住者身份履历，人文的因素决定了院落的布局和建筑物的风格。既注意到两进、三进占地在两条胡同之间的大型院落，或占地两三条胡同的王府，也没有把两合、一合不成格局的小院子漏掉。不同阶层的人构成了北京居民的成分和居所建筑的不同。北京旧城内、外城居民成分不同，内城多住满人，达官贵族府邸、王府多，大型四合院多；外城前门大街以西（宣武区）同乡会馆多，进京的汉人官员和士大夫多；前门大街以东（崇文区）工商会馆多，小手工作坊多，居住条件狭小，出现了"奴欺主"式的窄条形四合院，但建筑物的细部往往有精致装饰，说明他们社会地位虽然不高，却不乏资财。除了阶层和地区的不同外，时代不同也在画册中显露出来，上个世纪初西式建筑出现在院落中，大街上的商铺门脸也有改用西式者，最典型的是西总布胡同协和医院的教授住宅，时代烙印极其明显。

郑先生调查作画时，也很留意院落建筑的类型和细部做法。院落建筑类型是反映城市功能的，除民居四合院外，还画了北新桥的恒兴木厂和板桥胡同的裕德粮店及其磨房，也画了不同形式的铺面房。建筑的细部做法，有些是不太被人注意的，譬如察院胡同25号后院带穿廊的"工"字形平面，尚存宋元以来之规式。新鲜胡同42号桂公府别院的"廊墙"，是唐代院落中常用的建筑。南池子灯笼库9号两厢与正房房脊的式样，类似川滇民居中"一颗印"式院落的屋顶而又有区别。凡此种种，都说明北京历史文化名城内容丰富，在长达七百余年的历史长河中，汇集沉淀了厚重的中国古代城市的物质文化遗迹，是极其宝贵的历史文化遗产。如何在保护这些历史文化名城中认清它们各自的历史价值，仍是亟待研究的课题。

本书所画的百余院落，郑先生告我已拆毁无存占五十九座，剩下的也多残缺不全。美术馆后街22号赵紫宸故居拆的最早，2000年10月被拆，当时侯仁之、吴良镛、郑孝燮、罗哲文等多名专家呼吁抢救而无效。东直门北沟沿胡同23号梁启超故居，是在谢辰生先生的关注下保护下来的。最著名的是西河沿街222号林家大院，完整的四个院落在2006年被拆毁了三个院，剩下一个院坚持到2008年6月，才以拆迁户"民告官"的方式打赢了官司，很不容易，被称为是"打赢文物保护第一案"。官司是打赢了，被拆毁破坏了的怎么办？谁来负责？文物管理部门为什么在诉讼程序中被排斥出局？暴露了文物保护法规方面还存在漏洞。朱寿全律师曾就此指出三点（见《北京晚报》2009年1月7日），很值得有关部门重视。以上所举的三个例子的院落图画都在本书之中，读者自可参阅。后附近年拆迁现场的几张照片，以见这段历史的全貌。

　　郑希成先生是一位北京普通的市民，为保护北京历史文化名城做了他力所能及的事情。在他的书即将出版的时候，我能先睹为快，写了几点感想谨表敬贺之意！

徐苹芳
二〇〇九年二月三日

　　注：徐苹芳，1930年10月生，国家文物局考古专家组成员，建设部、国家文物局全国历史文化名城保护专家委员会委员，中国考古学会理事长。

Preface

Mr. Zheng Xicheng began his sketches of Beijing courtyards in the year 2001. He had been shocked by the scale and speed of their demolition in the old downtown area. Though Beijing was listed among the first batch of China's Historical and Cultural Cities early in 1983, the debate over how the protect its old town lasted for half a century, meanwhile demolition inside the city never ceased.

At the same time Beijing was proclaimed a Historical and Cultural City, things changed: the government began to involve property developers in urban renewal, allocating urban land for property developers to invest and build. Demolition ran amuck on account of the huge profits to be gained. Against this background, Mr. Zheng started to race against the bulldozers to sketch the old courtyards of Beijing.

Mr. Zheng was nearly seventy years old when he started this undertaking. Though he suffered from a foot impairment from childhood, he rode his bike though the lanes and hutongs in both summer and winter, and with superhuman will power he finished over a hundred sketches of Beijing's fast-disappearing residential courtyards.

Born and raised in Beijing, Mr. Zheng had deep feelings toward the city, its homes, its neighborhoods and the simple folk customs pervading within the hutongs. All his nostalgia is embodied and reflected in his sketches and notes.

Mr. Zheng is a painter and sculptor, not an architect. His sketches are not exact diagrams; nor was he intent on recording courtyards from a relic protector's perspective, so the messy unplanned or unapproved structures inside the courtyards are not represented in the drawings. Mr. Zheng made his survey and spent time checking old photos and pictures, so that he might reconstruct the original courtyards in his sketches. Some courtyards which he knew well were sketched based on his own memories. He has presented the most beautiful things to the readers. Mr. Zheng saw with his own eyes how some courtyards were demolished ruthlessly, and yet he has dispassionately represented the history and beauty of Beijing. And this is essentially the eternal theme of the book.

The author attaches special importance to the identity and background of the courtyard's owners or residents because it is their personality and tastes that determined the courtyard's layout and architectural style. The sketches include not only the large, two-courtyard or three-courtyard compounds, or the princely residences that cover two or three hutongs, but also include the tiny two-sided or even single-sided courtyards.

Different types of people occupied the Inner and Outer cities. The Inner City, sometimes referred to as the Tartar City, was populated chiefly by Manchu ethnics, dignitaries or aristocrats who lived in larger courtyard compound. Whereas in the Outer City, to the west of Qianmen Street, are many guild halls and residences of officials or literati from other parts of China, while to the east of Qianmen Street are business guild halls, and small handicraft workshops. Due to limited space, the courtyard compounds are relatively narrow, and we see courtyards described as "servant teases master"[1], but the buildings are exquisitely decorated and adorned, showing that people living there were not poor, even though their social status might not be high. Besides the variation due to social and geographic differences, changes along with the times are also reflected in the album, for example, early 20th century western-style buildings appeared in the courtyards, street shops with western style decorations, and the professor's residences of the PUMC Hospital in Xizongbu Hutong are typical of this period.

When surveying for his sketches, Mr. Zheng also pays attention to the courtyard

---

1 A style in which the East and West side wings block light from reaching the end rooms of the main north wing.

type and detailed work. Courtyards have many functions, for example, in addition to the residential courtyards, he has made sketches of the Hengxing Wood Workshop at Beixinqiao, Yude Grain Shop and its flour mill at Banqiao Hutong, as well as courtyards with shop fronts. The detailed treatments often go unnoticed, for example, the "H" shaped back courtyard at No. 25, Chayuan Hutong with its covered corridor linking front and back wings, retains the layout common after Song and Yuan Dynasty. The "passage / corridor wall" leading to the side courtyard of Guigongfu at No. 42 Xinxian Hutong is typical of Tang Dynasty construction. At No. 9 Nanchizi Denglongku, the way the roof ridges of the side wings and main wing join reminds one of the "chop" style courtyards in Sichuan or Yunnan provinces. All this goes to show that Beijing, the famous historical and cultural city, has rich and invaluable deposits of tangible cultural relics among ancient Chinese cities. How to appreciate the historical value of all this heritage during preservation efforts is a question that needs further study.

Of the over one hundred courtyards sketched in this album, Mr. Zheng tells me, 59 have been totally demolished while only a few of the rest remain intact. No. 22, Meishuguan Houjie Street, former residence of Zhao Zichen, was the first courtyard to be demolished back in October 2000. At the time Hou Renzhi, Wu Liangyong, Zheng Xiaoxie, Luo Zhewen and many other experts called for its preservation to no effect. No. 23 of Dongzhimen Beigouyan Hutong, former residence for Liang Qichao, survived thanks to the attention of Mr. Xie Chensheng. The famous Lin Family Courtyards, at No. 222 of Xiheyan Street, consisted of four courtyards, but three of them were demolished in 2006, and the remaining one was saved in June 2008, when a "civilian against officialdom" law suit against illegal demolition was won. This was hailed as the "first cultural relics protection case ever to wins". The case ended favorably, but what about the already demolished courtyards? Who is to blame? Why was the cultural relics administration authorities excluded from the legal proceedings? Obviously there are loopholes in the cultural relics protection legislation. Lawyer Zhu Shouquan expressed three concerns (*Beijing Evening News*, July 1, 2009) that should be considered and addressed properly by official departments concerned. The book contains sketch drawings of all three examples cited for the readers' reference. Also several photos of demolition that has taken place in recent years are included (see page 3), just for history's sake.

   Mr. Zheng Xicheng is an ordinary Beijinger who done his part to protect this famous historical and cultural city. Personally I am delighted have had the chance to read this book before publication, so write these thoughts to congratulate the author.

Xu Pingfang
February 3, 2009

Note:Xu Pingfang, born oct 1930, is a member of the Archeological Experts Team of the China Cultural Relicts Bureau, member of the Expert Advisory Committee for Historic and Cultural City Protection, under China's Ministry of Construction and Cultural Relicts Bureau. He is also a Board member of the China Historical Society and Chairman of the Board of the China Archeological Society.

自　序

　　我出生在鼓楼前的小四合院里，又在北新桥自家小院中成长。在小院中，我体会到了老北京人与人之间的深厚情谊。

　　邻里间的真诚相助，是北京胡同文化的精髓，这是北京胡同文化的"神"。胡同中各种形态的民居宅院，是北京胡同文化的基础，是胡同文化的"形"。

　　神形兼备的存留，才是真正保存了北京的胡同文化。

　　进入市场经济的初期，人们似乎都疯狂了。很多人只认钱，没了信仰，忘了父母，少了亲情，缺了友情，北京胡同文化之"神"渐渐丢失了。

　　我因之而悲，再加重病，而想远离社会，在自家小院静修，不问世事。

　　2001年推土机的喧闹声将我吵醒。北京胡同里的"神"已经缺损，开发商又向北京民居文化最集中、最美好的宝库——北京的胡同民居宅院"开刀"了。

　　胡同文化之"神"缺损之后，又欲将其"形"摧损吗？！

　　睁开眼看到很多人为保护北京的胡同文化在抗争，还看到只有四分之一中国血统的法国人华新民也在为此奔波，而深受感动。

　　站在已被拆毁的院落前，想起了雍和宫吐布丹老师讲的话："世界万物都有灵。"看到颓垣断壁，我突然见到了它们的灵，想起了：

　　是它们见证了明灭清亡；

　　是它们见证了人们由盘头到辫子，又变成分头；

　　是它们见证了窗纸变玻璃的变化，见证了由矿石收音机到彩电、冰箱；

　　是它们见证了一些古老的院落建起了卫生间，向现代化生活转变……

　　在这院落里，胡同文化之神见证了这一切一切！

　　这种文化，一代一代在这些古老的房屋及院落里传播；

这种文化，是我们北京的文明，是我们北京的灵魂。

这灵魂，就存在于这些院落里，就存在于这些房屋里，就存在于北京人的心灵中！

眼看这文化、这灵魂，就要随着这些房屋、这些院落的消失而消失，我坐不住了。

我不能再坐在自家的小院中修身养性了。

我走出了封闭的小院，端起了摄像机、照相机，拿起了画笔，面对即将消逝的民居小院和多弯的胡同，开始了对我家附近"新太仓民居文化"的研究，想用自己的画、照片，体现北京民居宅院之美，引起开发商的关注，请其手下留情。

走出去以后看到，这是几十年积攒的问题。四合院破败成大杂院，这是摆在我们面前的实际问题。老百姓希望改善居住环境，而开发商想挣钱，两者都想到一块儿了，但最根本的一条却被忘记了：我们中国是一个穷国，又是一个文化大国，不能为了面子上好看，受"穷国心态"左右，将我们的文化埋葬，去修建面子工程。在销毁了北京民居文化的地基上"改善"百姓的居住条件，用北京民居文化下面的土地去发财，是对中华民族的犯罪！

很多人为了保护这些北京民居文化找到了我，希望能将他们院落的复原图画出，用此告诉开发商，这些民居原来是这样的美好，只要不拆，逐步恢复，将是一笔多么丰厚的遗产。

我不懂建筑，学着《北京四合院》书中的画法，为居民们画起了宅院的复原图，没有蓝图，得在满是违章建筑的院落里瞎转，找出规律，有时还受到误解与驱逐，我只能用速写、用照片、用DV记其特点，并勾画其平面图，回家后再一笔一笔将其画出来。

起初，我是想用这些图配合居民的抗争，保存下这些院落，将这些实物保存下来，而不仅仅留下这些画。这些画是赶着画的，有的原想画细一点，也是给开发商看的，希望他们看到这些好的院落手下留情。

现在好多院落已经没有了，大家关注起了这些画，我的心里很感凄凉。这些画中有的宅院是我亲眼看着它们消失的。因此，请您不要品评我的画的"匠气"与

"细致"了吧。只希望您通过这些画看到祖先留给我们的宝贵遗产——北京民居文化。她实在是太丰富、实在是太完美了。

有朋友非要我说说是怎样画的。

我过去是搞工艺美术设计的,工笔白描是青年时代的基本功。曾有人建议我用毛笔和宣纸画,用界画来画,将来可以赚大钱。我也曾想过这样画。但是保护京城民居需要我尽快及时画出,所以,最后我还是选择了用钢笔来画。

我青年时代就很喜欢英国人比亚兹莱的黑白画,他独特的画法是吸收了日本的"浮士绘",而浮士绘又是受到中国木刻版画的影响而形成的。我昔日的工作是搞象牙雕刻"小活",即山水、风景、建筑的设计,自然要临摹芥子园等中国传统绘画,尤其黑白木刻版画为我所爱。王弘力在《黑白画理》中说:"从汉画像砖开始,以高视位表现广阔视野和斜平行线表现建筑物的方法,逐渐成为中国风景画的传统"。

在我的设计工作中,用高视点和斜平行线画法,画山、画水、画树画人,但那时只是工作。

在画这些民居复原图时,怎么画?想的不多,只是将设计稿的方式用于画民居。这些画,只是凭感觉画,画个大概,不能细究。透视、结构都不够准,而且不好交代的地方,都用树来遮盖,说好听点儿叫艺术手法处理,实际就是取巧。这些画究竟算什么画?真没想过,应当归"黑白画"吧。

以上谈的多是技术问题。下面根据书名《老北京民居宅院》谈谈我为什么对北京的民居这样感兴趣。

从儿时起,这四九城的大小宅院就给我带来许多神秘的遐想。幼年我的脚不好,家人外出从不带我。一次,母亲和哥哥从大翔凤胡同某厅长家中回来,讲述起这家的深宅大院、美丽的廊子,使我充满了无限的向往。还有一次,哥哥从山石专家的同学家回来,讲起那院落之美,勾得我心仪神往。在我当时的想象中,那些宅院一定比鼓楼前同兴长绸缎庄过年贴窗户的年画还要漂亮。

母亲送我上小学时,当她见到前圆恩寺小学的校舍一道一道的过厅,高兴地告诉我,这院与她湖北江陵老家的院子一样,只是小了点,没有树和竹林。

我大姨家的养蜂场,即在香饵胡同中间的承恩公府中,花园、廊子就是我们儿时嬉戏的地方。

1949年以后,我哥哥他们驻军在东城什锦花园胡同原吴佩孚的府邸中,那里曲折优美的游廊给我留下了深刻的印象。后来认识了马旭初老人,他说这院的游廊最有特色,是北京民居中少有的。我有幸在其中游历过,可惜当时太小。

从工作伊始,我就在崇文区南北羊市口的几处民居小院中学徒,那些各具特色的小院同样给我留下了不可磨灭的印象。后来工厂又搬进了同仁堂乐家老母亲曾经住过的大宅院,那里有抄手游廊、有地炉、有水会,还有鹿苑,真是美不可言。

我与北京各类民居宅院的缘分太多太多了,这也是我为什么不只是画画街景、画画门楼的缘故。刚开始的时候,我在竹杆胡同也是画街门的速写,画完后,我在想,院里是什么样?房主还在吗?这院落是什么时候买的?这种欲知其详的心理促使我走进院落,见到了这家主人。男主人告诉我,这院是他父亲盖的,并详细地介绍了院落的原貌。我一一记录下来。由此,也确定了我的作画方向:那就是一定要进院!

是日,在南竹杆胡同25号,就是这种寻宅作画的开始。当时我在院落里发现,虽然地界不好,但经过主人巧夺天工的构思,达到了天圆地方的境界。从此后,我就把画民居特色作为了绘画的重点。可惜的是,竹杆胡同之类各具特色的民居已被高楼大厦所取代。

一提起北京的民居,人们总会与豪宅大门的四合院联系在一起,实则不然。

老北京的民居,是以原皇城为中心的民居建筑群,不仅有四合院,还有三合院、二合院,即使是一居小院,也各领风骚,别具特色。

在这本画册里,我基本按所画时间之顺序,将这些年所画的比较有特色的宅院选出99张,以供大家欣赏。

在此要感谢马旭初老先生。他是古建筑大师,是六百年"哲匠世家"的第十四代，也是最后一代传人。多年来马老不顾自己八十多岁高龄，在马家花园内为我们讲解指认花园里建筑结构、花园格局。通过他的指导，我才能在已是私搭乱建、杂乱无章大杂院一般的马家花园中将此院的复原图画出来。还有很多胡同里的院落、门脸房及其建筑格局、历史背景、住宅人物，也都是经马老指教，我一一记录下来。有的住宅院落虽然还没来得及画出来，但给我留下了将来绘画民居宅院的宝贵历史资料。近几年来马老身体不好，还为我的书出版题写了宝贵的题字，在此专门表示感谢。

我还要特别感谢谢辰生老先生，他身为著名文物专家、原国家文物局顾问、中国文物学会名誉会长、全国历史文化名城保护专家委员会委员，为保护老北京民居民宅做了大量的工作、在病中还为我这本画集出版题写了"留住城市记忆"的题字。

我还要万分感谢年已八十高龄的徐苹芳老先生。作为国家文物局考古专家组成员、全国历史文化名城保护专家委员会委员、中国考古学会理事长，他在百忙中一直关注着老北京民居民宅的保护工作。我与他素不相识，经人介绍，我请他给我的画集的出版提些指导意见。他要我从出版社调回画集的校样稿，非常认真地逐字、逐句、逐图地校对，还向我讲解了很多有关古建筑方面的知识，对一些人名、地名、建筑物等的名称进行了修订，甚至还为画集的一些图画撰写了说明文，并为我的画集的出版撰写了"序"，使我非常感动。

在这几年当中，对我帮助过的人太多了。他们说："帮你就是为保护北京民居文化尽一点力。"都是无私的帮助！这使我又深深地体会到，老北京胡同文化的"神"还在，还存在于北京各年龄层人们的心中。哦，不只是北京人，保护北京民居文化的，还有外省市的人，还有鄂温克等少数民族的人，还有外国人……

谢谢！谢谢！谢谢一切帮助过我的人们！

郑希成

2009年1月15日

老北京民居宅院

松竹剧社忆童年

（东城区九道湾西巷小大院）

这是我的第一张画胡同的回忆画，记忆我们的童年。

我家对面是九道湾 17 号（画中右侧的院落），我少年时代的朋友黄世俊爱好天文，自己做了一个天文望远镜（见图右侧）。

7 号院中坐在台阶上吹笛子的是我。

A Childhood Memory

Location: Courtyard Houses in Jiudaowan Xixiang, Dongcheng District
This is my first sketch depicting a hutong, helping to recall our childhood days.
Opposite to my house is No.17 Jiudaowan (the courtyard on the right in the sketch). Huang Shijun, a childhood friend of mine, was keen on astrono my and made a telescope for himself (see the right side in the sketch).
The one sitting under the eaves in No. 7 courtyard playing the flute is me.

(2002年绘)

前店后厂义盛号

（东城区新开路北口）

这座民居的特点是：前为店铺，中间是作坊，后院是老板的宅院。在老北京民居中，是颇有特色的。

门脸都是硬杂木窗框，装着进口的西洋厚玻璃，楼上以及后宅，都用雕花挂檐板，窗台门楼则是磨砖对缝。

Yishenghao with Shop and Residence all in one

Location:The North End of Sinkable in Dongcheng District

This courtyard features a shop on the street front, workshop in the front courtyard and the boss´s living quarters in the back. It is distinctive among traditional courtyard houses in Beijing. The shop front window frame is made of hard wood and set with thick glass imported from the West. Eaves-hung boards with carving were used on the upstairs and back courtyard house. The window sill and the gateway were built of polished bricks with tight joints.

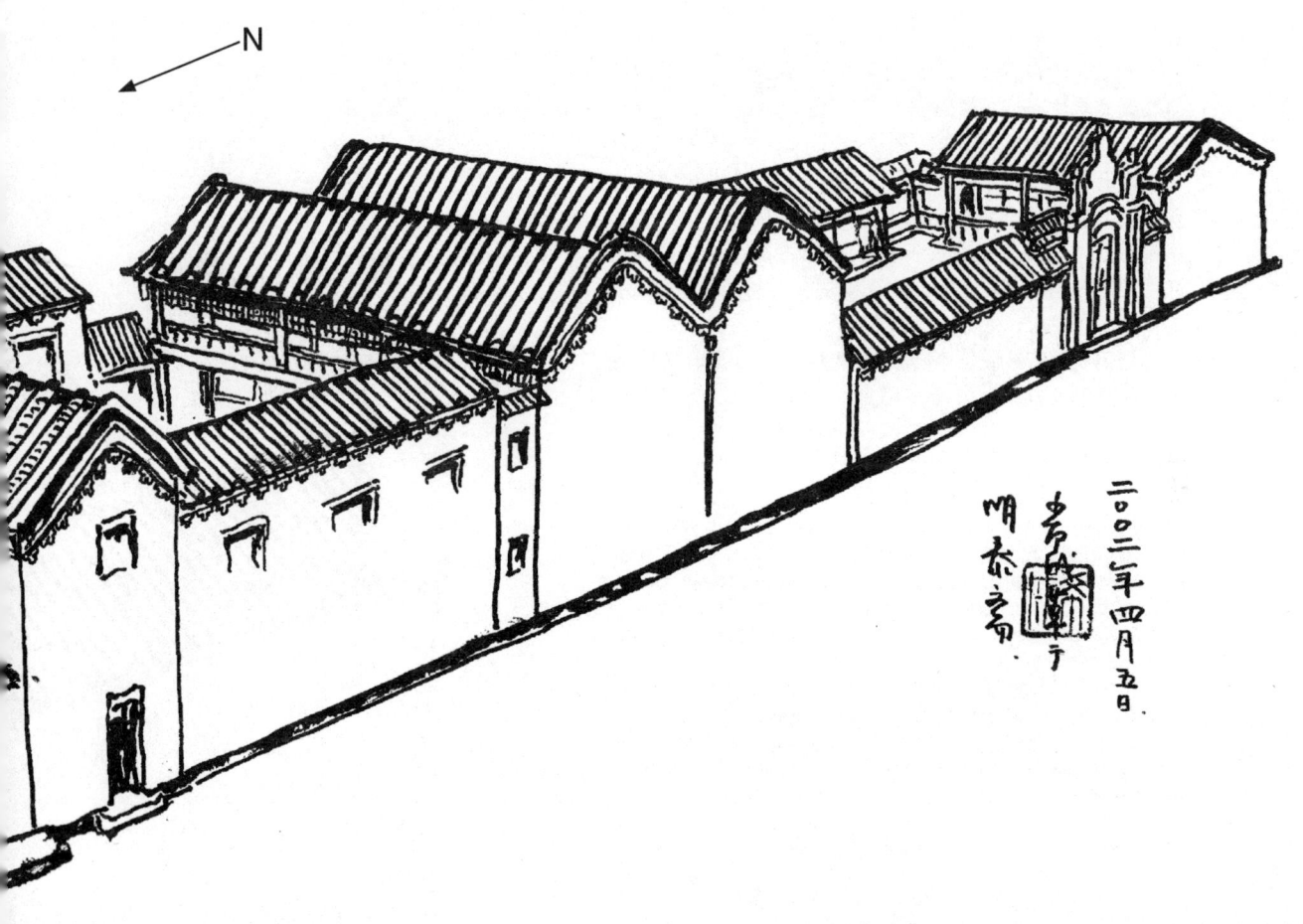

(2002年4月5日绘)

晋陕风格"奴欺主"

（崇文区）

在清代至民国，外地来京的商人多，尤其晋陕人多，将其家乡宅院窄长之风格带进了北京。

这种房屋的特点俗称"奴欺主"。

老北京四合院一般是正房为主，左、右厢房为奴。东、西厢房不能挡着北房的阳光，一定要闪在正房的左右。而南城的这类房屋，正房三间（主房），厢房在正房的下方，只将正房中间一间留为明间，正房左右两间都可以被遮挡，厢房遮挡了主房，因而叫"奴欺主"。

与老北京传统民居不同的是，正房不见得以北为上，东、西、南屋都可以建得高大做正房。

Servant Trumps Master

Location: Chongwen District

From the Qing Dynasty (1644-1911) to period of the Republic of China (1912-1949), there were many businessmen from other parts of the country in Beijing, especially Shanxi and Shaanxi provinces. They brought the style of the narrow and long courtyards from their hometown to Beijing.

In the traditional courtyard in Beijing, the principal, south-facing north wing is compared to the master while the eastern and western wings are likened to the servants. These rooms should not block the northern rooms from the sunlight. Whereas the Shanxi and Shaanxi style courtyard houses in southern Beijing, the East and West wing rooms are right in front of the end rooms of the principal wing, blocking its sunlight. Therefore such courtyards are called Servant Trumps Master（"奴欺主"）.

Another difference from Beijing tradition is that the principal wing does not always face south, but may face any other cardinal direction.

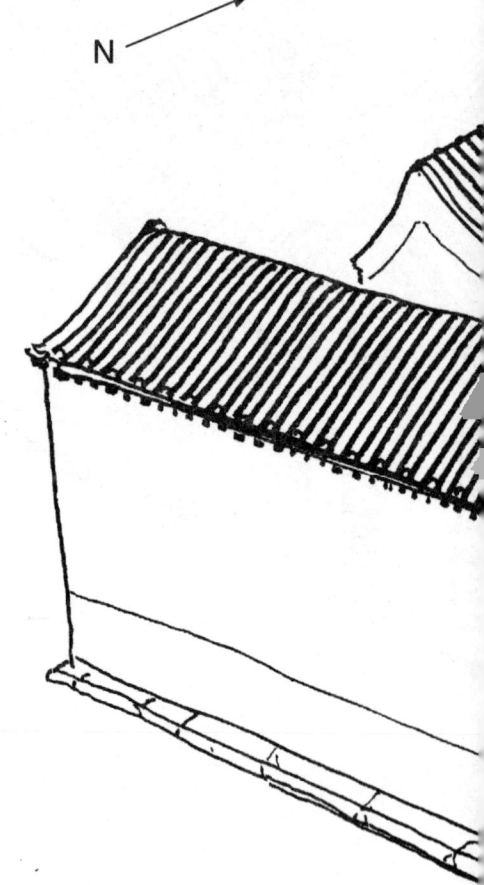

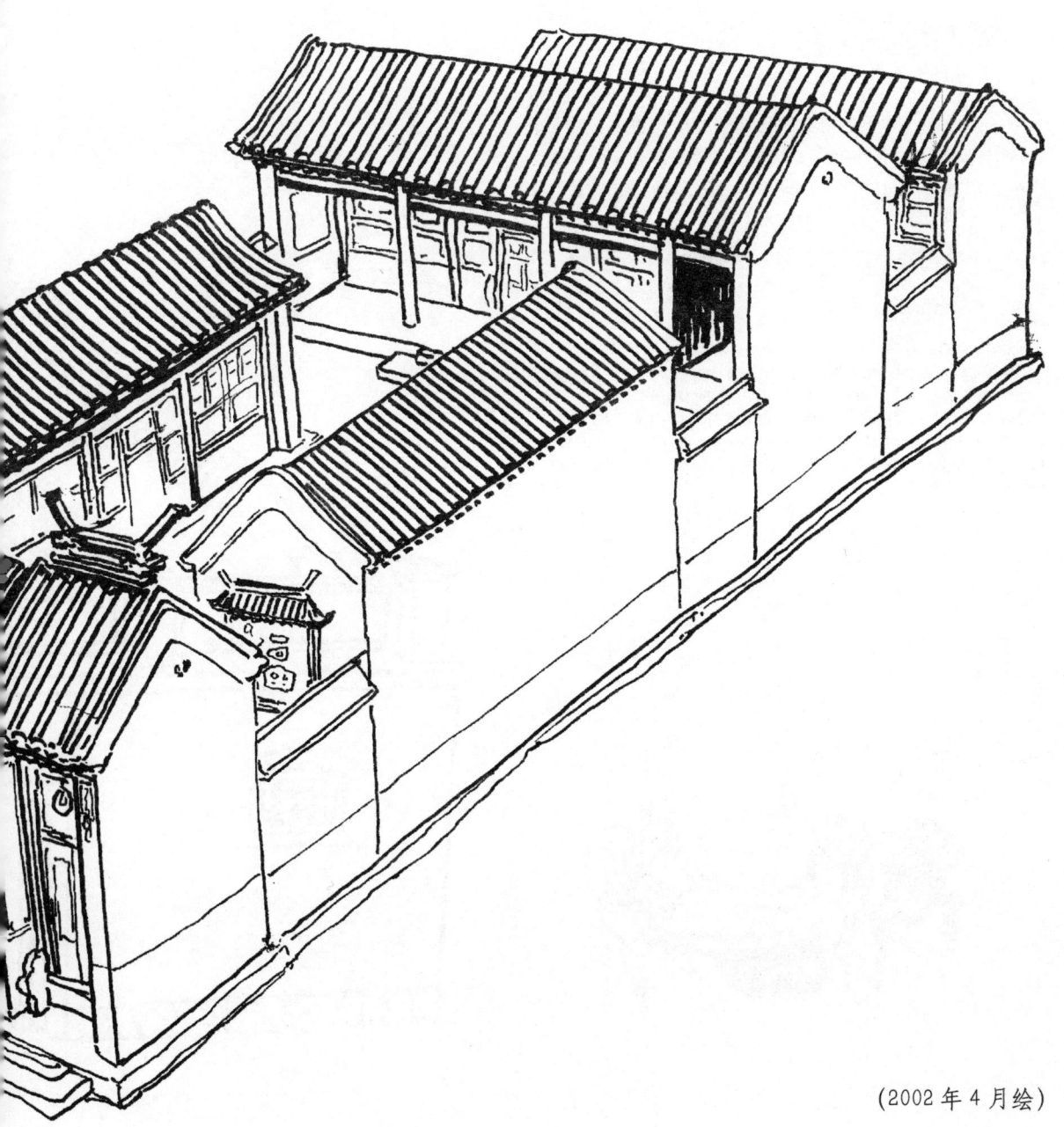

(2002年4月绘)

裕德粮店有磨房

（东城区板桥胡同）

此店在东城区北新桥地区板桥胡同的中部。这里原来是明代著名粮仓之一的"新太仓"的西仓墙，清代弃仓，后依仓墙及仓门建民宅，此粮店即在仓墙边上建起的房屋。

此院落建成时间较早，当在清朝中期，现仍遗存。

Grain Shop with Mill

Location:Banqiao Hutong in Dongcheng District
Here originally was the western wall of the "Xintai Granary", one of the famous imperial granaries in the Ming Dynasty. This granary was abandoned in the Qing dynasty. Later courtyard houses were built against the granary walls and gates. This grain shop was one such house.
This courtyard house was built fairly early, probably in the mid Qing Dynasty (1644–1911). It still stands.

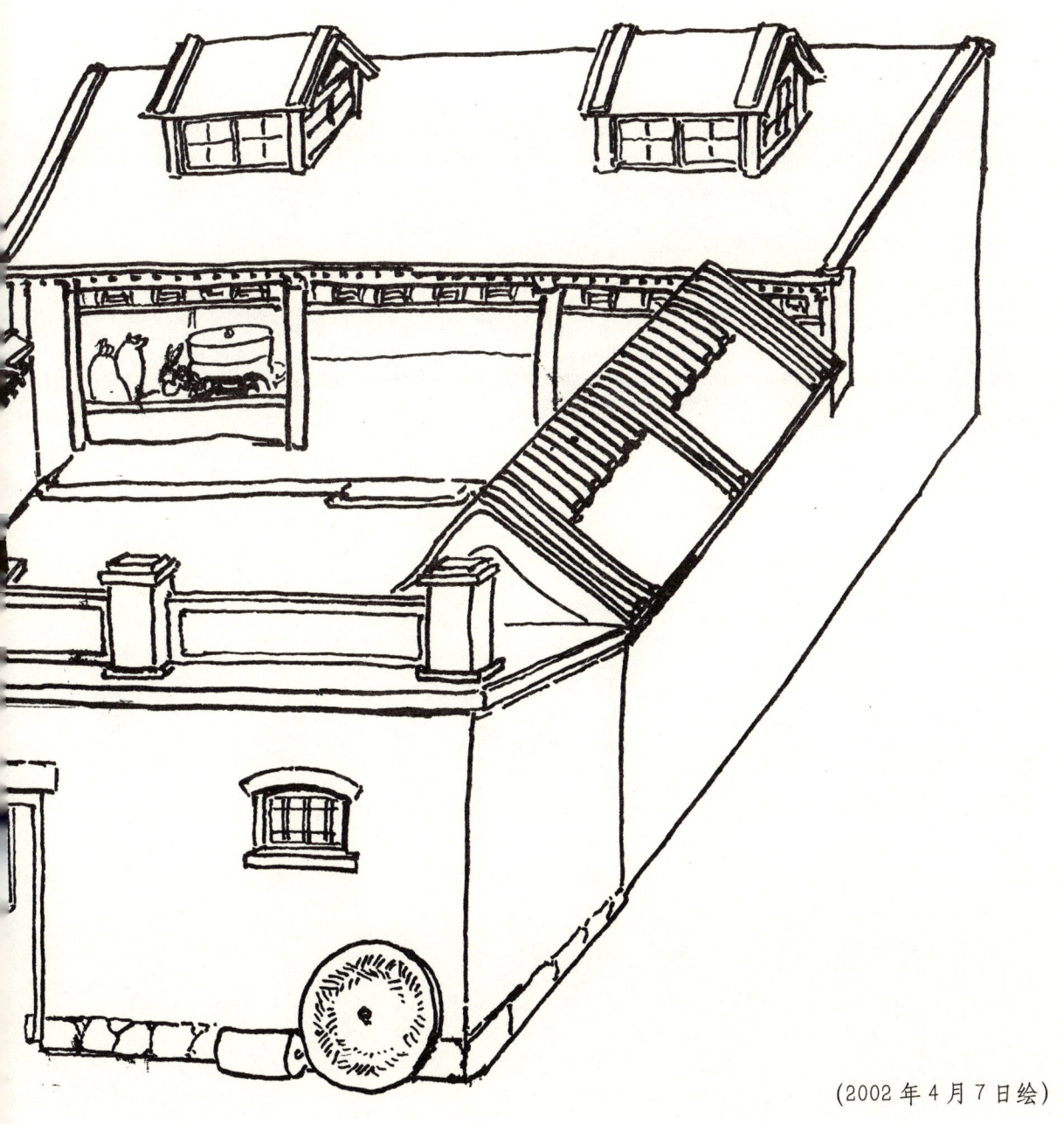

(2002年4月7日绘)

恒兴木厂大门洞

（东城区北新桥地区）

明、清两代，东直门是京城进木柴之门。北新桥到交道口一带是建木材场的首选之地，集中了六七家大木场和棺材铺。这些大木场进料时，要用大马车拉着木材直接进入大门，因此在这条大街有许多大门洞的院落。这种大门洞，全北京只在北新桥到锣鼓巷之间才有，尤其在北新桥到交道口这一段最为集中。

Hengxing Timber Yard with Wide Gate

Location: Beixinqiao Area in Dongcheng District

In the Ming and Qing Dynasties, Dongzhimen Gate was a gate through which timber was transported into the city, so the area from Beixinqiao to Jiaodaokou was the first choice for the building of lumberyards. There were six or seven big lumberyards. When these big lumberyards laid in goods, the lumber had to be brought by cart directly through the entrance gate to the yard inside. Therefore there are many courtyards with big gates opening on to this street. Such big gates could only be seen between Beixinqiao and Luoguxiang, but mostly in the section between Beixinqiao and Jiaodaokou.

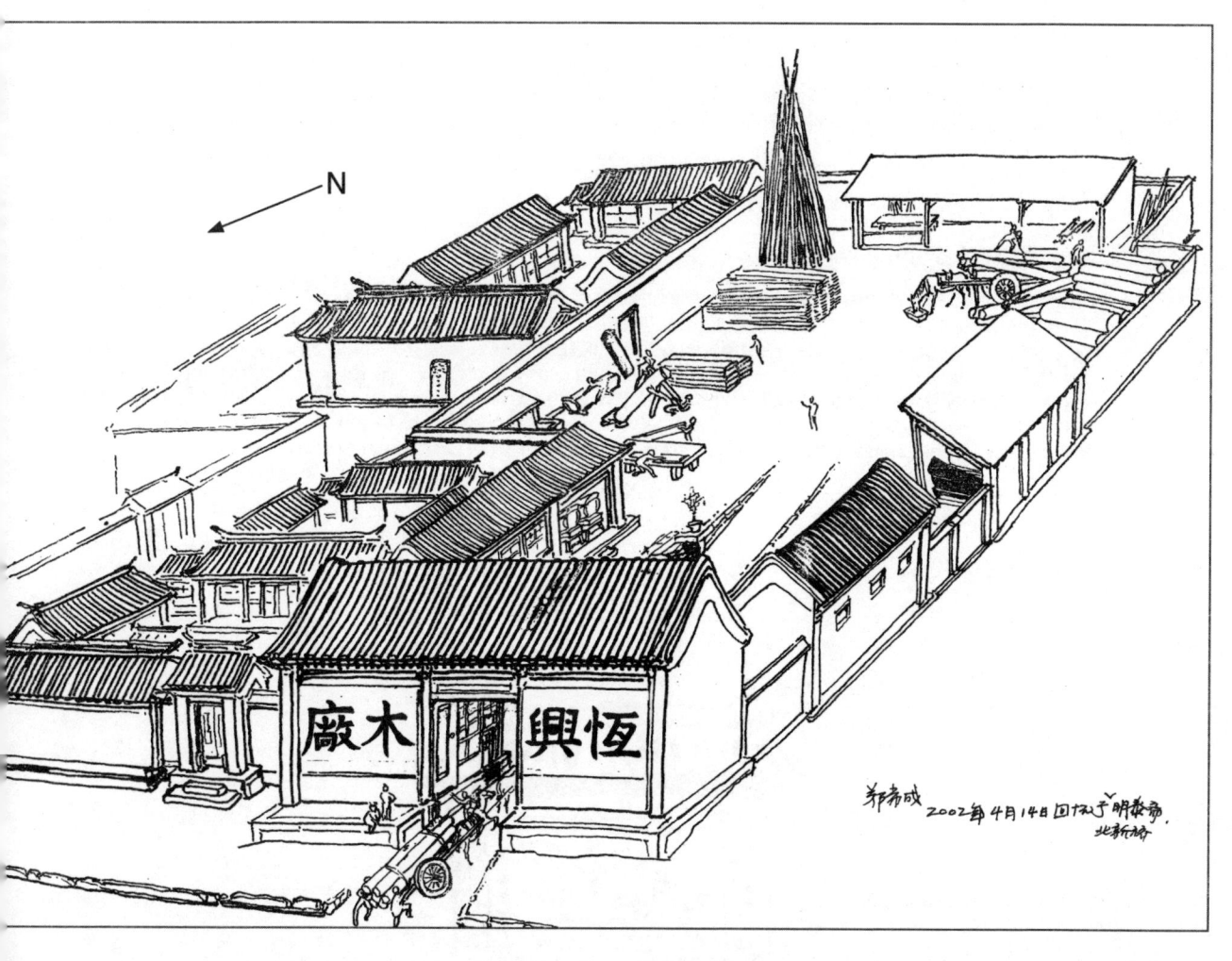

(2002年4月14日绘)

地界不利墙找方

（东城区南竹杆胡同25号）

这是一幢清末民初比较典型的中间开门的小院落，充分体现了建筑师巧妙的构思。

中华文化讲究"天圆地方"，院子方方正正是中国院落的传统。25号院缺了西南一角，为了弥补这一缺憾，主人在自己院东房的南山墙与27号北房的东山墙之间修了一堵东西墙，并开一门。这样，此宅五间北房前即形成了一平整的长方形院落，显得十分舒展。

Regular Yard on Irregular Plot

Location:No.25 Nanzhugan Hutong in Dongcheng District

"Round sky and square earth" is a basic concept in the tradition of ancient Chinese culture. This is a small courtyard house with the front door in the middle, which was relatively typical in the late Qing Dynasty and early of the Republic of China. The plot was square, except for a piece missing from the southwest corner belonging to No.27. To make up this lack, the master built an east–west wall between the south gable wall of the east wing and the east gable wall of the north room of the No.27 and put a door in it. Thus, a spacious rectangular courtyard was formed in front of the 5-room master wing.

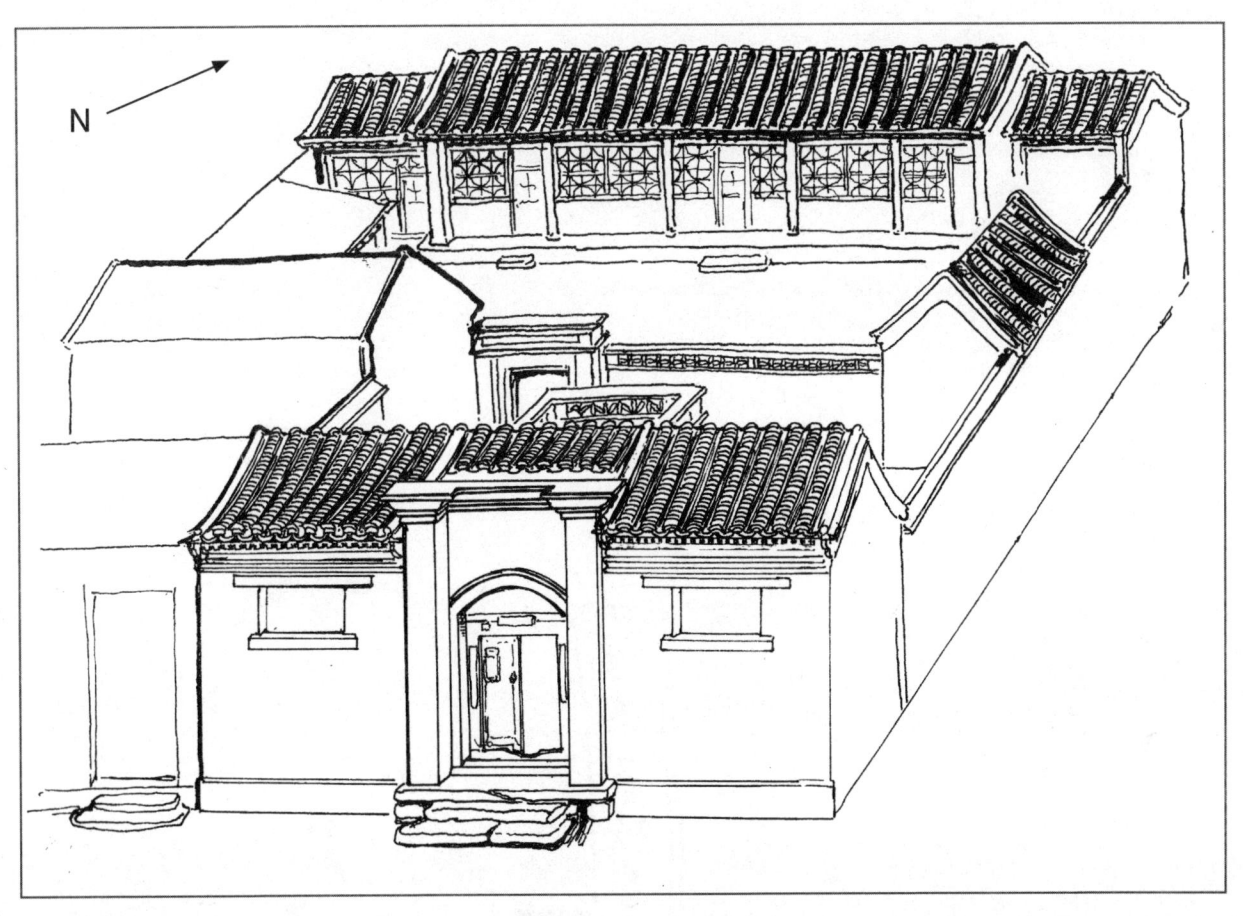

(2002年5月24日绘)

民俗遗韵泰山石

（东城区九道湾南巷7号）

这是一座保存尚完整的典型两进四合院，坐北朝南，其南房墙上尚遗留"泰山石敢当"的石碑。在胡同里若见此碑，则表明前面是活胡同，可以通行。从风水讲，此碑又可压着对面胡同的气，不至于直冲。

在过去京城胡同里，如果院墙恰好面对"丁"字形交会的另一条胡同口，一般会认为不吉利。正对胡同口的墙上或墙脚要立一"泰山石敢当"的石碑。

这个院落的大门、二门、影壁保存尚可，院中的太湖石保存完好，院外墙上的"泰山石敢当"在京城现已难找了。

Taishan Stone to Ward off Evil

Location: No.7 Jiudaowan Nanxiang in Dongcheng District

This is a well preserved courtyard house with two courtyards, gate opening to the south. The main gate and second gates and screen wall are fairly well preserved and the ornamental Taihu rock in the courtyard is in good shape. The Taishan Stone (a stone with the inscription Taishan *Shigandang*) embedded in the south wall outside the courtyard is now seldom seen in Beijing.

Note: A shigandang is often placed by corners, or facing south-leading roads to ward off evil.

(2002年5月26日绘)

宅地凹陷墙遮眼

（东城区演乐胡同21号）

这是清末官员马玉昆在京的宅院。

此宅院坐北朝南，建在一凹地内。宅院大门外的路高于此院。一出家门就看到自己的院子在一坑中，会很不舒服。于是建筑师在临街路边盖一片墙，挡着路边行人的视线；在东边墙上另建一门，门内建简单的垂花门，再修下降之台阶；迎л西边种大树，遮挡东西深沟的视线，又富于变化。此院可称适应环境变化之典型宅院，体现了建筑师精巧的构思。

说明：为了使大家看的明白，我把外墙画成了透视图。

A Wall to Hide a Sunken Yard

Location:No. 21 Yanyue Hutong in Dongcheng District
This is a traditional-style courtyard house of Ma Yukun, an official in the late Qing Dynasty, in Beijing.
This courtyard house facing south was built on sunken ground. So the architect had a wall built along the front to keep the house out of sight of passers by. On the east wall a door was set, inside which was a simple Chuihua gate and downward steps. A big tree was planted west of the gate both to hide the deep trench running in the east-west direction, and for variation.

(2002年5月26日绘)

二门筑廊开双道

（东城区东四十四条19号）

这是在旧粮仓"新太仓"南仓门之东建起的一座三合院，坐北朝南，小门楼、影壁都很规矩。老北京民居的二门一般开在中间，为一个门，而此院将二门的墙改成一有座的廊子，在廊子左右各开一个四扇屏门。在普通的小三合院中，两个绿色的四扇屏门和横在北边的廊子，就能让你感受到大宅院穿廊及在游廊中小坐休息的感觉。

在二道墙之内，街上喧闹都听不见，可静静品茶。此主人真聪明，巧用了廊门，此三合院在北京民居中确有独特的味道。

说明：图下部两个四扇门中间应是墙，为了说明墙后有廊，所以我画成了透视图。

Two Gates Set in a Corridor Between the Courtyards

Location:No. 19 Dongsi Shisitiao in Dongcheng District
　　This is a courtyard with buildings on three sides, the principal one facing south. Its small gatehouse and spirit screen wall were both built according to established practice. A second gate leading to the inner courtyard was generally placed in the middle of the south wall of the courtyard proper. However in this courtyard, there is a wall and corridor linking east and west wings, at each end of which is a screen door of four panels.
　　Inside the second wall, noise can not be heard from the street, so the master can quietly drink tea. The master made skilful use of the corridor!. This courtyard is quite unique among the Beijing courtyard houses.
　　Note: The space between the two four-panel gates on the lower part of the sketch is a wall. To reveal the corridor behind the wall, I have omitted the wall, and inscribed the word "墙" – (wall) in the space.

(2002年5月31日绘)

正房前后勾连搭

(东城区南池子大街82号、84号)

从布局看，82号、84号原为一整套宅院。院为四进，房是卷棚硬山式，三进正房为两个硬山勾连搭，用平廊与后院相连，中院有一棵两人抱不过来的大树，这种结构在北京的老民居中亦是罕见。

此处是清末保存完好的四合院。

Two Buildings Back-to-back

Location:Nos. 82 and 84 Nanchizi Dajie in Dongcheng District
From the layout, Nos. 82 and 84 were originally a single courtyard house with four courtyards. The houses have round roof ridges and flush gable roof. The north wing of the third courtyard has two roof ridges back-to-back, with flush gables connected, and the third courtyard linked through a flat corridor to the back courtyard. There is a tree so big that two people could not around its trunk inside the middle courtyard. The layout is rare among the old houses in Beijing.

This courtyard house built in the late Qing Dynasty is well preserved to this day.

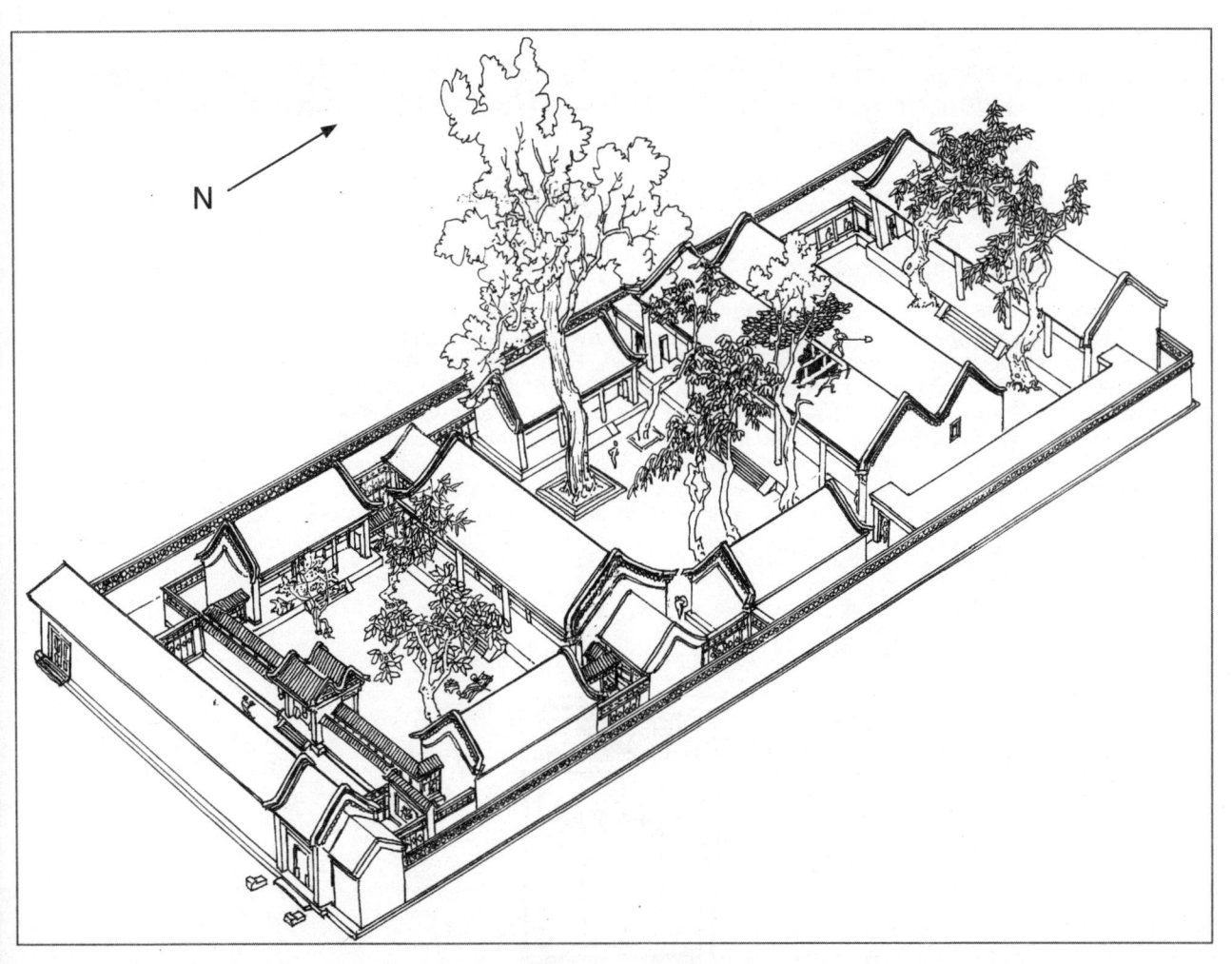

(2002年6月8日绘)

紫气东来经营巧

（东城区南池子大街普渡寺西巷45号）

　　这个院落坐西朝东，南北两居，因而在绿色屏门上用金字书写了"紫气东来"。建房时，南北房只用了灰梗阴瓦，没有阳瓦，是为了省点钱。而在大门外全用整砖（在当时，普通民居多为碎砖墙），上面还有高高的女儿墙、门楼，还用了筒瓦，说明此宅主应当是很讲究外表的，但并不太宽余的小户人家。把钱用在了脸面上，经营巧！

　　此院是北京老民居文化中小门小户的一种典型，很有特点。

Purple Haze from the East

Location:No. 45 Pudusi Xixiang, Nanchizi Dajie in Dongcheng District
This courtyard opens to the East, and has just two wings— south and north, therefore four golden characters "Ziqidonglai" meaning the Purple Air Coming From the East were inscribed on the inner green screen door. The reason why the roofs of the south and north wings were covered with concave tiles without convex tiles was just to save money. However, its street front wall was built from whole bricks (at that time, most houses of common folk had walls built from broken bricks), with a tall parapet wall and its gatehouse had an awning covered with semi-cylindrical tiles. This indicates that the master of this house paid much attention to face, but was not well-off. He skillfully spent money on the face job.

This courtyard house is a typical of old small houses in Beijing, with unique characteristics.

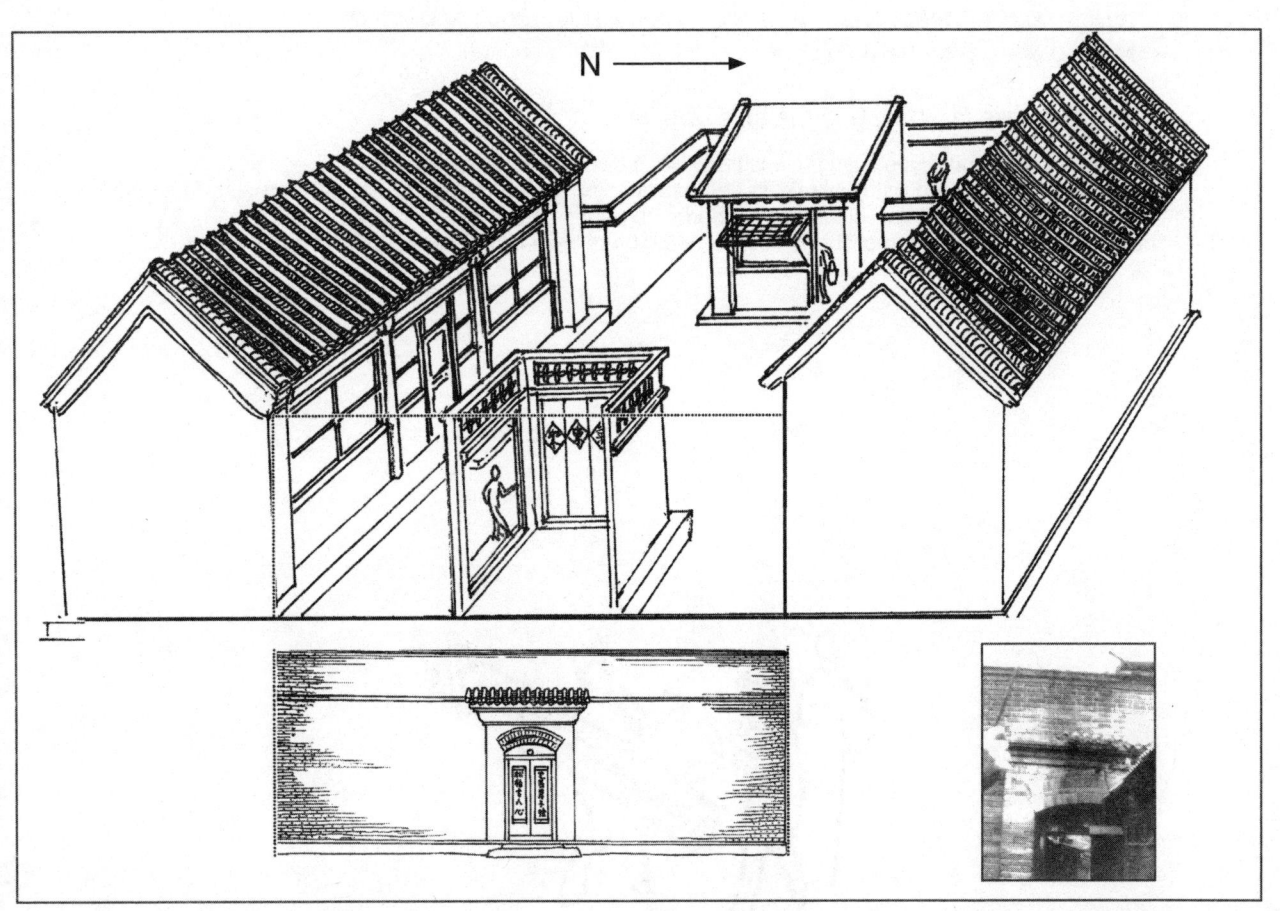

(2002年6月25日绘)

皮之不存毛焉附

（东城区南池子大街普渡寺东巷16号）

这是一个只有东西房的小院落，坐东朝西，二门内侧挂着两块像对联样的竖牌。
随着院落被拆，这副对联也不知去向。

When the House Is Gone, Can Plaques Live on?

Location:No. 16 Pudusi Dongxiang, Nanchizi Dajie in Dongcheng District
This is a small courtyard with only west and east wings. The courtyard opens to the west. Inside the second gate used to hang two plaques inscribed with poetic couplets.
The courtyard was later demolished, and the two tablets have disappeared without a trace.

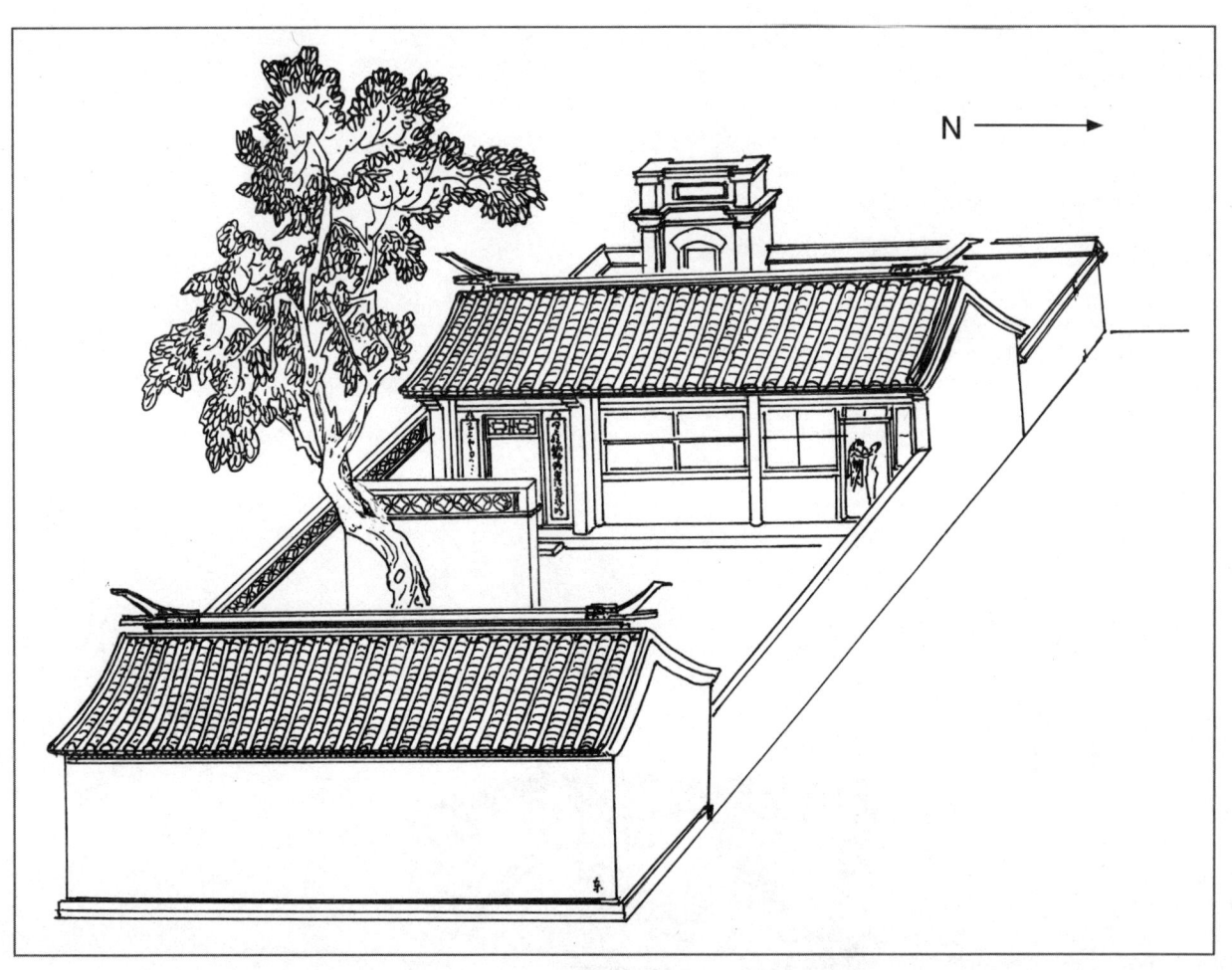

(2002年6月25日绘)

少堵多隔成四合

(东城区南池子大街66号)

此院坐东朝西，北房与东房之间西北角少一处地界，主人就在两房之间修了一道墙，将缺少的地界堵上。而南房之东又多出一处地界，主人便在东房与南房之间修一道墙并加个门一隔，另出来一小东院。这样，大院则变成一方正的四合院落。

经过主人的刻意设计，原本不规则的小院变成了"天圆地方"的典型，舒适、多变又幽静，别具一格。

Block and partition to Make It Square

Location:No. 66 Nanchizi Dajie in Dongcheng District
This courtyard, which opens to the west, was missing a piece of land at the northeast corner between the north wing and east wing. So the master built a wall between the two wings, thus blocking off the missing land. But this meant that to the east of the south wing there was an additional piece of land. So for symmetry, the master built a wall between the east wing and south wing, and set a door in it, thus creating a small eastern courtyard. In this way, the courtyard came to be bounded by buildings on all four sides.

Thanks to the master's painstaking design, the originally irregular courtyard became perfectly symmetrical.

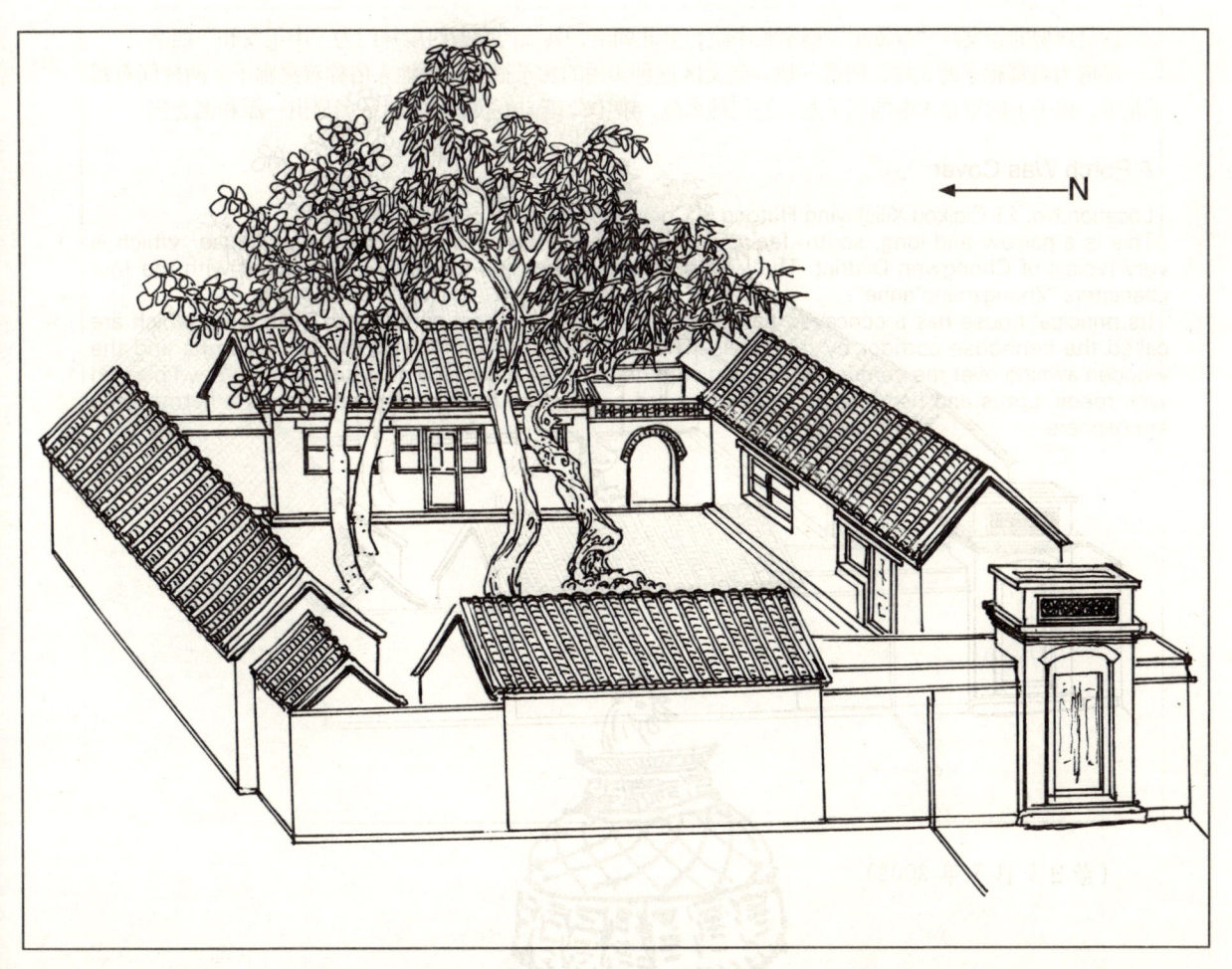

(2002年6月28日绘)

鸡窝廊子拐子罩

(崇文区磁器口西利市营胡同11号)

这是典型的崇文区"奴欺主"型窄长小院，坐北朝南，其二门西面四扇并门为"中正安和"四字。

正房为鸡窝廊子的式样，凹进一块。崇文区这种实用的廊子很多，当地人俗称鸡窝廊子。两柱间有拐子花罩，廊子上的罩是木雕的拐子龙。迎门种水葱，院中荷花、鱼盆一片生机，彰显出一派和谐之气。

A Porch Was Cover

Location:No. 11 Ciqikou Xilishiying Hutong in Chongwen District

This is a narrow and long, south-facing little "Servant Trumps Master" courtyard house which is very typical of Chongwen District. The western screen door has four panels inscribed with the four characters "Zhongzheng'anhe".

Its principal house has a concaved part. There are many practical corridors of such kind, which are called the henhouse corridor by the locals. There is carved awning between two columns and the wooden awning over the corridor is a carved with dragons. At the welcome gate is a large bowl planted with reeds. Lotus and fish bowls in the courtyard give vigorous signs of life, creating a harmonious atmosphere.

(2002年7月3日绘)

北方园林好庭院

(东城区东直门内北沟沿胡同23号)

文化名人梁启超故居。

梁启超、梁思成父子在中国文化史中的地位,以及名人故居的历史价值暂先不提,仅从宅院的结构看,亦有很多独特之处。例如,在大门北侧,一片似是办公用的客房,有别于清末以前的四合院;小巧的垂花门及三门的两廊都是通道,它是全院的交通枢纽;再有全院的水道设计,一到下雨,全院的雨水都很自然地流入花厅前的水洼中;后院假山下,有通道可直通花厅……此院主体结构清楚,房屋保存完整,恢复原貌,此宅院将既是一处有历史文化价值的名人故居,又是一处非常优美的北方园林式宅院。

A Northern Garden Set with Stately Courtyards

Location: No. 23 Beigouyan Hutong, Dongzhimennei in Dongcheng District

Former Home of Liang Qichao, the great reformer of the late Qing dynasty.

The layout of this courtyard has many unique features. For example, to the north of the entrance gate is a row of office-like guest rooms, which is different from the courtyards built before the late Qing period. The small and exquisite Chuihua gate obliquely facing the main gate is linked through corridors with the third gate. These passageways constitute the transport hub of the courtyard. Also remarkable is the design of the drainage in the courtyard such that when it rains, the rain water naturally flows into the pools before the Flower Hall. At the foot of the rockery in the back courtyard there is a channel leading to the flower hall. This compound has clear structure and the rooms are well preserved. If it were restored to its original state, this courtyard house would be not only the former residence of a celebrity of historical value, but also a very beautiful garden-style courtyard house in North China.

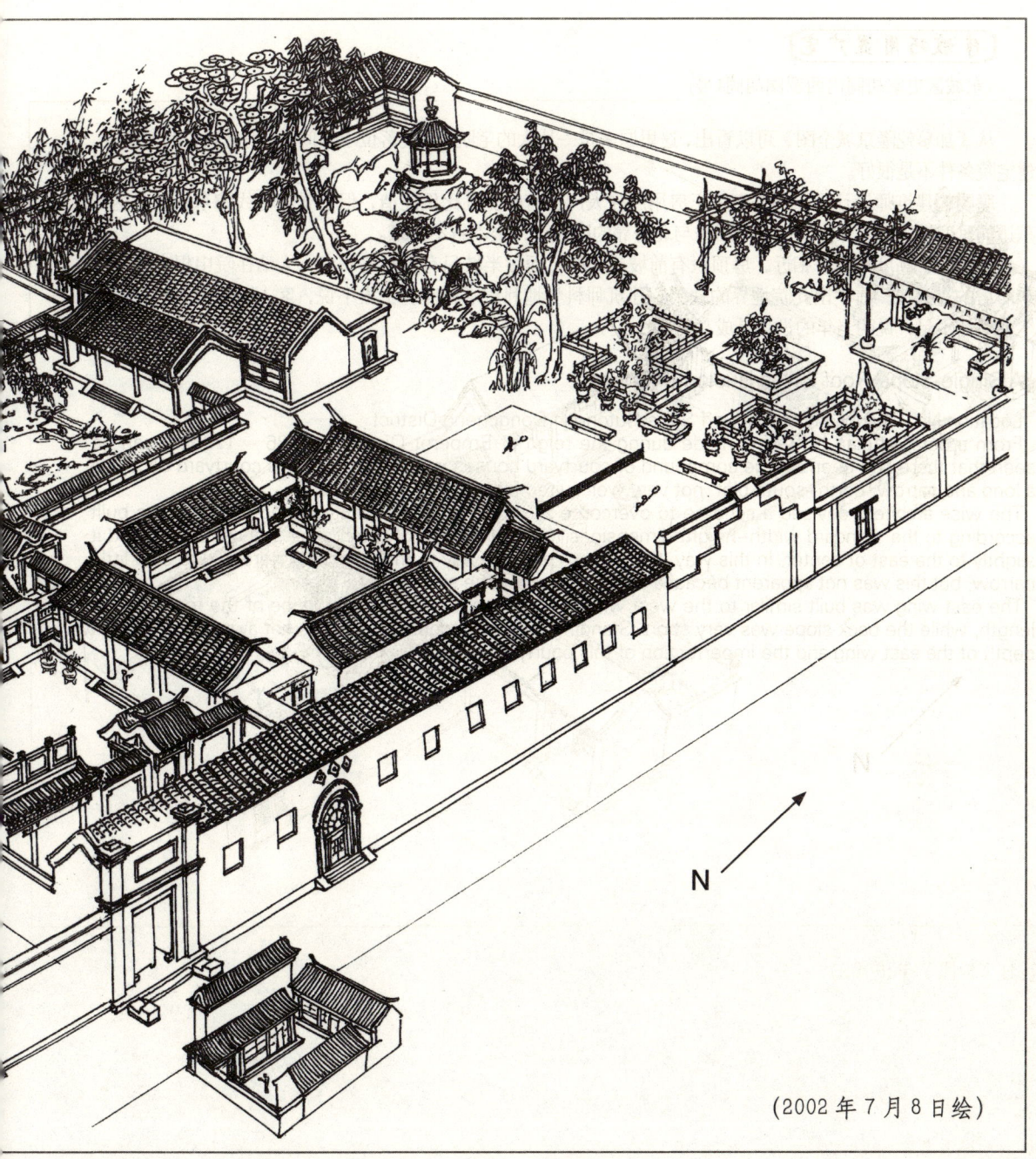

(2002年7月8日绘)

半坡巧用显广宅

(东城区史家胡同内西罗圈胡同1号)

从《加摹乾隆京城全图》可以看出，这里原来是一片大的宅院，此院落位于其间，为南北狭长的宅基地，建宅院条件不是很好。

聪明的建筑师设计了一种方案：正房用广亮大门应有的宽高比例建造，但位于中心线偏东一点。这样东边的耳房过道窄一点，但由于东西房与北房靠的比较近，根本看不出来。

东厢房，高度与西房相近，房顶只有前坡是满的，而后半坡只有短短的一点。人站在院中根本看不出东厢房的进深浅，看不出此院地界的缺欠。建筑师科学地利用了视差，主人不说，客人一般根本感觉不到宅基地的不足，说明当年的设计是成功的。

A Single-Slope Roof Gives Illusion of Space

Location:No. 1 Xiluojuan Hutong, off Shijia Hutong in Dongcheng District

From a detailed plan of Beijing made during the reign of Emperor Qianlong (1736 – 1796), it can be seen that there had been a large compound of courtyard houses in this location. This courtyard occupies a long and narrow, north–south plot not very well suited for building courtyards.

The wise architect devised a scheme to overcome this constraint: the principal central wing was built according to the standard width–height dimensions to suit the style of the main entrance, but located it slightly to the east of center. In this way, the eastern passageway to the inner courtyard had to be a little narrow, but this was not apparent because it was hidden by the side wings.

The east wing was built similar to the west wing in height, but only the front slope of the roof was full length, while the back slope was very short. Standing inside the courtyard, one is not aware of the short depth of the east wing and the imperfection of this courtyard at all.

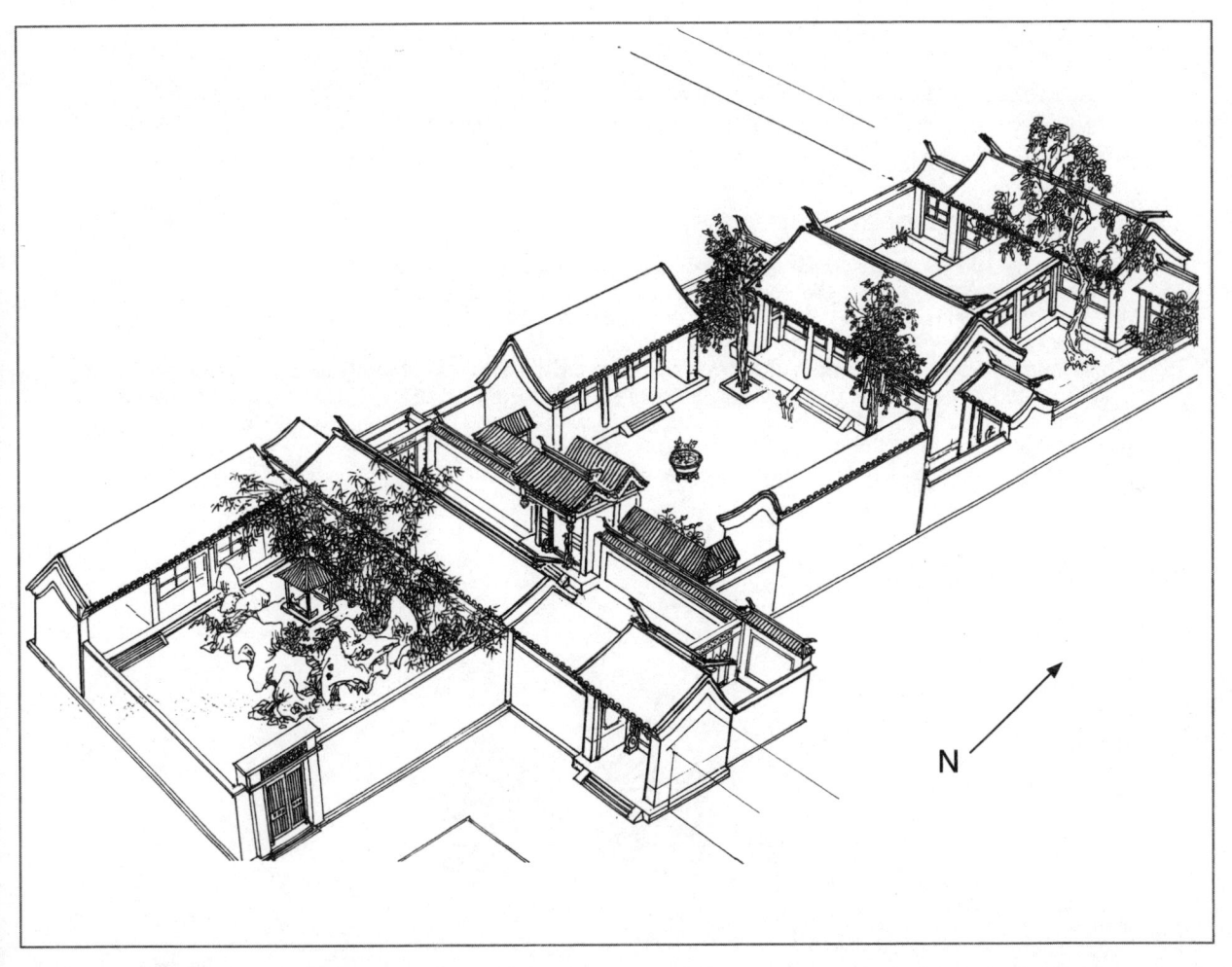

(2002年7月13日绘)

切割亦留整体美

(东城区南池子大街普渡寺后巷10号)

此院原是清初亲王多尔衮管家的宅院。此房格扇精美,木架粗大,尤其是大门的砖雕,很有特点。

此院两廊有门可通左右两院,正房前廊后厦,可知此院绝不是只有北房、东房的小院,原来定是包括8号、12号……的一个大宅院,这院只是花园的一部分。院中石榴、葡萄、玉簪花营造出幽静、清爽的环境。

Beauty Remains Despite its Breakup

Location: No. 10 Pudongsi Houxiang, Nanchizi Dajie in Dongcheng District

This courtyard was originally the courtyard house of the steward of Dorgon, a prince in the early Qing Dynasty (1644–1911). The partition doors of this house are exquisite and wooden frames thick and big. The brick carving on the entrance gate is very unique.

This courtyard has doors set in the two corridors on either side, leading to the two neighboring courtyards to left and right. There is also a covered corridor areas at the front of the principal wing. Clearly this courtyard was not only a small courtyard with only east and west wings, but part of a big compound including the Nos. 8 and 12, this courtyard being a part of its garden. The pomegranate trees and grape vines and plantain lily create a serene and fresh environment.

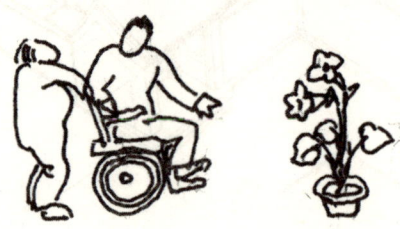

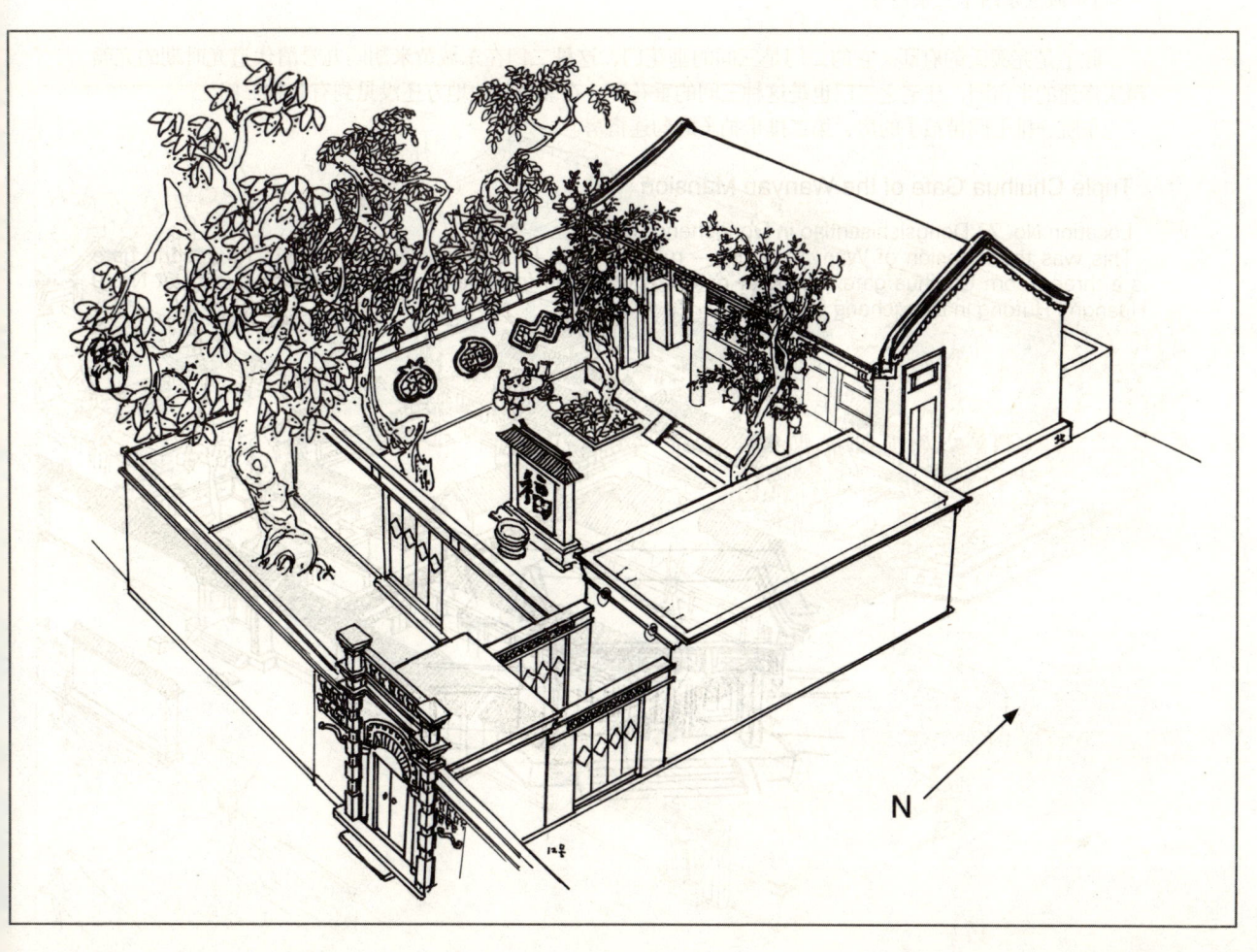

(2002年7月15日绘)

完颜府里三垂花

(东城区东四十三条77号)

　　此宅是完颜氏的府邸。它的二门是三间的垂花门，这种二门在东城黄米胡同九号清代道光时期的完颜麟庆修建的半亩园，住宅之二门也是这种三间的垂花门，在北京其他地方还没见到有此种二门。

　　东院一排七间带拍子的房，第二排带拍子的勾连搭房。

Triple Chuihua Gate of the Wanyan Mansion

Location:No. 77 Dongsishisantiao in Dongcheng District

This was the mansion of Wanyan family – rulers of the Jin Dynasty (1115 – 1234). Its second gate is a three-room Chuihua gate. No other gate like it can be found elsewhere in Beijing except at No. 9 Huangmi Hutong in Dongcheng District.

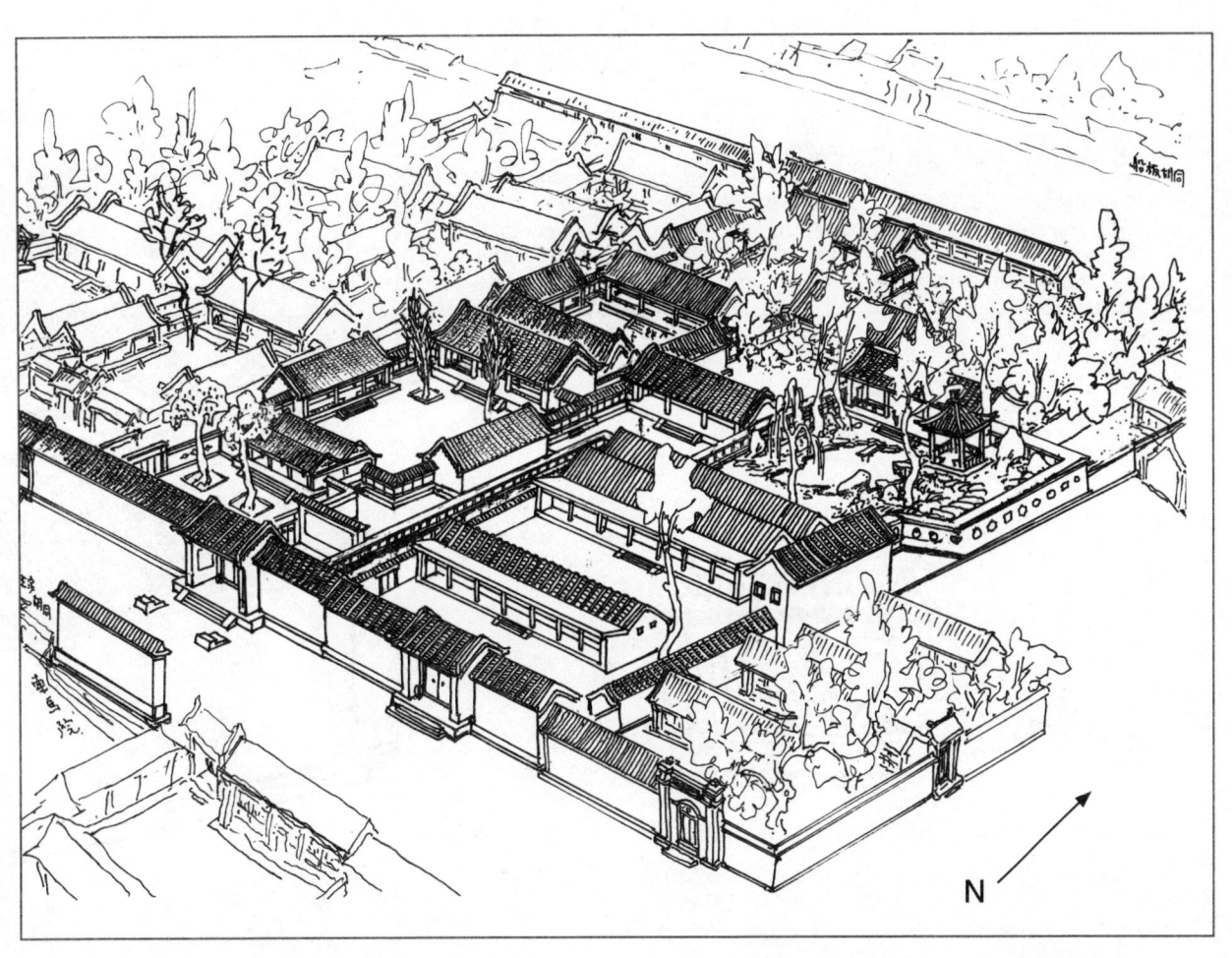

(2002年7月草, 2008年8月补完)

完颜新宅静安居

（东城区柴棒胡同55号）

主人为东四十三条77号主人完颜氏的后人，姓王。王家在卖了东四十三条77号宅院之后，在此院住。院内影壁及如意门上的砖雕非常精致，很有特色。

A Quiet New Dwelling for the Wanyan

Location:No. 55 Chaibang Hutong in Dongcheng District
The master of this courtyard, surnamed Wang, is a descendant of the Wanyan Family which owned No. 77 Dongsishisantiao. The brick carving on the screen wall and the Ruyi gate, is exquisite and unique.

(2002年8月3日绘)

临街经商铺面房

（东城区朝阳门内南小街367号）

这种店铺大概是布铺等小商号。楼上是仓库，楼下是门市，还有后门。一家在此，既商且住。

二楼的万字花纹栏杆，是挂字号、招牌的地方，二楼上还有挑杆，用来挂幌子。

A Shop Front Dwelling

Location:No. 367 Nanxiaojie, Chaoyangmennei in Dongcheng District
The ground floor was a shop, while the second floor was a storeroom. There is also a back door. The family conducted business and also lived here.
The banister on the second floor with the swastika pattern is where the signboard hung. There was also a pole from which to hang the business banner on the second floor.

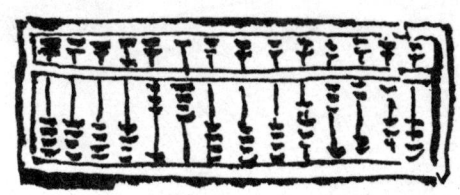

(2002年7月24日绘)

41

世代祖居进士第

（西城区复兴门内察院胡同23号）

此宅为古典诗词大师——叶家滢女士（满族）的祖宅。其曾祖为武官，祖父为皇宫中的医生、儒医，伯父亦是医生。大门上原挂有"进士第"之匾。门内影壁上挂有"华佗再世"等四块匾。

Ancestral Home of Jinshi

Location:No. 23 Chayuan Hutong, Fuxingmennei in Xicheng District

This courtyard is the ancestral home of Ms. Ye Jiaying, Manchu master of classical Chinese poetry. Her great grandfather had been a military officer, her grandfather a Confucian physician in the imperial palace, and her uncle was also a doctor. A horizontal plaque inscribed with "Jinshidi"–meaning successful candidate in the highest imperial examinations–originally hung over the entrance gate. On the screen wall inside the entrance gate hung four other plaques, one of which was inscribed with "Zaishihuatuo" meaning "Reincarnation of Hua Tuo ." (Hua Tuo was a legendary doctor from ancient times.)

(2002年7月31日绘)

【祁家行医睦邻里】

(西城区复兴门内大街96号)

　　祁宅，祁家世传行医，原门口有行医之匾。此院在幽静的小胡同里，房为整砖到顶的硬山搁檩式，颇有特色。

Doctors of the Qi Family Served the Neighborhood

Location:No 96 Fuxingmennei Dajie in Xicheng District

The courtyard is the home of the Qi Family, who practiced medicine from generation to generation. A horizontal plaque inscribed with "Medical Practitioner" originally hung over its entrance gate. This courtyard house is in a quiet hutong. The house, flush-gable-roofed, purlin-framed, had end walls entirely of brick – a unique feature.

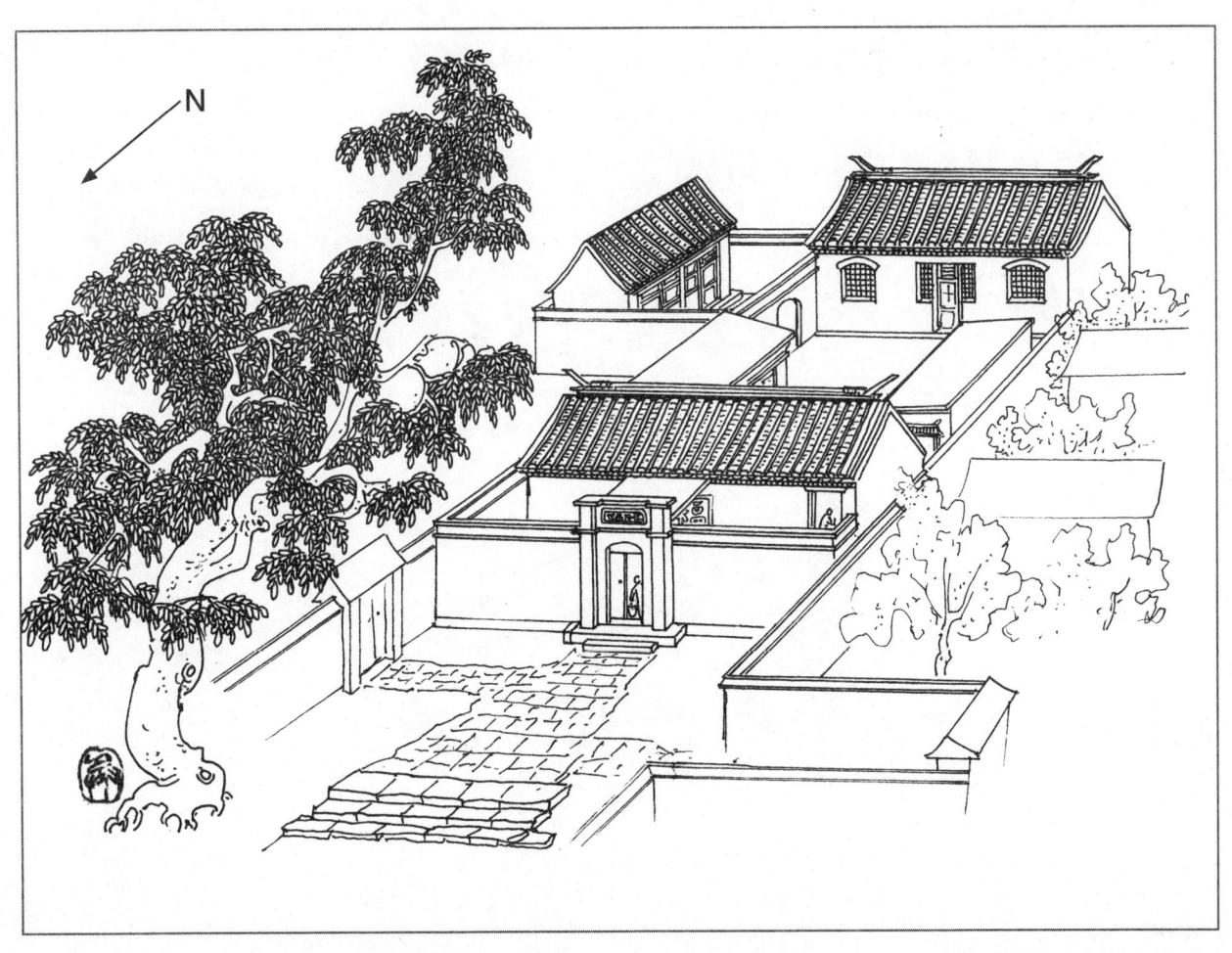

(2002年8月7日绘)

小门小户亦欢颜

（东城区南池子大街缎库胡同1号）

此院坐南朝北，北房三间半（门占半间），南房三间半（在东南角留的半间），东西房为灰顶平房，院中一棵香椿，是一座舒适清雅的小院。

A Happy Family Behind a Low Gate and Small Doorway

Location:No. 1 Duanku Hutong, Nanchizi Dajie in Dongcheng District
This courtyard opening to the north has only three and a half rooms (the gate occupying a half) facing south, a north-facing south wing with three and a half rooms (a half at the southeast corner reserved), and untiled, rendered gray flat roofed wings on the east and west sides. There is a toon tree inside the courtyard.

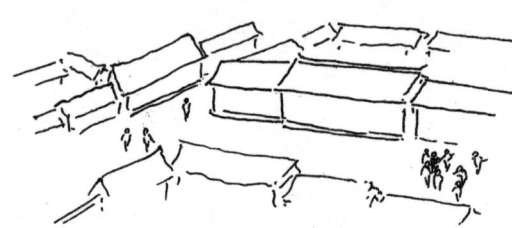

(2002年8月12日绘)

格扇二门独此家

（西城区复兴门内大街58号）

此宅曾是袁世凯侄子的住宅。此院以南为上，但所有的房屋均高大、整齐，保存完好。平廊的望板上，绘有勾子莲及团福、寿字，它的格扇二门在京城民居中是罕见的。

An Inner Gate with Unique Screen Door

Location:No. 58 Fuxingmennei Dajie in Xicheng District
This courtyard house once belonged to a nephew of republican president Yuan Shikai. The principal wing of this courtyard lies to the south, but all the buildings are tall and neat and well-preserved. The roof boarding on the flat-roofed corridor is decorated with auspicious patterns of hook-shaped lotus, bats in a circle(meaning good luck), and the Chinese character "Shou" (meaning long life). Its inner gate with screen door is also rarely seen among houses in Beijing.

(2002年8月15日绘)

八月十五云遮月

(西城区复兴门内大街90号)

　　广亮大门，东院是平顶抄手游廊的整齐四合院。院中大白海棠树的叶伞，遮盖了大半个院。西院将正房及倒座房拆除后，改造成西式瓦房，并用磨砖对缝墙辟成另一院，洋房与院中之门像是后开的。东院正房之西耳房的过厅内，除了有与两厢相连的游廊有门，在其西山墙的北面还有一个旧的穿廊门洞，原为并连之东西院相通的廊子。这是一座中西建筑合璧的民居院落。

The Moon Obscured by Clouds on Moon Festival

Location:No. 90 Fuxingmennei Dajie in Xicheng District
　　The main gate to this courtyard is a wide-open *Guangliang* gate. The east side is a regular courtyard behind a forecourt, with the main buildings connected by corridors. A big white begonia tree in this courtyard shades half the courtyard. On the west side, the north and central buildings having been demolished, a western-style tile-roofed house was built in their place and a separate small courtyard was created for it by laying a wall of polished bricks with pointed joints between the house and courtyard behind. The door linking the western-style house and the courtyard behind appears to have been made later. Back on the east side, the west side room of the principal building has an old covered doorway connecting the east side with the west.
　　This is compound combines Chinese and western architectural styles.

(2002年8月6日绘)

> 正月十五雪打灯

（东城区朝阳门内新鲜胡同38号）

这里原是桂公府的花园。桂公府系慈禧之弟桂祥的府邸，此为其花园部分，应属文物类的民居。

这院除假山石不存，其他主体建筑基本完整，戏台及逐步增高的看台很有特色，尤其花园中的花厅，前面的敞轩，及后面的建筑都很完好。

画此院时，想起了"云遮月"，想起了幼时正月十五灯节母亲带我们去大宅门里看"放盒子"的情景。我去的宅门小于此院，这样好的府门，正月必放盒子，故将童年的记忆画在此图中。

注："放盒子"是中国花炮艺术，是已失传的一种文化遗产，比西洋的礼花弹更有情趣，更贴近喜庆之主题。例如放花放到最后，像变魔术一般，花炮再一炸响，一条红红的祝寿喜单，随即徐徐落下。

Lunar January fifteen a light snow

Location:No. 38 Xinxian Hutong, Chaoyangmennei in Dongcheng District

Originally this was the garden of the mansion of Duke Gui Xiang, younger brother of Empress Dowager Cixi. It is a folk dwelling classed as a cultural relic.

Except for the rockery, which no longer exists, all the structures of the courtyard are well preserved. The theatre stage and gradually rising stand are a unique feature. The flower hall in the garden, the open pavilion in the front and buildings in the back are all preserved well.

(2002年8月21日绘)

廊墙围绕作何用

（东城区朝阳门内新鲜胡同42号）

此院为桂公府靠西边的一个别院，坐南朝北，两排七间高大的北房在北京并不出奇，与众不同的是其他三面都是围成圈的"廊墙"，与北房是断开的，并不相连。

此种"半坡围圈"，实际上是一种"廊墙"，即内做成围廊，外则为围墙，唐代的大寺庙中多用廊墙。

Why the Cloister?

Location:No. 42 Xinxian Hutong, Chaoyangmennei in Dongcheng District

This courtyard's entrance faces north. It has just two buildings: each one a row of seven big rooms. These are not special in Beijing. What is different from the others is the cloister-like corridor-lined walls running along three sides, which are disconnected from the house.

This kind corridor wall,with a single slope tiled roof,was commonly found in big monasteries built in the Tang Dynasty (618-907).

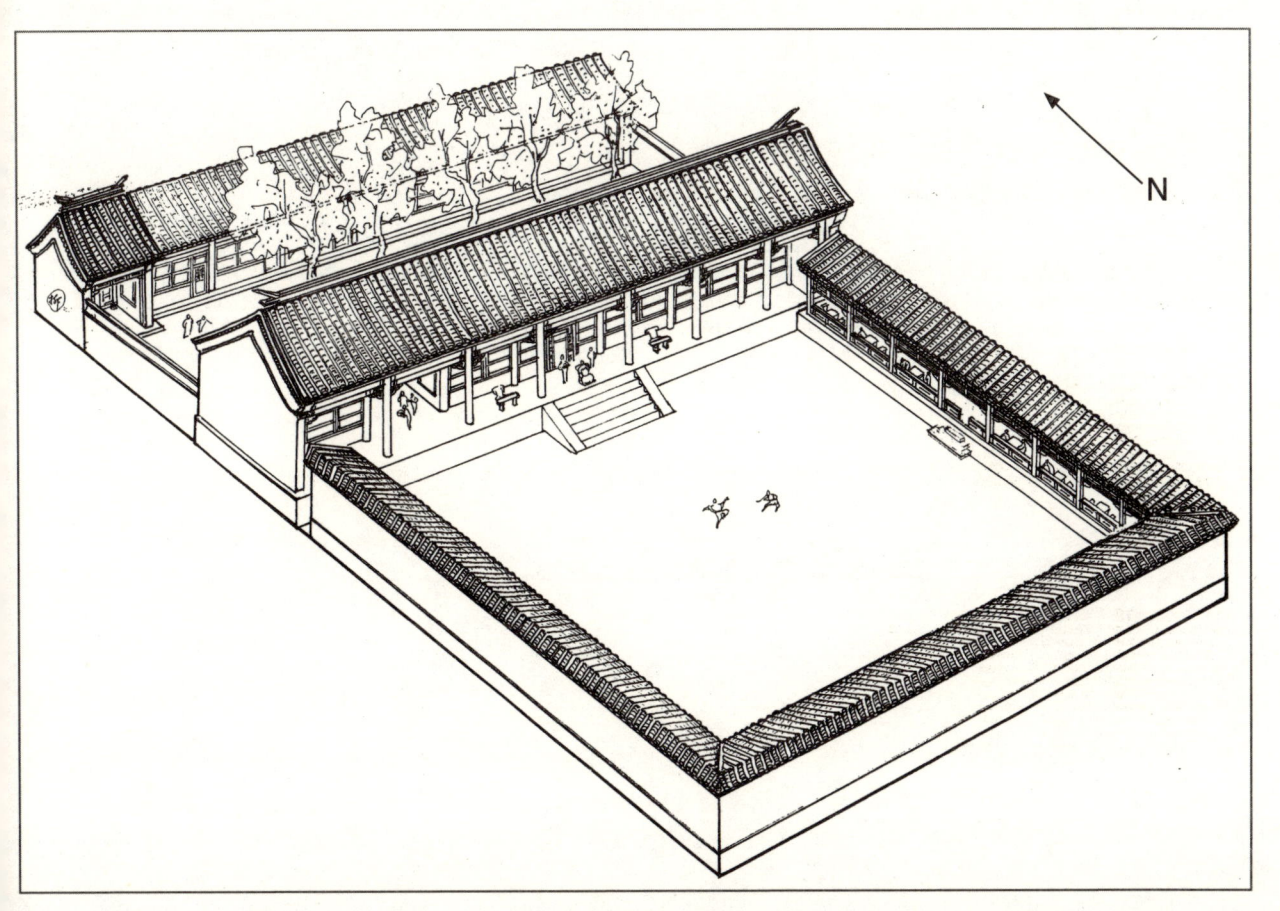

(2002年9月5日绘)

知是风水详不解

（东城区草厂胡同二条××号）

此院坐东朝西，东为上。东房的房顶南北有两个镇物：一个是在两房脊蝎尾之间立一方砖，另一个是在房脊中用小瓦做成银锭花纹。

东房内的精美木雕落地罩保存得如此完好。清水脊上完好保存下来的两组镇物，也是研究北京民俗史不可多得的实物。

Mysterious Objects to Contend with *Fengshui*

Location: No. XX Ertiao, Caochang Hutong in Dongcheng District

This courtyard with its entrance facing west has east wing as principal wing. At the southern and northern side on the roof ridge of the east wing there are two items for suppressing evil: one is a diamond shape standing between the two scorpion tail decorations on the ridge and, and the other the pattern of silver ingots made of small tiles on the ridge.

The exquisitely carved wooden partition screen in the east wing is well preserved. The two items on the roof ridge for suppressing evil are preserved well and are rare material items for studying the history of folk custom in Beijing.

(2002年9月28日绘)

标准外院求严谨

（西城区学院胡同39号）

此院第一进院为标准院，这标准是要制造出等级与严谨。给人一种压抑感是中国四合院设计者最基础的目的，抑扬交错，主次分明。

这是一座比较典型的二进四合院，但在二门（垂花门）及抄手游廊的建造上有点简单，垂花门内不是三副四扇屏门，而是对正房者为四扇屏门，两边为两扇小门。游廊到正房，不是用一拐弯，而是将游廊直通耳房，从廊子的侧边进入正房。

此院一进门，从南房廊下走外院西侧廊子进入内院，可从廊子直通正房。

Conventional Outer Courtyard Leaves More to be Desired

Location: No. 39 Xueyuan Hutong in Xicheng District

The forecourt of this courtyard house is a very standard one, aiming to show rank and precision.

This is a fairly typical house with two courtyards, but construction of the second gate (Chuihua gate) and the veranda connecting the principal and wing houses is a little simple. Behind the Chuihua gate are not three sets of four-door screen doors, but only one set, facing the principal wing. There are only two-door openings on each side giving onto the side wings. The corridors do not bend toward the central doorway, but lead directly to the lower, side rooms of the wing. Entry to the central rooms is through the side of the corridor.

Entering the gate of this courtyard, one can walk along the corridor under the eaves of the south (street side) building, and go along the west corridor in the outer courtyard directly into the inner courtyard and the principal wing.

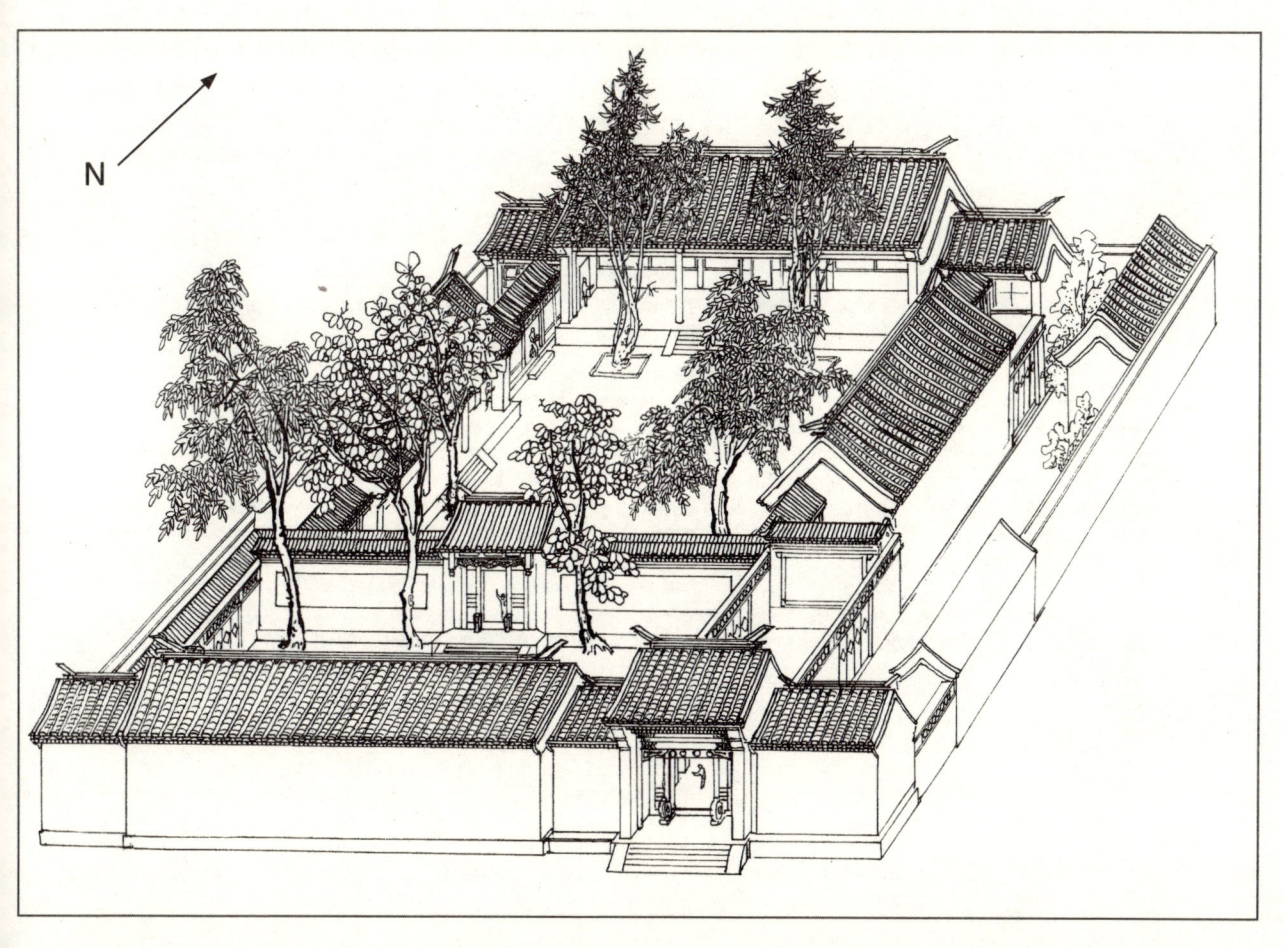

(2002年8月25日绘)

宽敞外院有豪情

（西城区复兴门内察院胡同25号）

　　一般的四合院，大门与二门之间是紧凑扁长的小院。而此院不同，第一进院是一片宽广的平地，宽敞之院没有了压抑感，还可产生豪情，使人有舒畅的感觉，似乎四合院从封建等级制度的桎梏下走了出来。

　　此院进大门为外院，二门内才是住宅。进内院后，有正厅与东西厢房，正厅三大间，与五间北房之间有穿廊相连，平面构成"工"字形。这种"工"字形的平面建筑是自宋元时期寺庙、官廨和府邸中最流行的平面建筑。明代以后多省去了穿廊变成加厢房的四合院。北京城民居很少见到带穿廊的"工"字形平面建筑，但是在一些大的衙署府邸中还有存留（见《加摹乾隆京城全图》）。

　　此院可以说是北京民居中保留穿廊的孤例。

——徐苹芳

A Wide Forecourt Offers Breadth of Feeling

Location:No. 25 Chayuan Hutong, Fuxingmennei in Xicheng District

In most courtyard houses, the forecourt between the main entrance gate and the second gate is a narrow, compact courtyard. But this courtyard house is different. The forecourt is a spacious yard.

Here the entrance gate leads to only to the outer courtyard, it is the second gate that leads to the living quarters. The central courtyard consists of main hall and west and east wings. The three-room main hall is connected with the five-room rear wing by a covered corridor in the middle, in an "H" shape layout. This kind of layout could often be found in temples, government offices and mansion houses built in the Song (960-1279) and Yuan (1206-1368) Dynasties. After the Ming Dynasty (1368-1644), the covered corridors mostly disappeared, and left and right wings were added creating a four-sided courtyard. This kind of architecture with a covered corridor in the middle is now rarely found among the folk houses in Beijing.

This courtyard may be unique in Beijing for having a covered corridor in the middle.

——By Xu Pingfang

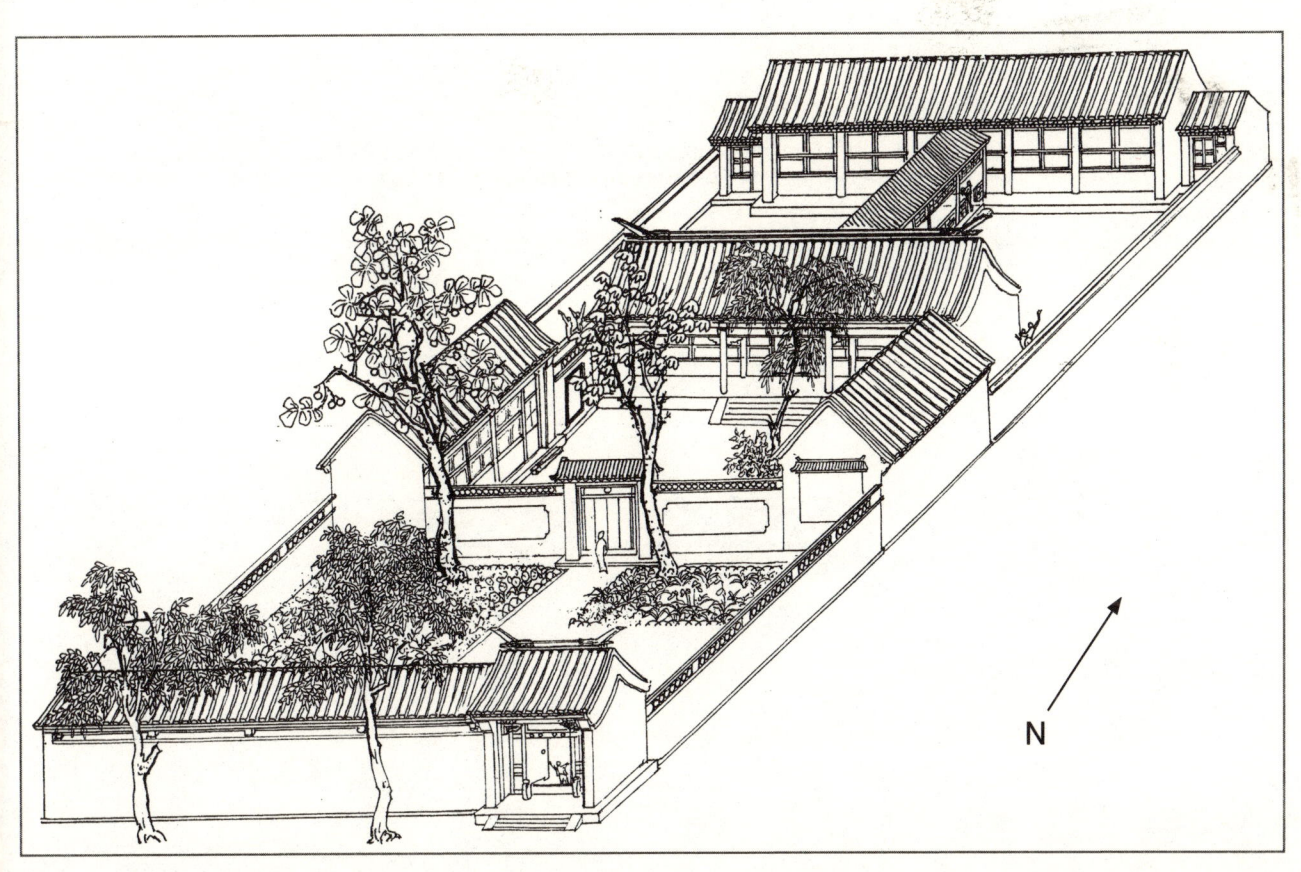

(2002年8月28日绘)

倒座房上风水墙

（西城区太平桥东街1号）

此院坐北朝南。

可以想象，原来在此院之南一定另有一院，其房屋比此院的高，因而此院倒座房上的花墙应当是风水墙。

A Fengshui Ridge atop the Front

Location:No. 1 Taipingqiao Dongjie in Xicheng District
This courtyard faces south.
It can be deduced that there must originally have been another courtyard to the south of this courtyard, with buildings taller than those in this one. Therefore, a lattice ridge was built atop the south building to ward off evil.

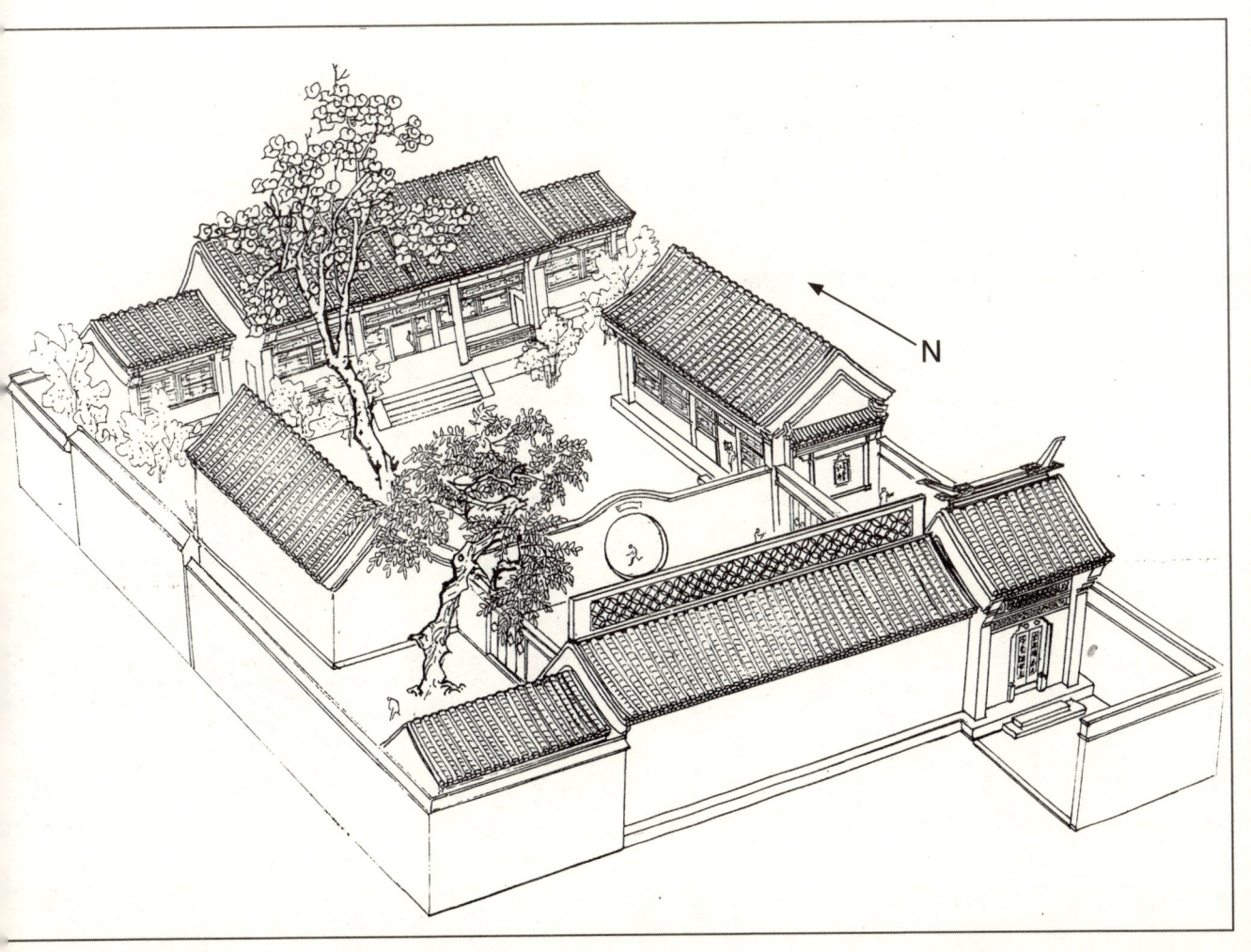

(2002年9月4日绘)

马家致富购三宅

（东城区石雀胡同15号、17号、19号）

北新桥石雀胡同15号、17号、19号，当地人称之为"四棵槐马家"，是马家发家后逐步购置的。

选此三院，只是想说明北京的四合院不都是四方的，比如马家，还没有来的及将三个院子拆了统一修建，有的院子修建了，其地界也并不是方方正正的，由此可证。

The Wealthy Ma Family Buy Three Courtyards

Location:No.15,No.17 and No.19 Shique Hutong in Dongcheng District

No.15, No.17 and No.19 in Shique Hutong, Beixinqiao are called by the locals "Four-Chinese scholar tree House of Ma Family". They were gradually acquired by the Ma Family as it built up its family fortune.

The selection of these three courtyards is to show that not all courtyard houses in Beijing are square. Take the House of Ma for example: They never got around to rebuilding the property in its entirety, although some buildings were rebuilt. The plot is not at all square.

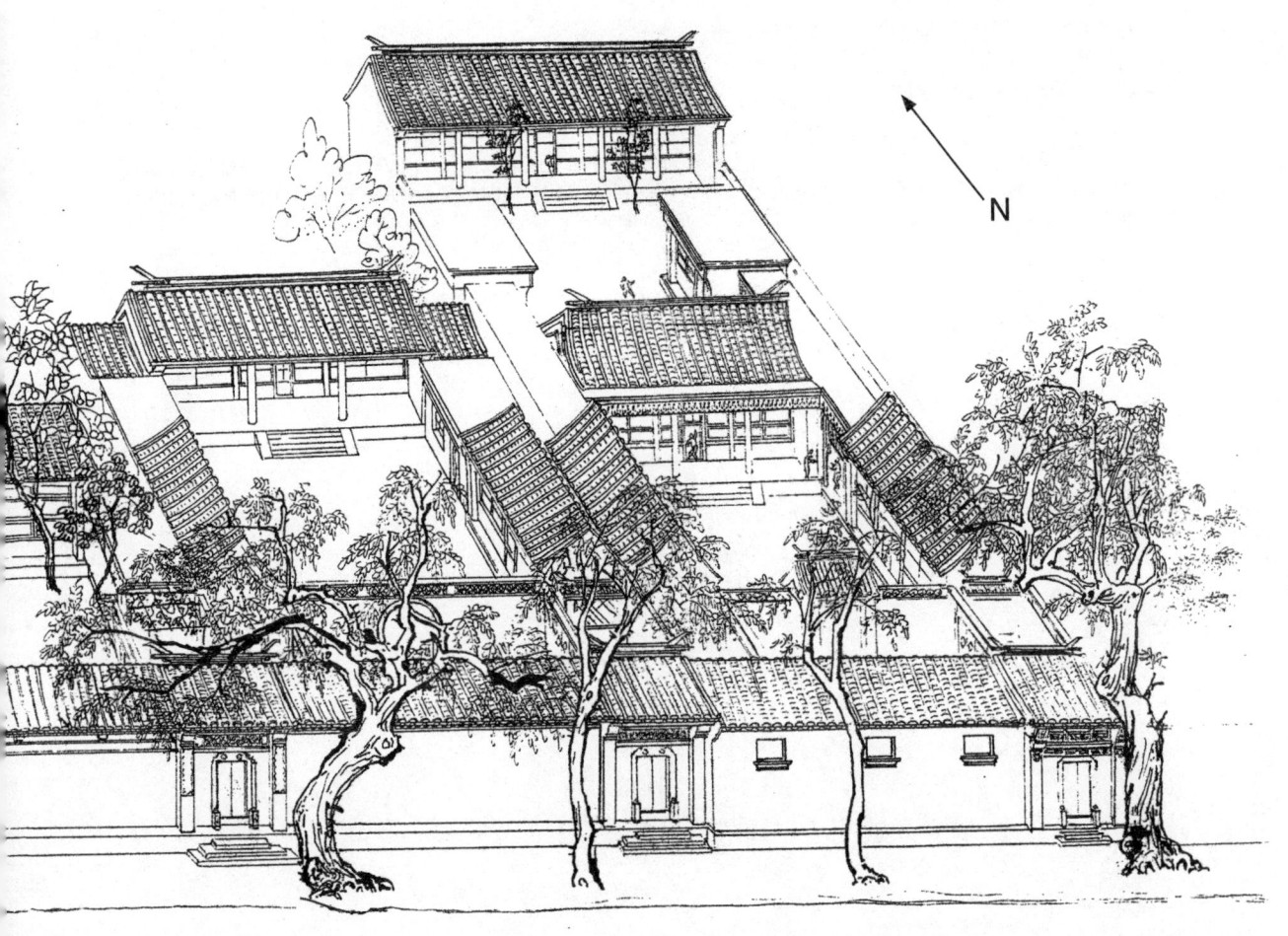

(2002年10月12日绘)

深藏不露小住宅
（东城区九道湾西巷5号）

此院坐北朝南，在东南角有朴实无华的随墙小门楼，而二门则是很讲究的蛮子门。院内是精致的硬山顶小三合院，明亮大窗，屋内是进口的小花瓷砖地。

在僻静的小胡同中常能找到富人在这些地方修建的小外宅，就与此相似。

再有，由此院向西的九道湾西巷7号，是北京民居小院中常见的一居小院，小门内只有三间北屋，方顶为棋盘心的灰瓦结合的顶子，属于老北京下层居民的住房。

A Gem, Tucked away Inconspicuously

Location: No. 5 Jiudaowan Xixiang in Dongcheng District
This courtyard opens to the south. At its southeast corner there is a simple outer gate in the wall while the second, inner gate is a highly respectable *Manzi* gate. The inner courtyard is surrounded by gable-roofed houses on three sides with big and clear windows. Inside the house, the floor is paved with imported ceramic tiles with small flower patterns. One can often find such houses built by the rich as second homes in quiet little hutongs.

And if one were to head west past the gate to No. 7, one would find a tiny courtyard with only one building consisting of just three rooms. Its roof covered only partially with tiles, leaving squares of untiled rendering. This was typical of dwelling of the poor lower classes.

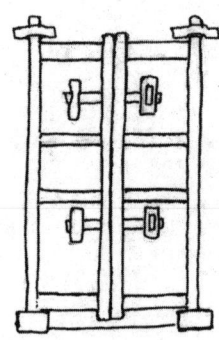

(2002年10月23日绘)

西藏活佛自家院

（东城区九道湾中巷13号）

九道湾形成始于明末清初，因粮仓"新太仓"低洼积水而弃仓后，开始形成宅院。直到20世纪20年代，仓的西北部还是一片很大的广场，当地人称之为"大院"，现在的西巷13号前的小广场则被称为"小大院"。

这个院子坐北朝南，位于仓西北部的中心，是房主于20年代在"大院"边建起的自家院。房主是西藏的活佛，在雍和宫"工作"，自己一家人住此。50年代就经常有蒙古、藏族等少数民族友人来访，这里一直是民族友好之院。

门前广场曾是煤铺，在图中将"摇煤球"的全过程画出。这是过去北京人冬季取暖的主要方式，留给后人知晓。

A Tibetan Living Buddha's Residence

Location: No. 13 Jiudaowan Zhongxiang in Dongcheng District

Jiudaowan neighborhood came into being in the late Ming Dynasty (1368–1644) and early Qing Dynasty (1644–1911) after the imperial granary "Xintai Granary" was abandoned because it had become water-logged, due to its low elevation. Until the 1920s, the northwest part of the former granary was still a spacious square which was called the "big yard" by the locals while the space before present-day No. 13 Xixiang was called the "little big yard".

This courtyard house facing south is located in the center of the northwest part of the granary. It was built for private use in the 1920s next to the "big yard". The owner was a living Buddha from Tibet who "worked" at the Yonghegong Lama Temple. He lived there with his family.

The yard before its gate was once a coal shop. I have included in the sketch the whole process of making coal balls so that future generations will know how it was done. This was the main source of winter heating for Beijing residents in the past.

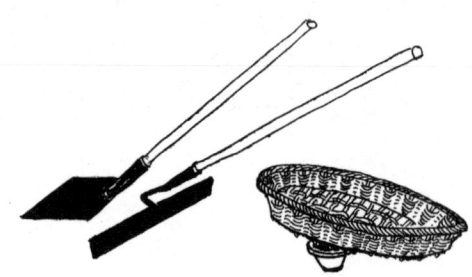

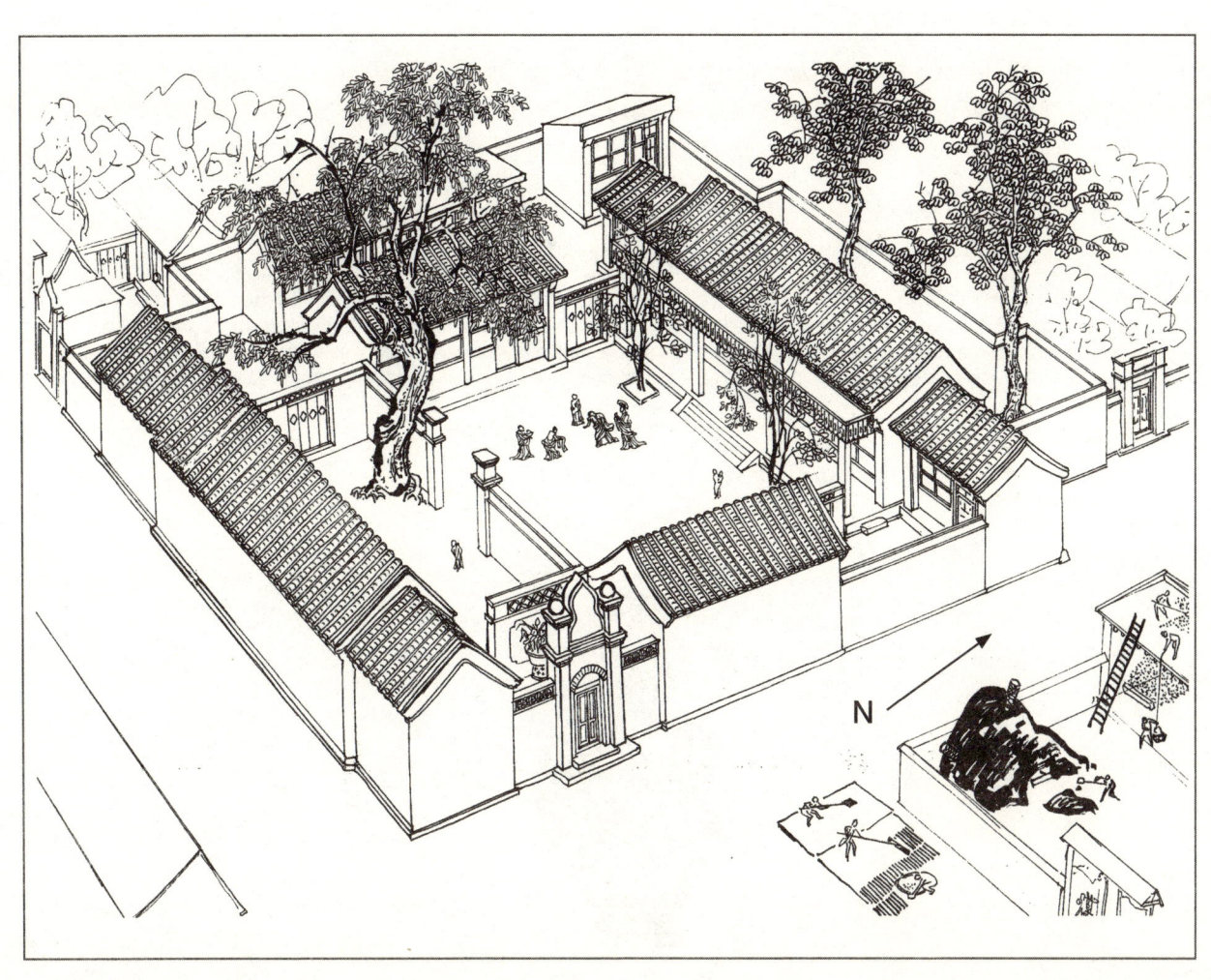

(2002年10月26日绘)

多设屏门遮欠缺

（东城区九道湾西巷13号）

左边院子的门楼上原有飞鹰浮雕，门柱上是一对瓜果花篮。进门后三面是绿色屏门，再左转又是一扇绿色屏门。进此门后南北各三间精致的小房，向西迎面又见南北两个绿色屏门。你一定认为屏门后面应当是三正两耳的另一间耳房藏在此处，其实没有。此院地界小，里面只有小棚，但欠缺就被遮住了。

Extra Screens to Cover up Inadequacies

Location:No. 13 Jiudaowan Xixiang in Dongcheng District

The gate tower of the courtyard on the left originally had a relief carving of flying eagles and the gate posts were carved with baskets full of fruit, melons and flowers. Entering into the entrance gate, there are green screen doors on three sides. Turning left, there is another green screen door. Passing through this door, there is a small exquisite three-room house each on the north and south sides. Walking westwards, one can see two green screen doors respectively on the south and north sides. (The courtyard on the right is No. 11)

(2002年11月5日绘)

祈福遇福共赏福

（东城区九道湾南巷31号）

从九道湾西巷转到南巷，这里是最绕人的地方，没有出口，只能再绕回去。

有的人走到此处不但不急，反而面对院门上的蝙蝠雕刻，高兴地说，"没白走，要不走到这里怎能遇到这'福'。好！好！有福，有福！"房主为自己祈福，给路人送去了福，祈福与遇福心态不一，但共同赏福，让福给我们带来欢乐。这就是老北京的胡同文化。

Seek, Encounter and Enjoy Good Fortune

Location:No. 31 Jiudaowan Nanxiang in Dongcheng District
Turning from Xixiang to Nanxiang is very confusing. This is where many people get lost. There is no exit, so one has to turn back.

Yet when they reach this place, some people are not anxious, instead they gaze up at the carved bat above the gate leading to this courtyard and say, "I did not walk in vain, for otherwise I would not have encountered the gigantic bat (pronounced 'Fu', which also means good fortune)! Great! I will have good fortune!" While the master of the courtyard house begs for good fortune, he also gives fortune to the passer by. The one who begs for good fortune is in a different state of mind from the one who encounters good fortune, but they both seek good fortune. Let good fortune bring us joy. This is the hutong culture of the old Beijing.

(2002年11月14日绘)

| 符合标准有厨卫 |

（东城区南池子大街46号）

在这个古老的四合院中，主人为自己安置了现代化的厨房、卫生间，房屋建筑完好，既保持了古老院落的风貌，又让日常生活方便舒适。

All Modern Conveniences

Location:No. 46 Nanchizi Dajie in Dongcheng District

In this old courtyard house, the master installed a modern kitchen and toilets for themselves. The house is well preserved, not only keeping the style and features of the old courtyard, but also making the daily life convenient and comfortable.

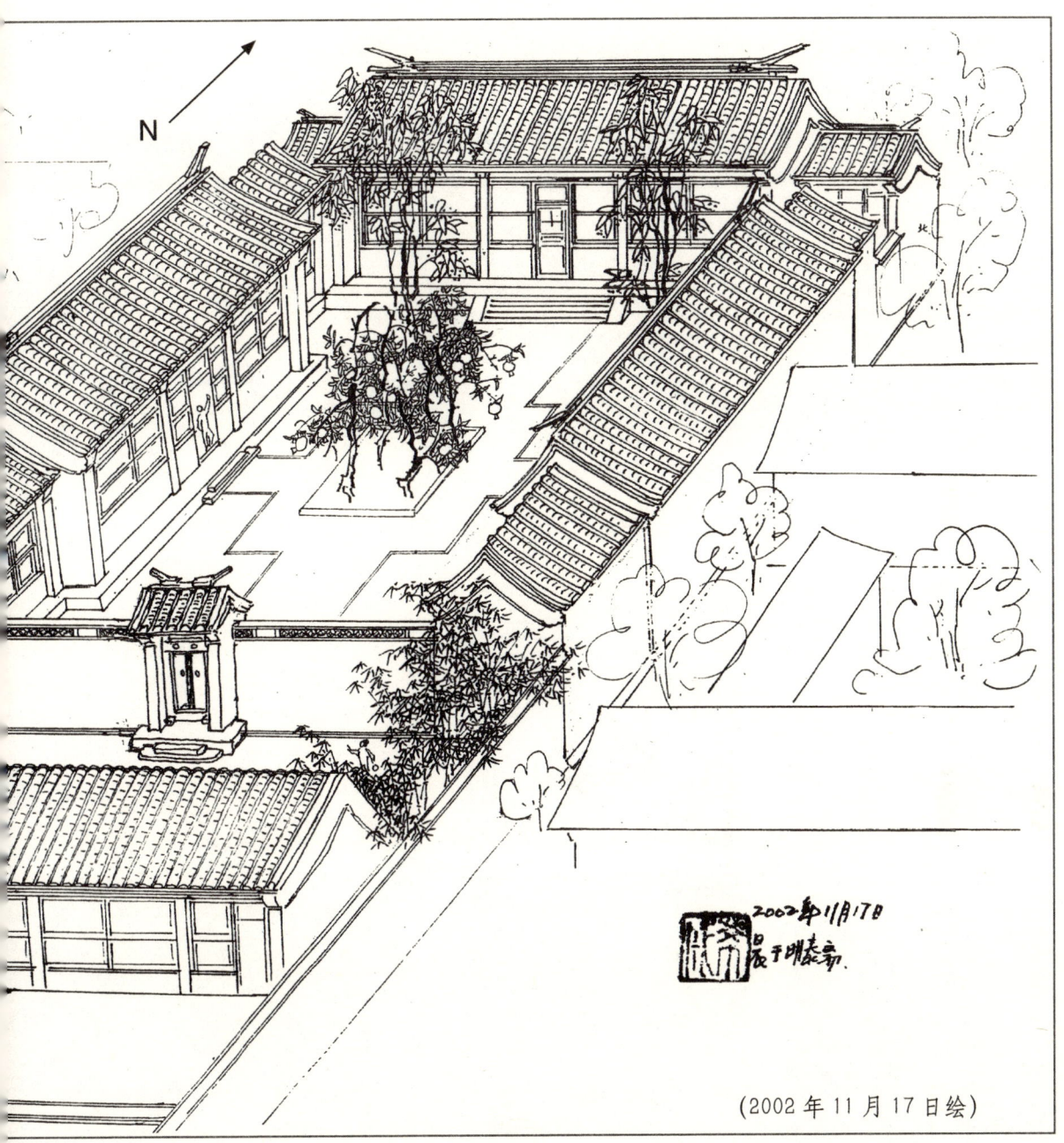

(2002年11月17日绘)

| 标准二进四合院 |

东城区石雀胡同43号

此院院门为栏板式如意门，门道内天花板有团鹤彩画，影壁为麒麟砖雕方心，四周有草花抱角的精美砖雕，全院花窗、屋门有木雕裙板，后院为佛堂，是一座标准的二进四合院。

A Standard Double Courtyard

Location:No. 43 Shique Hutong in Dongcheng District

The gate of this courtyard is in the style of a Ruyi gate (i.e. the door is set at the front of the gate room). Inside the gate room, the drop ceiling is decorated with square boards paintings of circling cranes. The diamond shaped brick in the center of spirit screen is carved with a Kylin, and around it are corner bricks exquisite carved with floral patterns. The lattice windows and doors are all set in carved wooden skirt boards. The back courtyard is used as a family shrine. It is a regular courtyard house with two courtyards.

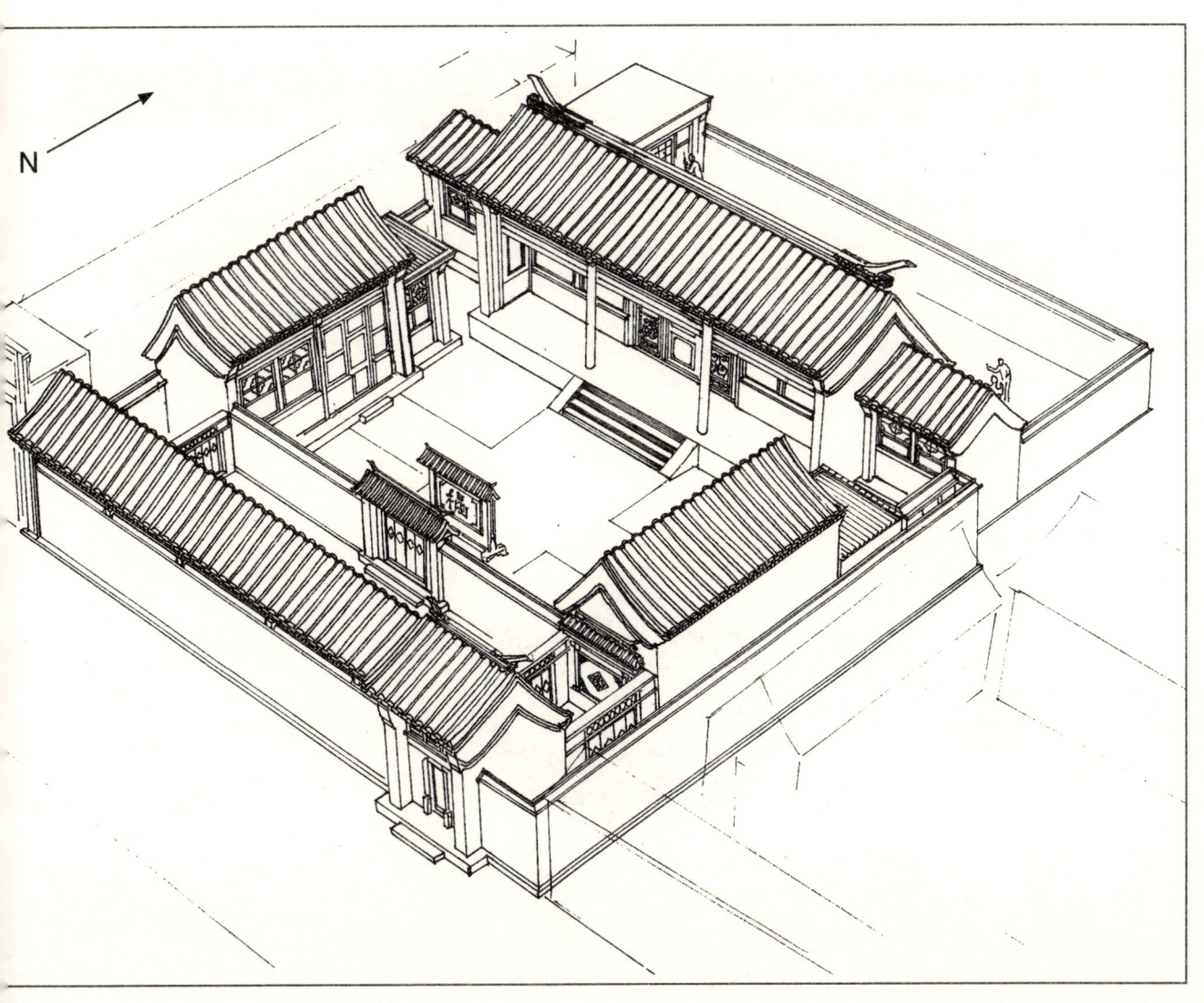

(2002年12月25日绘)

兄弟三宅院连院

（东城区八宝坑胡同37号、39号、41号）

此三个院落坐西朝东，是顺义进城的农民三兄弟置的产业。虽然三个院子各自有门，但院内又有门彼此相通。院子大门为农村的大梢门，可由老家的大车直接将粮食拉进院。

该图是女儿郑欣习作。

Three Brothers in Three Adjoining Courtyards

Location:Nos. 37, 39 and 41 Babaokeng Hutong in Dongcheng District

These three courtyard houses facing east are properties purchased by three farmer brothers who came to the city from Shunyi. The three courtyards each have their own entrance, but are also connected to each other. The main entrance gate to the courtyards is a wide gate popular in the countryside through which carts from their hometown bring grain into the courtyard. (This sketch was made by the artist's daughter Zheng Xin)

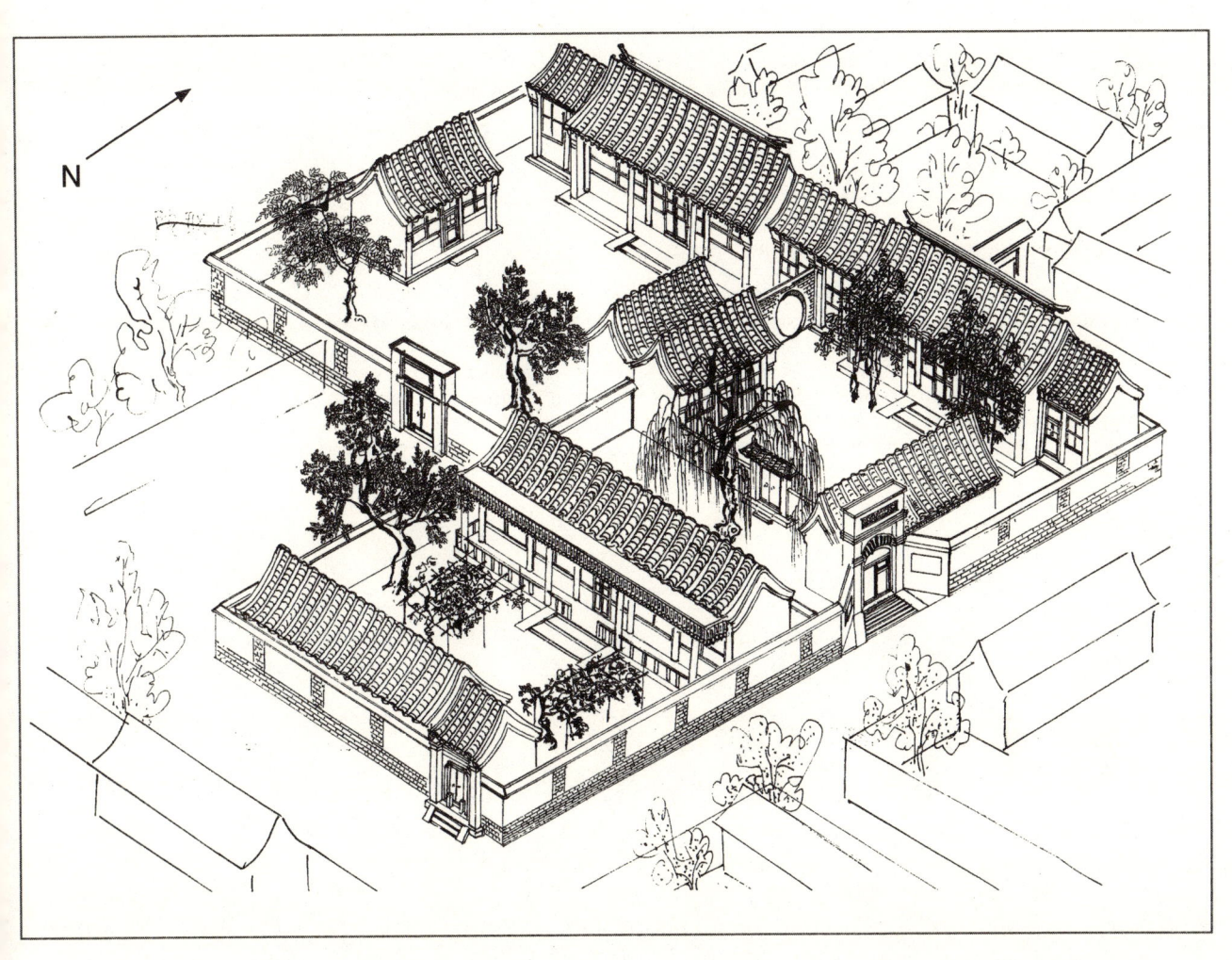

(2003年1月10日 郑欣绘)

山东叔侄一家亲
（东城区东四五条138号）

据说此院为清代一位官员的宅子。因孩子年幼，故定产权人为叔父。叔父将三兄弟供养成人，三兄弟为不负叔父养育之恩，将此院产权按比例分了，一家人以一家亲为重。

此院在五条胡同中间路南一小胡同的尽头，北部、东部都有宅院。若从东留通道，由东南吉位开门，则不能形成规整的四合院；若从正房后留通道由西北开门，则影响了里院为正的规矩；于是此门开在了东北角，此处地势低洼，门外留了台阶。

A Northwest Gate-Most Unusual!

Location:No. 138 Dongsiwutiao in Dongcheng District
It is said that this courtyard house was the mansion of an official in the Qing Dynasty.
This courtyard is located at the end of a small hutong leading south off the central portion of Wutiao Hutong. There are courtyards to both its north and east. If a passageway were left to the east of the compound, and a gate built in the auspicious location of the southeast corner, it could not constitute a regular courtyard house; if a passageway were a passage were to run behind the principal house so as to have a gate built at the northwest corner, it would break the rule that the inner courtyard is the main one. So it was decided to build the gate in the northeast corner. This part was low-lying so steps were built outside the gate.

(2003年2月24日绘)

| 四周更道保平安 |

（东城区东四二条21号）

　　李培基之宅。李曾任原为国民党政府河南省主席，解放后为中央文史馆馆员。

　　听本家后人说，此院的前院为客院。前院没有廊子。后院四周的主房外不是做成抄手游廊，而是做成四间像是平房一样的廊子，有柱，有倒挂楣子、花牙子雀替，下设坐凳栏杆。楣子上有彩画，两耳房前与廊子间有空距可透光，西边院有车库、厨房，四周有更道，颇具特色。

Watchman's Passage all Around to Guard the Peace

Location:No. 21 Dongsiertiao in Dongcheng District
    This was the mansion of Li Peiji, who once served as chairman of He'nan province for the Kuomintang government.
    According to his descendants, the front courtyard was used for guests and had no corridors linking the buildings, whilst the rear courtyard, instead of corridors linking the buildings, had four flat-roofed, broad corridors with pillars, hanging lattices, carved buttresses and bench rail. The lintels are decorated with color paintings. There is space between the two side rooms and the flat-topped corridors allowing light to pass inside. To the west of the courtyards there is a garage and kitchens and all around the courtyards there is watchman's passage.

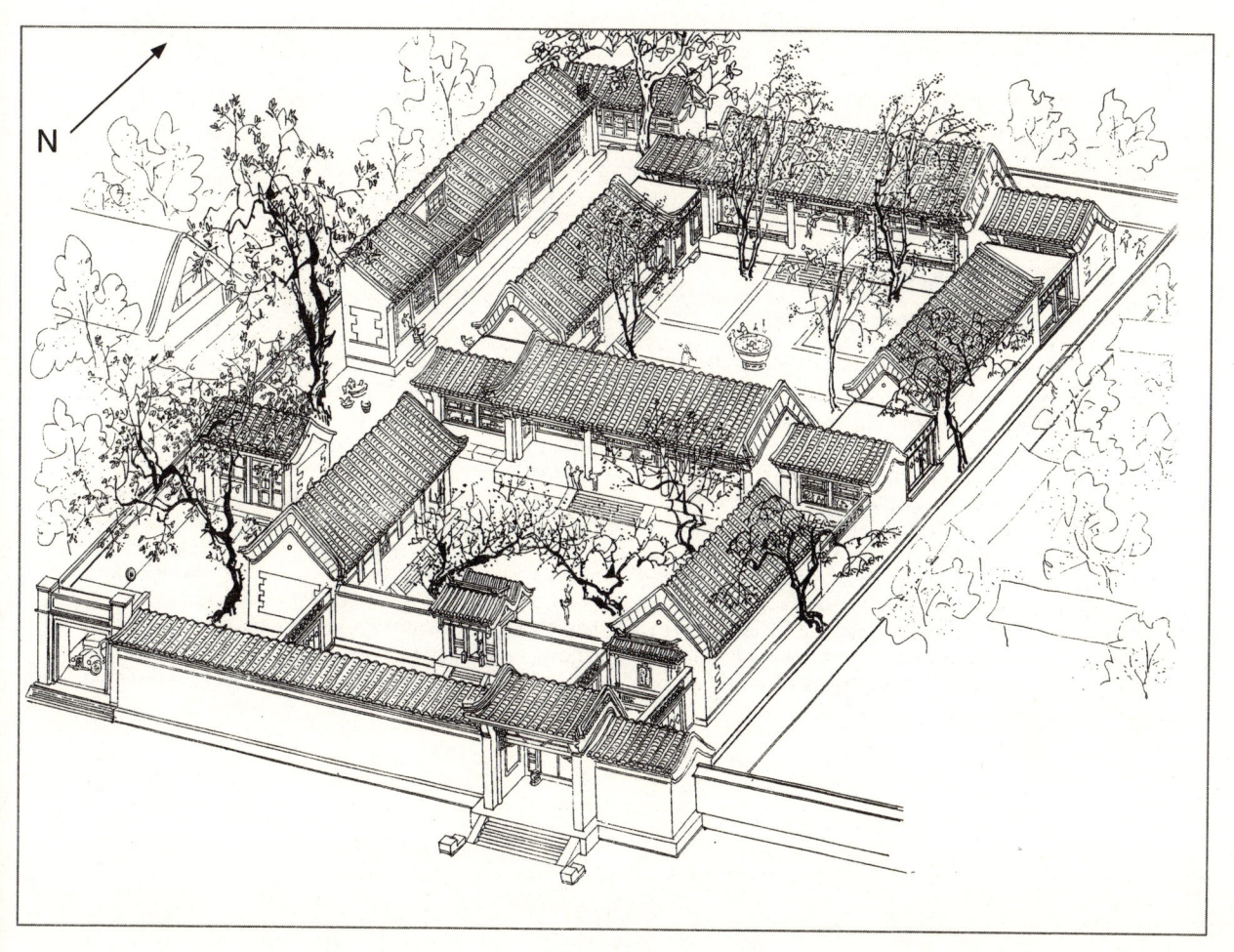

(2003年3月19日绘)

| 田家祖宅名人住 |

（西城区菜市口丞相胡同41号）

此宅为田学景先生的祖宅，清末其曾祖父在南方为官。此院位于南、北方向的两条胡同中。后门在米市胡同，坐东朝西，广亮大门，雕花影壁，倒座房五间为客厅，外院北房两间为学馆。第二进院，进垂花门有抄手游廊，北房五间为其曾祖父住，南房五间为其祖父住，东房为勾连搭式双排房，中间过厅为全家吃饭处所。第三进院东房为供奉先辈主人画像之所，北房前为搭戏台处，东北小耳房为存放物品之库，冬日所有的廊子都用木板封起，廊内放花，夏日将木板藏在库内。此院南房背后又勾连搭建北房五间，前面是花园，有假山、水池和多种树木、花草。花园之西为厨房院、厕所及上菜的走廊。

The Tian Family's Ancestral Courtyard

Location:No. 41 Chengxiang Hutong, Caishikou in Xicheng District
This is the family home of Mr. Tian Xuejing. In late Qing Dynasty (1644-1911), his great-grandfather had served as an official in South China. This courtyard is located between two north-south Hutongs. Its back entrance opens west toward Mishi Hutong, with a wide-open Guangliang entrance gate and carving spirit screen wall. The five rooms next to this entrance was used as reception rooms and the two rooms on the north side of the outer courtyard was the clan school. Inside the second courtyard, beyond the Chuihua gate, covered corridors runs all the way around the courtyard. The five rooms to the north were for his great-grandfather, while the five rooms to the south were for his grandfather. The east wing was a two-row building with the central hall being the family dining hall. Inside the third courtyard, the east wing had portraits of the ancestors for worship. Before the north building is a space where a stage could be put up. The northeast side room is used as a storeroom. In winter all the corridors would be boarded up and flowers would be places inside. In summer, these boards were stored in the storeroom. The south building of this inner courtyard has a north five-room house built adjacent to it, in front of which is a garden with a rockery, a pond and various trees, flowers and grass. To the west of the garden is the kitchen courtyard, toilets and corridor used for carrying food from the kitchen to the dining hall.

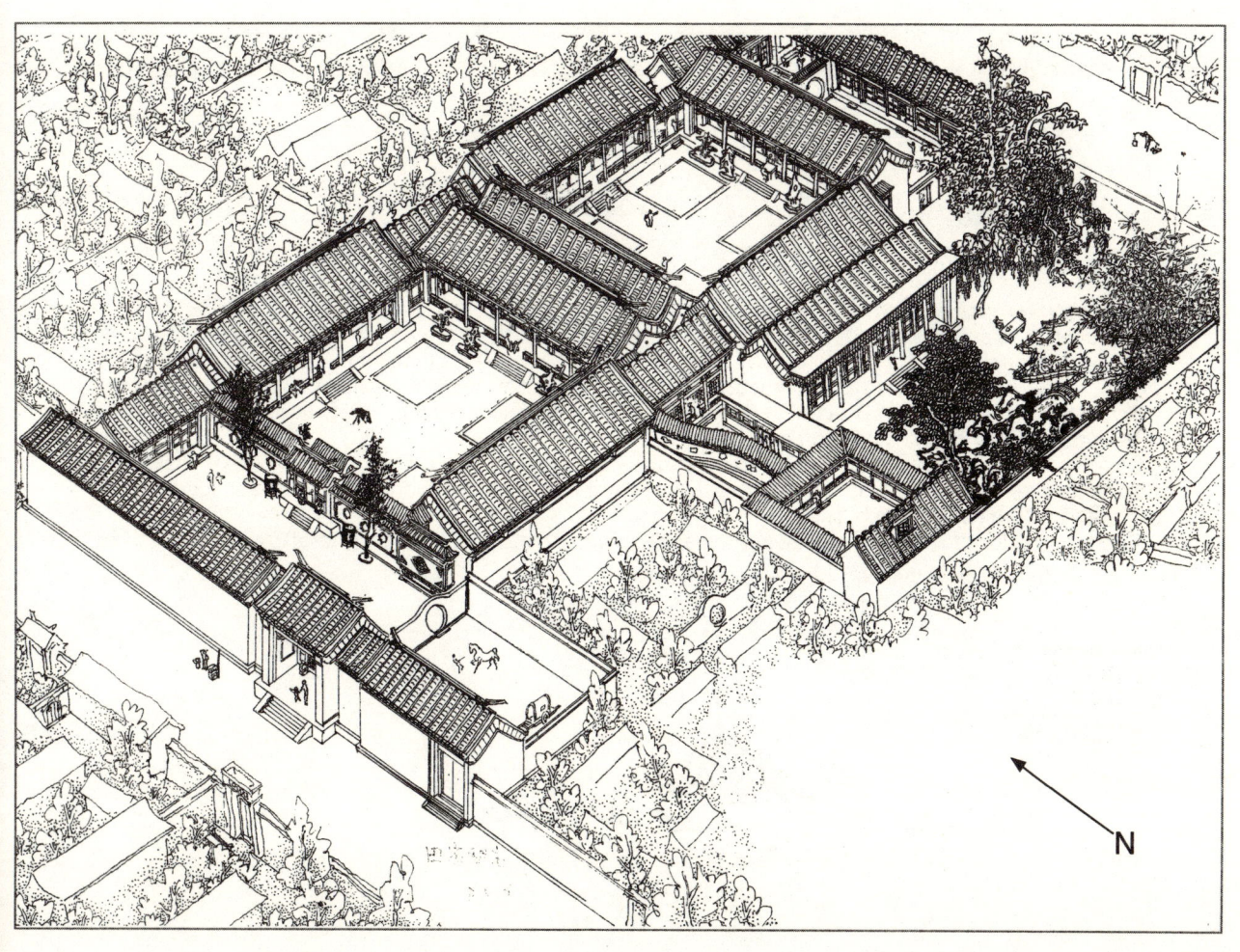

(2003年3月26日绘)

陟山门外观景楼

（西城区陟山门街13号）

听老人讲，陟山门街13号原为清末太监李莲英九姨太太的宅院，后为法国人办的助产士学校。门楼已改为西式大门楼（现存），日本侵略中国时为"八周旅馆"，现已成大杂院。主体建筑还在，有些廊子还保留，此院经友人介绍，并根据他考察的平面图绘出此复原图。

此院为靠北海东门最近最大的一所宅院，全院都有廊子相通，第一进院的廊子与第二进院的廊子不是在一条直线上。

观景楼位置选的太好了，向西可看北海的白塔，向东可观景山。

A Two Story Building with a View

Location:No. 13 Zhishanmenjie in Xicheng District

According to some elders, No. 13 Zhishanmenjie was once the mansion of the ninth concubine of Li Lianying, a eunuch of the late Qing Dynasty (1644–1911), and later it housed a school for midwives run the French. Its gate tower was changed to a western-style one (which is extant). During the Japanese occupation, it housed the "Bazhou Hotel". It is now a compound shared by many households. The main buildings still stand, and some corridors remain.

This is the largest courtyard house close to the east gate of Beihai Park. All the houses inside the courtyard are connected by corridors. The corridors in the first courtyard and those in the second one are not built on the same straight line.

The location for the two-story viewing tower is so good that the White Pagoda of Beihai Park can be seen to the west and the Jingshan Hill to the east.

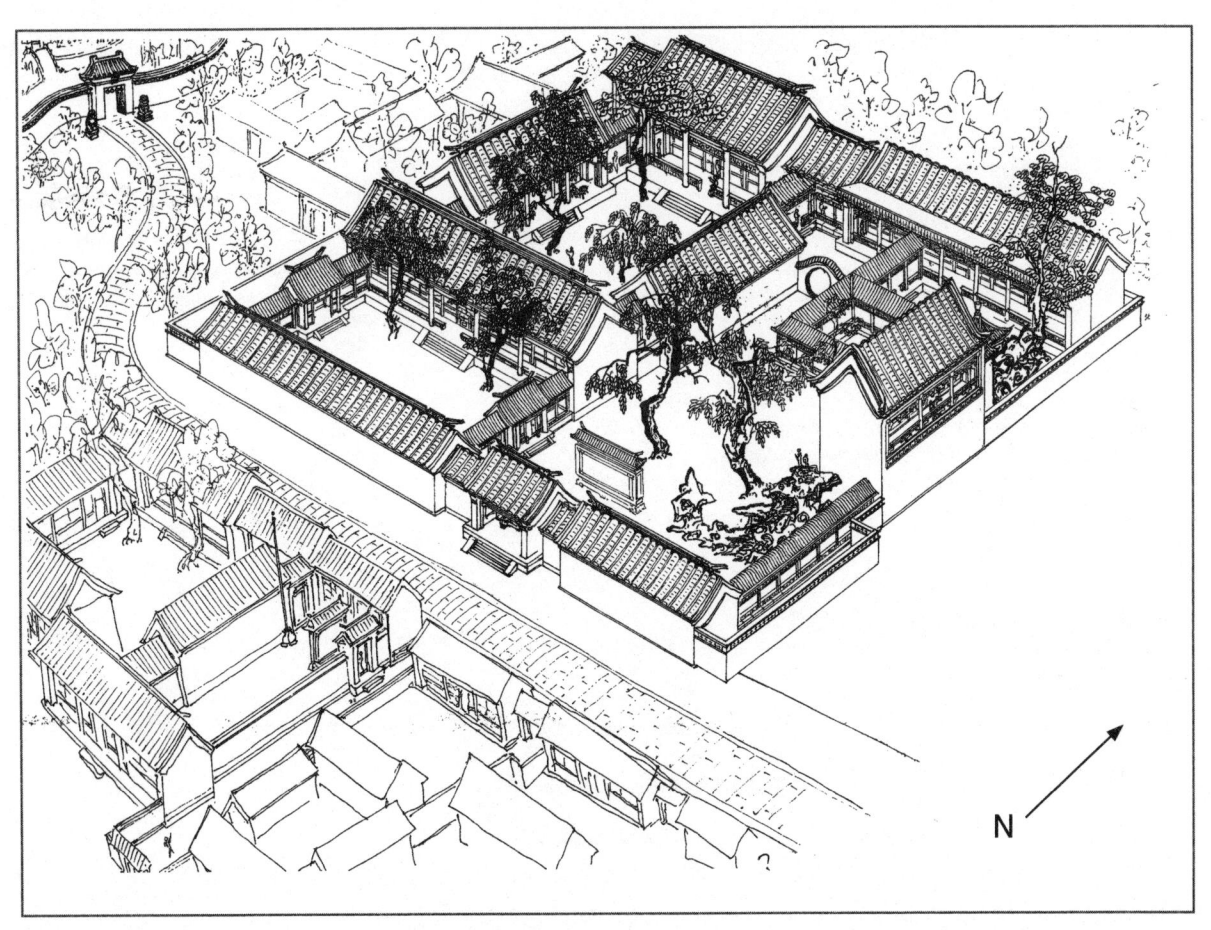

(2003年3月30日绘)

御使衙门院深深
（西城区陟山门街5号）

此处明代为内务府衙门，清代为御使衙门。此院坐北朝南，门前为陟山门街，石板路直通往北海陟山门。据几代世居于此的老人讲，清末四大奇案中的"杨乃武与小白菜"案就是在此做的终审。

此院正殿西头的戗檐砖雕是十几年前后补的，与西房戗檐的精美砖雕相差太远。此院大门两边的拐角廊子比较特殊，尤其它的房脊更是少见，转角处没有蝎子尾，两边做两个 ⸺ 亦很有特色。

An Imperial Magistrates Court

Location:No. 5 Zhishanmenjie in Xicheng District

This was the magistrates court (Yamen) of the Ministry of Internal Affairs in the Ming Dynasty (1368–1644) and that of the Imperial Envoys in the Qing Dynasty (1644–1911). This courtyard house face south and in front of its gate is the Zhishanmen Street where a flagstone path leads to Zhishanmen Gate of Beihai Park. According to the elders whose folks have lived here for several generations, it was here that final judgment was passed for the case "Yang Naiwu and Xiaobaicai", one of four *causes celebre* of the late Qing Dynasty.

The carved brick eaves prop at the west end of the main hall was replaced about a dozen years ago. The replacement is far from the exquisite brick carving on the eaves prop of the west building. The angled corridors on the two sides of entrance gate are very special. Especially their roof ridge: atop each corner there are no scorpion tails, but instead there are two downward pointing "⸺" –most unusual.

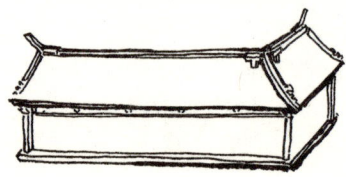

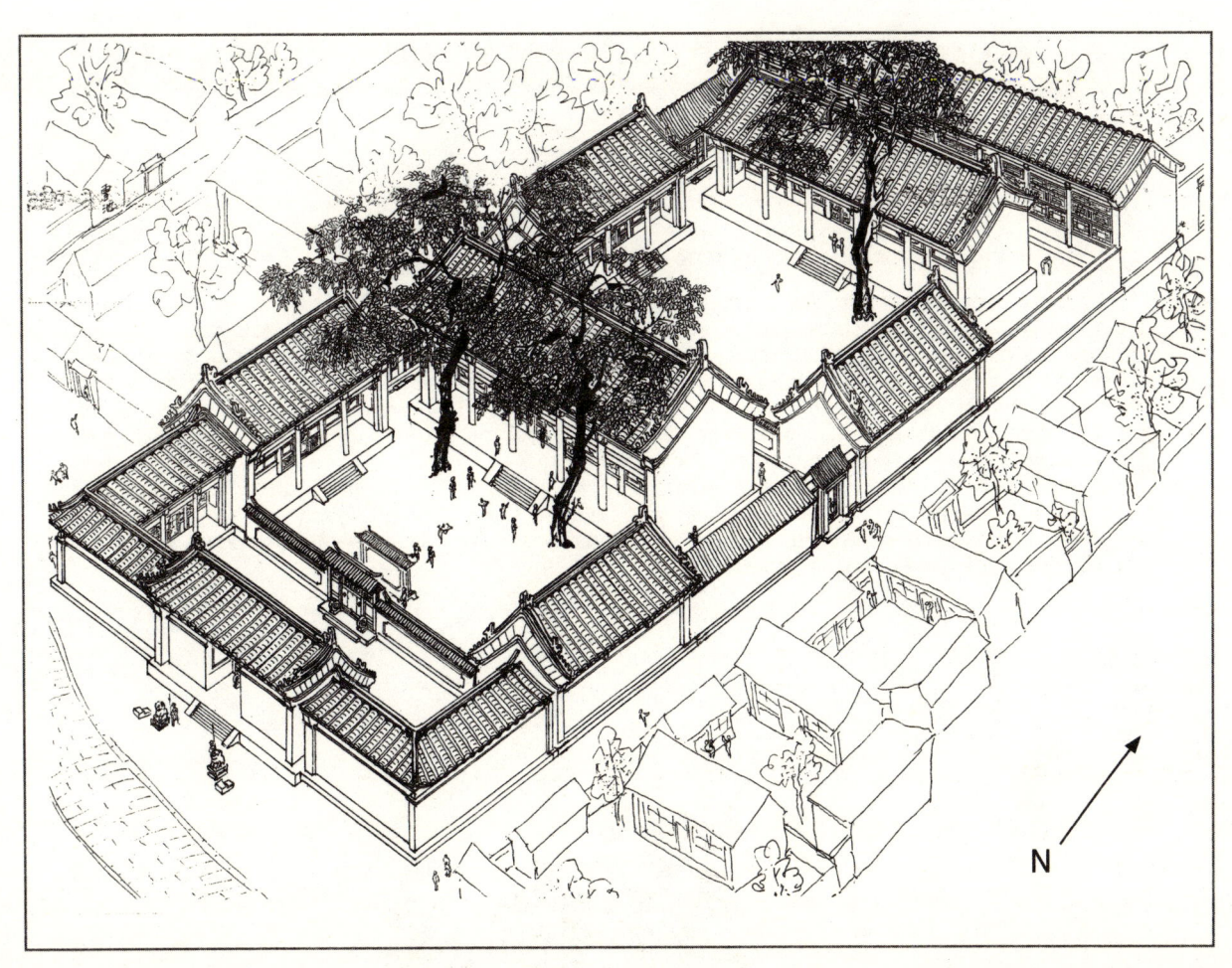

(2003年4月14日绘)

传统外衣现代囊

（东城区建国门内宝盖胡同3号）

这是一座保存很好的宅院，广亮大门，外院为花园，从大门内北侧的小门可穿过外院的小东房，再经过勾连搭的东房，通过北房廊子直到西屋。此院北房与东、西房不对称，但经建筑师的巧妙安排，让人们感到是方正对称的宅院。

此院应是清末民初将洗澡间、舞厅之类的现代化生活方式带入传统四合院的一种建筑，地板、花瓷砖地、洋式窗户及烧火排水气的通道、烟道，都安排得井井有条。

Traditional Exterior - Modern Interior

Location: No. 3 Baogai Hutong, Jianguomennei in Dongcheng District

This is a well-preserved courtyard house with a wide-open Guangliang entrance gate. Its outer courtyard is a garden. One can walk through a small door inside the entrance gate, pass through the small building running along the east side in the outer courtyard, through the double-roofed eastern building, and through the corridor in front of the north building all the way to the west building. The north building is not symmetrical with regard to the east and west wings, but the artful designing by the architect gives people impression it is a square and symmetrical courtyard.

This courtyard is typical of the kind of architecture when modern amenities such as bath room and ballroom were brought into the traditional courtyard house in the late Qing Dynasty and early Republican period. The floor was paved with ceramic tiles with floral pattern. The western-style windows, plumbing, and chimney vents were arranged in perfect order.

(2003年4月30日绘)

春松小院南北居

（东城区建国门内春松胡同6号）

此院在南北走向的春松胡同中，坐东朝西，小洋门楼。小院中只有南、北各三间房，东面为平顶厨房。房屋结构为硬山搁檩，西式门窗。

North and South Wings

Location:No. 6 Qingsong Hutong, Jianguomennei in Dongcheng District
This courtyard house is located on the north-south running Qingsong Hutong. The entrance gate facing west is western-style. Inside the courtyard, there are three-room buildings on the north and south sides. On the east side is the flat-roofed kitchen. The buildings has flush gables, with eaves resting on walls, and western-style doors and windows.

(2003年5月2日绘)

| 中西结合小巧院 |

（东城区建国门内盛芳胡同3号）

此院门前胡同很宽，有很多树，颇有些郊野的味道。院门坐北朝南，西式门楼在东南。进门后，经宽宽的门道在室内向西一转弯，走出屋子北门，进入外院。二门上有一弧形铁花门饰，有一门灯。东、西房为西式硬山搁檩式，有砖雕的西式门窗；北房为合瓦，带拍子。此院虽然很小，在北京民居中却是很有特色的一例。据房主讲，戏剧大师梅兰芳曾在此院居住过。

East-West Fusion

Location:No. 3 Shengfang Hutong, Jianguomennei in Dongcheng District
　The hutong before this courtyard house is very wide and lined with many trees, creating a suburban atmosphere. The western-style gate tower of this courtyard, facing south, is at its southeast corner. Upon entering the wide gatehouse, turning westwards in it, one walks out of its north door and into the outer courtyard. Over the second gate there is an ornamental iron arc on which there is a lamp. The west and east wings are western-style, with flat roofs and western-style doors and windows decorated with brick carving. The roof of the north house is covered with furrowed tiles. This courtyard is very small, but it is characteristic among folk dwellings in Beijing. According to the owner, Mei Lanfang, a master of Peking Opera, once lived here.

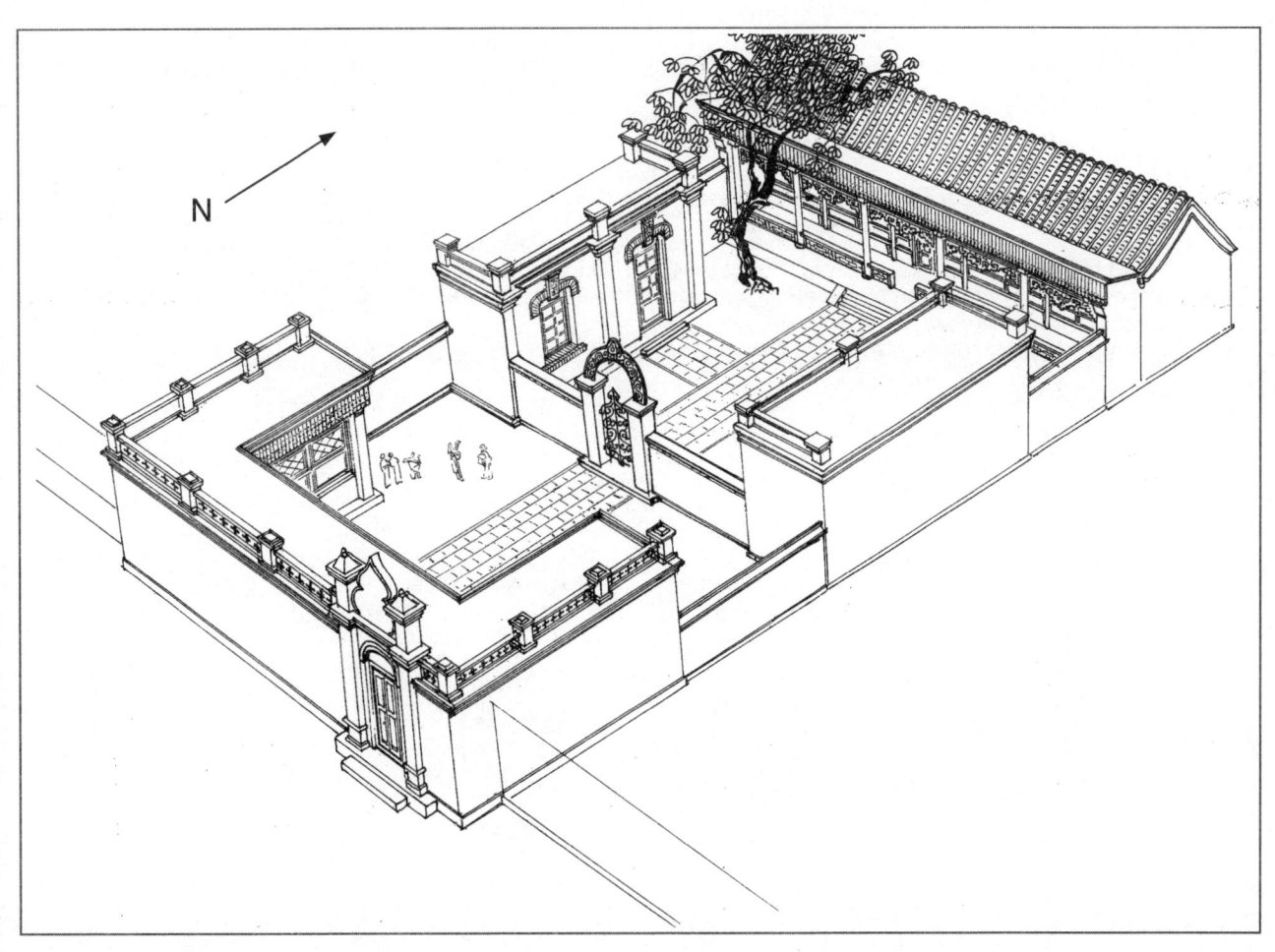

(2003年5月6日绘)

[庙之西界不开门]

（东城区南池子大街普渡寺西巷35号）

按当地的民俗，庙的西面宅院不能开正对着庙的门，所以原来35号的门开在普渡寺庙基高台之南。

注：图中的院门是按最初的样式画的。

No Gates to Face a Temple from the West

Location:No. 35 Pudusi Xixiang, Nanchizi Dajie in Dongcheng District
According to the local folk custom, the gate of any courtyard neighboring the west side of a temple cannot face toward the temple. Therefore, the former gate of the No. 35 was built to the south of the raised foundation of Pudu Temple.
Note: The gate of the courtyard was sketched according to the original pattern.

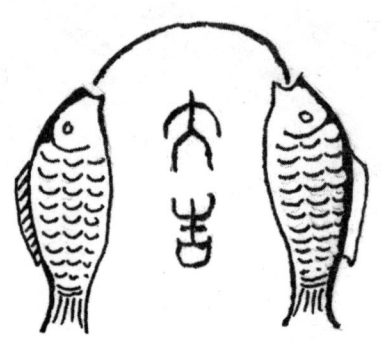

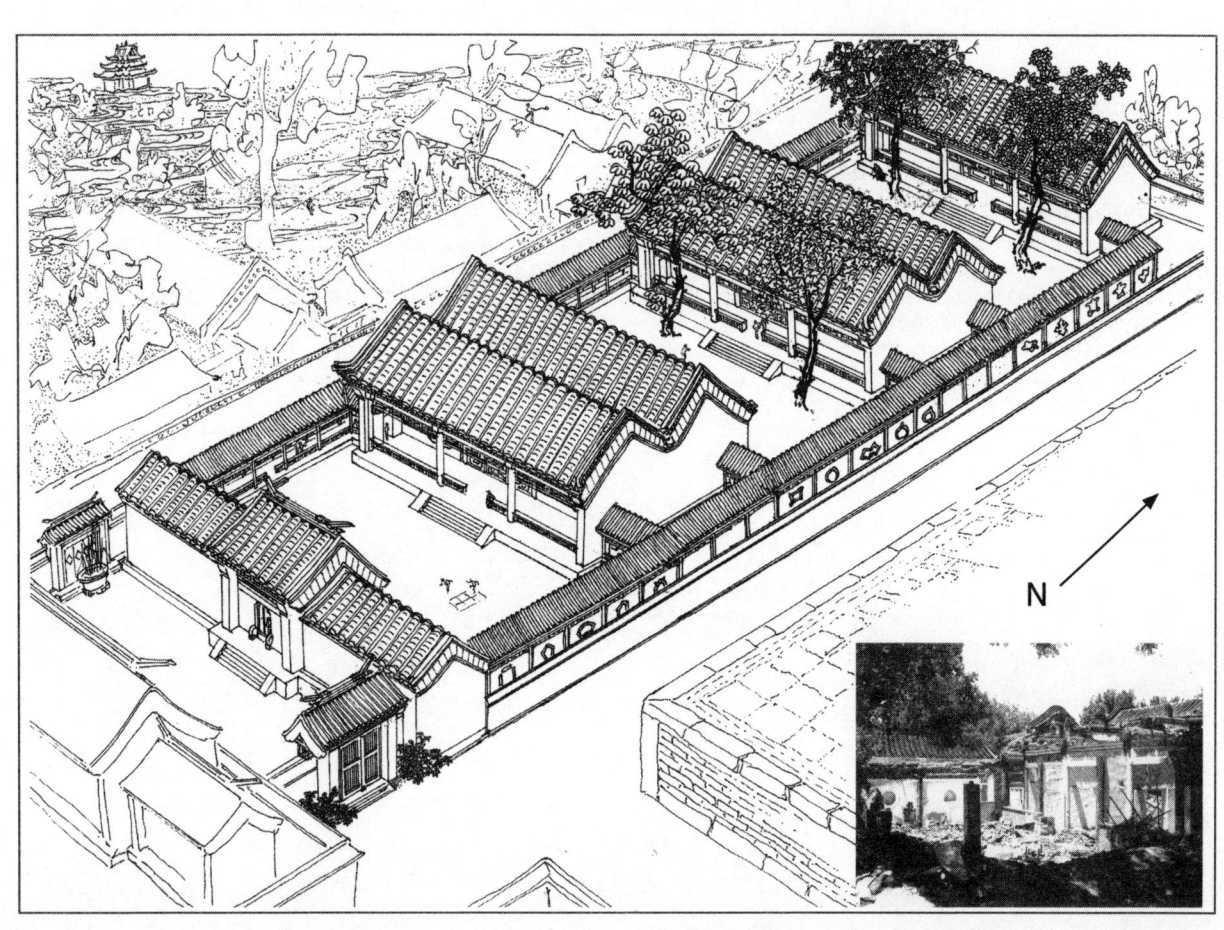

(2003年5月9日绘)

亲睹先辈扩宅院

（东城区南池子大街68号）

此院在南池子路东的一个小分岔内，坐南朝北。房主王姓，祖上在安徽凤阳做官，民国时期做买卖。其后人现年91岁，少年时他亲眼看到了先辈们首先扩建了80号院，后又扩建了78号院。

由此可以说明，北京的四合院不一定都是整整齐齐的方正之院，有钱了可以扩建，败家分家又可以切割。北京民居的变化与每个家庭命运有着密切的关系。

Witness to Courtyard Expansion

Location:No. 68 Nanchizi Dajie in Dongcheng District

This courtyard, facing south, is located in a tiny branch lane running east off Nanchizi Dajie. Its master, aged 91, is surnamed Wang. Some of his ancestors had been officials in Fengyang, Anhui Province and did business in the Republican period (1912–1949). He saw with his own eyes the expansion first of No. 80 and then No. 78 during his childhood.

This shows that courtyards in Beijing are not all regular squares. When wealthy, one can expand, while in decline one can divide the house. Changes in Beijing's courtyards are closely linked with the changing fortunes of every household.

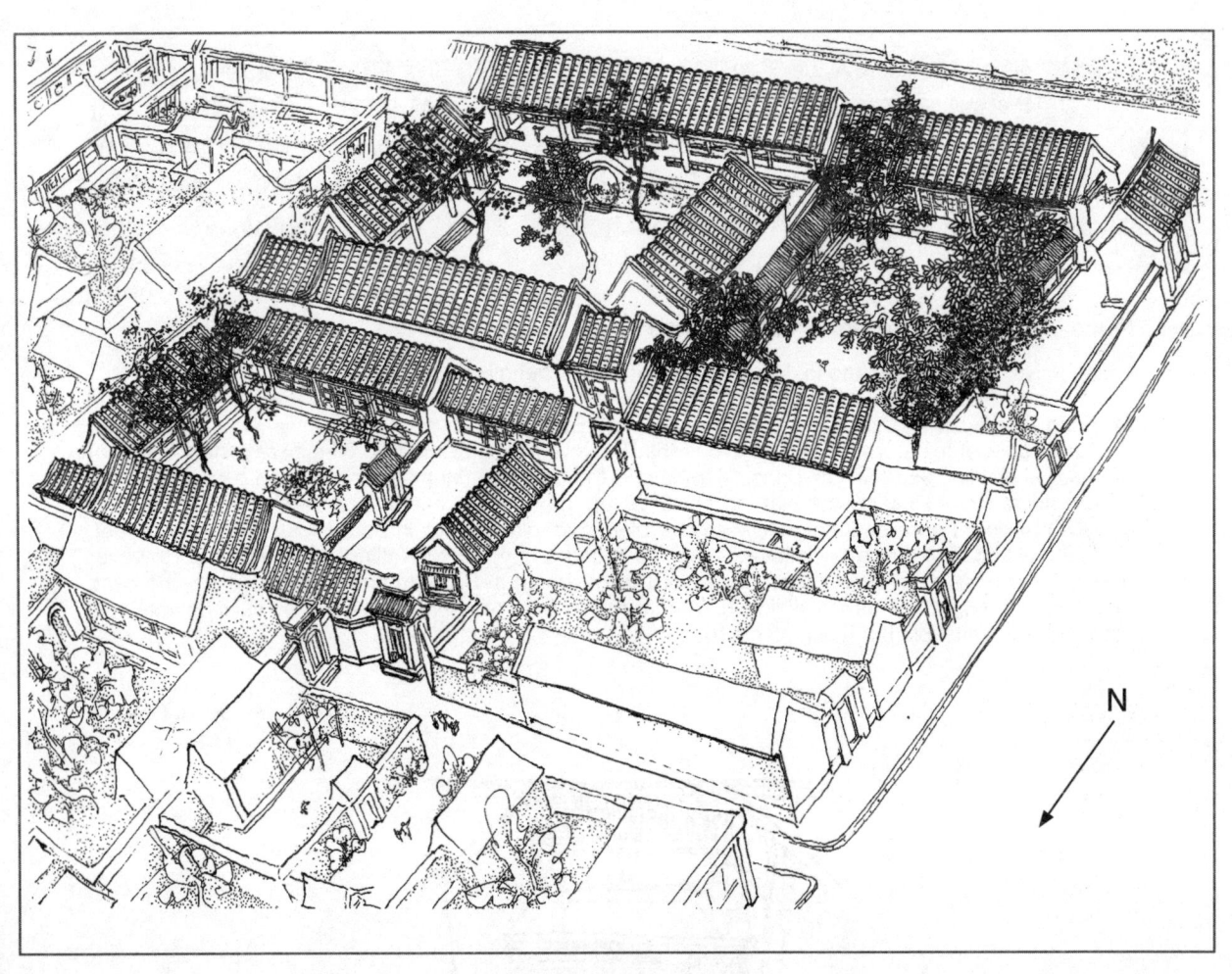

(2003年5月12日绘)

房顶烟道烧暖炕

（东城区南池子大街灯笼库胡同9号）

此院为祖籍山东的宋显庭的父亲在20世纪30年代修建。此种庭院的形制在北京比较少见。

此院最特殊是两厢房脊都戗接于正房脊上，使正房与两厢的室内空间连接贯通，室内用炕取暖，在北京民居中确属少见。我在韩国古建筑中见过几处两厢脊戗接正房的例子，都是比较正规的厅堂建筑。似乎山东民居中亦不见此式样，只有在四川、云南民居中有"一颗印"的封闭式院落，东西南北房围成一圈，犹如印章，其转角处，两脊相交，也不似灯笼库的式样．它建于20世纪30年代，应属模仿，但又不规范。

——徐苹芳

Flues in the Roof Bring Heat from the *Kang*

Location: No. 9 Denglong Hutong, Nanchizi Dajie in Dongcheng District

This courtyard house was built in the 1930s by Song Xianting's father whose ancestral home was in Shandong. The layout of this courtyard is rarely seen in Beijing.

The most special feature of this courtyard is that the roof ridges of the two wings are joined to that of the principal building and that the principal wing and the two side wings are connected each other. The house is heated with kang (a brick plat form bed heated from below), in a manner rarely seen among folk houses in Beijing. I once saw a house with this plan in an old building in South Korea – a very proper, classical building. This design I believe cannot be found among folk dwellings in Shandong. However there is what is called a seal-shaped courtyard to be found in Sichuan and Yunnan. There the east, west, south and north wings are all linked, so that the exterior resembles a seal. This building was built in the 1930s in imitation, but is not standard.

——By Xu Pingfang

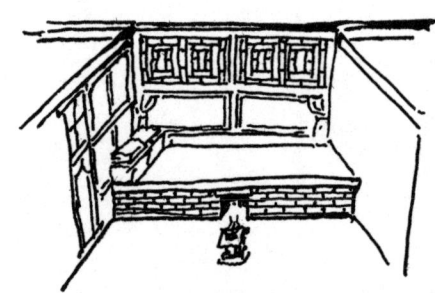

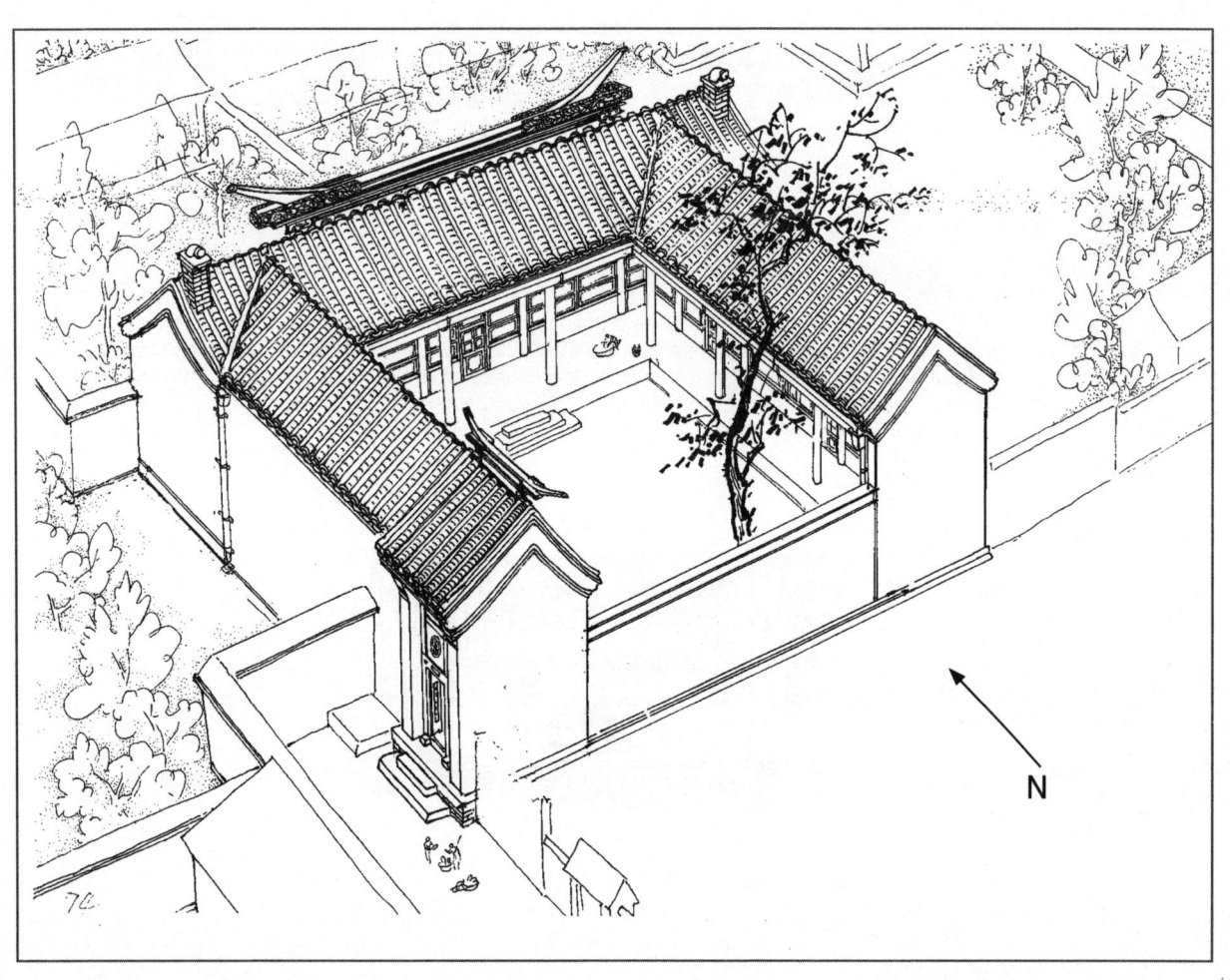

(2003年5月11日绘)

[清洁地炉古有之]

(东城区南竹杆胡同82号)

　　这里的二门不是垂花门，后在礼士胡同7号和灯草胡同36号又见了几个这种二门，虽然都残破了，但将几个完好的局部组合起来，画成此图之二门。

　　此院屋顶也有烟道，但这烟道不应是火炕的，应是地炉的，没找到生火口，这种地炉颐和园还有。据说解放后此院为文化名人夏衍先生的住宅。

Floor Heating from Below

Location:No. 82 Nanzhugan Hutong in Dongcheng District
The second gate of the courtyard house is not a *Chuihua* gate. I had seen several gates of this kind in other places. Though dilapidated, I sketched this kind of gate by combining their well preserved parts.
　　Inside the roof of the buildings in the courtyard there are chimney flues. But this chimney flue do not draw heat from *kang*, but from burners under the floor. I could not find the location of the burners. This style of heating can be seen in the Summer Palace. It is said that after liberation this courtyard was the house of Xia Yan, a famous writer.

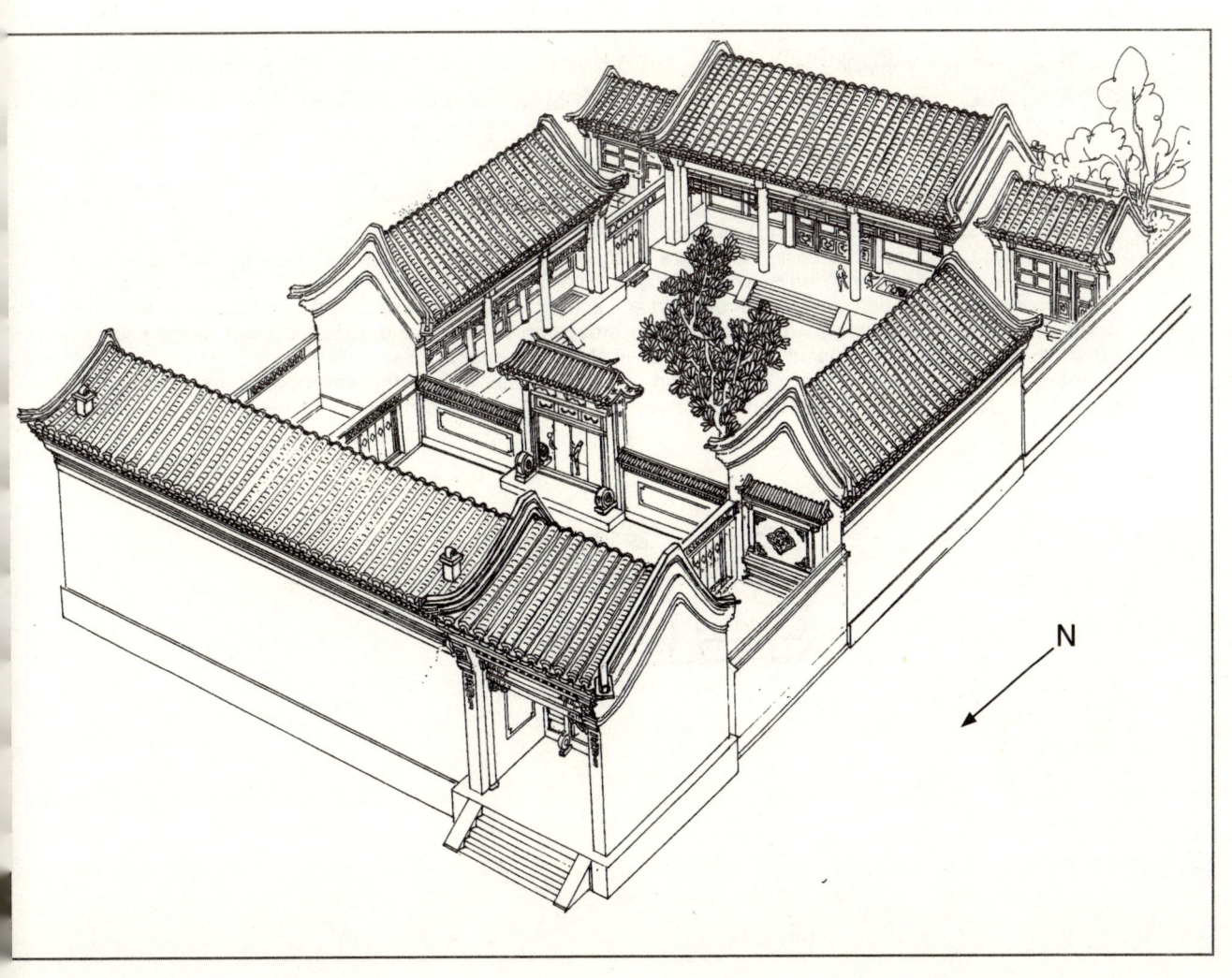

(2003年5月16日绘)

宅基不正分割巧

（东城区灯草胡同36号）

　　此院为东西街巷坐南朝北的院子，现有的地界很难做成门在西北角的四合院。设计者将此地基划分成两个矩型，形成一个北房独院及另一个三合院，并将南房北移，形成南北房，变成别具一格的幽静小院。

　　凸显出此院虽然是以南为上，但由于南房北移，南房又变成了明亮的北房，留出了一个室外活动的空间。

An Irregular Plot Cleverly Used

Location:No. 36 Dengcai Hutong in Dongcheng District
This courtyard located on a east-west lane opens onto the north. Given the irregular plot, it was impossible to build its gate at the northwest corner. The designer divided the plot into two rectangles, creating one courtyard with single north building and another courtyard surrounded by buildings on three sides. The street front building was moved northwards, with the north and south buildings facing each other. Thus a small quiet courtyard with unique style came into being.
　　Although this courtyard has a principle wing facing north, its south-facing wing was moved northwards and became a bright and airy wing, with plenty of space in front for outdoor activities.

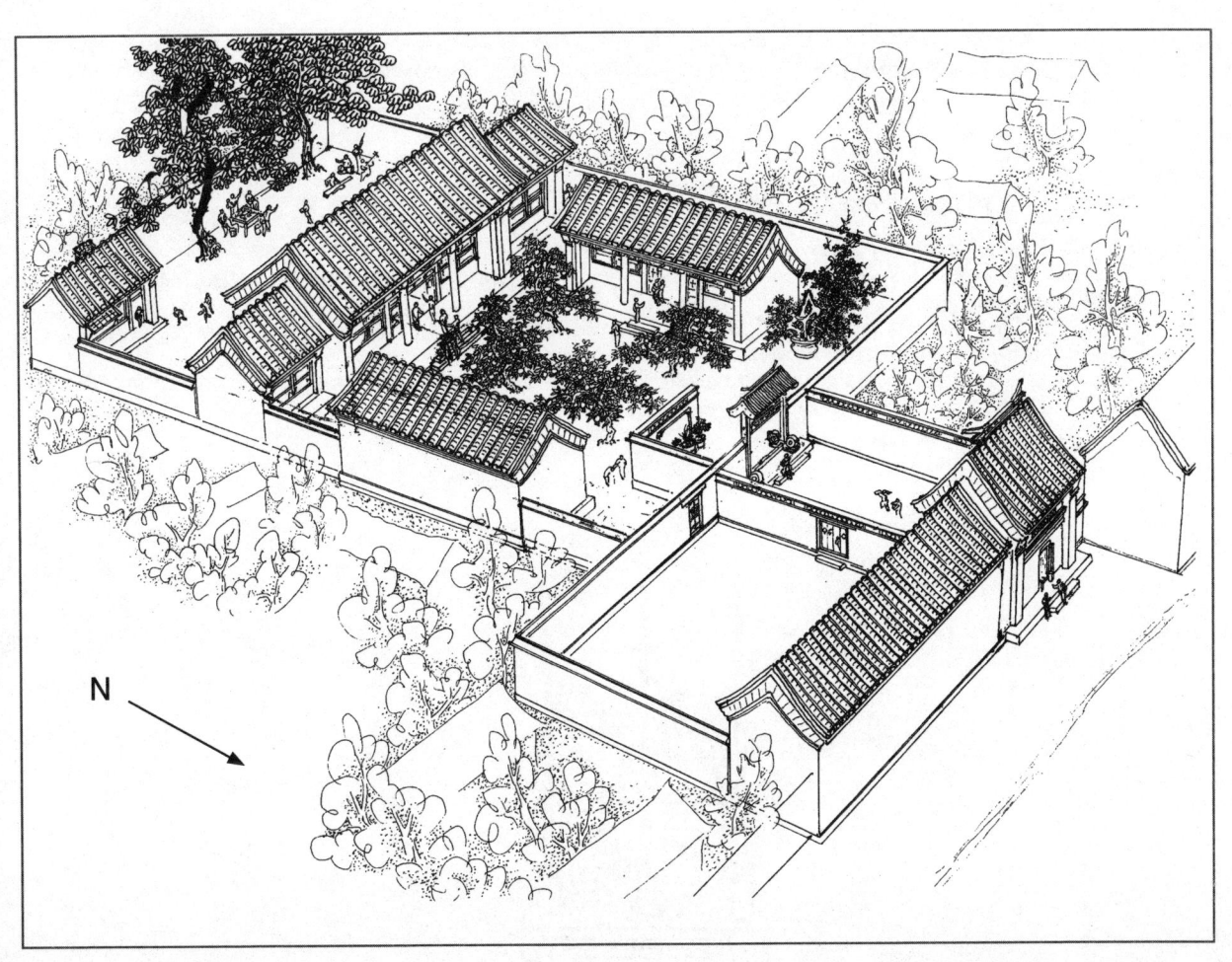

(2003年5月18日绘)

高耸商铺留国魂

（东城区朝阳门内南小街）

这里原是朝阳门内南小街北口坐西朝东的一座高耸的商店——宏兴号。

清末民初，西洋建筑风格融入了中国的民居中，民房、门楼、商铺，都有它们的影子，又都没有离开中国的元素。

此商铺基本是西式建筑，房顶有点中国的筒瓦。这种门面房是中西合璧的杰作。

A Scholar Tree behind the Tall Shop

Location: Chaoyangmennei Nanxiaojie, Dongcheng District

This was originally a towering shop called Hongxing Hao. It faces east at the north end of Nanxiaojie, Chaoyangmennei.

In the late Qing Dynasty (1644-1911) and the early Republican period (1912-1949), some features of western architecture were taken up in houses and shops etc.

This shop is basically a western-style building, but with some semi-cylindrical Chinese tiles on the roof. It is a masterpiece in the fusion of Chinese and western styles.

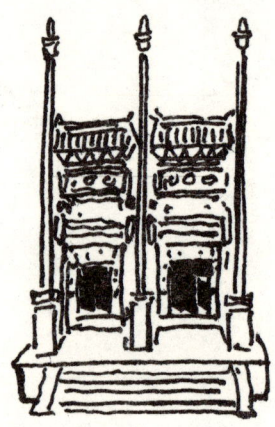

(2003年5月21日绘)

倒座北屋是正房

（东城区大菊胡同32号）

唐宅。此院坐南朝北，东院为正宅，五间北房为清水脊，其余为灰瓦房。西边二间比原建房高出约60厘米，并向后推了30厘米，当是后改建。西边这两间有后窗，可进阳光。

西院有北房三间，东西房各一间，西院原有大桑树，东院有枣树。此院门为三层砖的如意门，栏板式花卉雕砖。有一层连珠混，再下为万字不到头的檐板，门楼内有懒凳，上有天花板，可存物，影壁和东西屏门保存尚好，屏门上还有彩画。

Street-side Wing as the Main Wing

Location:No. 32 Daju Hutong, Dongcheng District

This is the Tang's Mansion, whose entrances faces north. The eastern part is the main courtyard. The north wing roof has a brick ridge along the top, the others have only tiles. The two western end rooms of the south wing are set back and about 60 cm taller than the other rooms on the south side. This was probably a later conversion. Thee two western rooms also have windows on the back side to let in light.

The western courtyard has three rooms in the north and one room in the east and west respectively. There had been a mulberry tree here and a jujube tree in the east courtyard. The gate into the western courtyard is decorated with carved brickwork, decorated with a pattern of strings of pearls and interlocked, never-ending swastikas. There are benches in the gatehouse with a ceiling above which one can store articles. The spirit screen wall and the eastern and western screen doors are still well preserved. There are also colorful paintings on the screen doors.

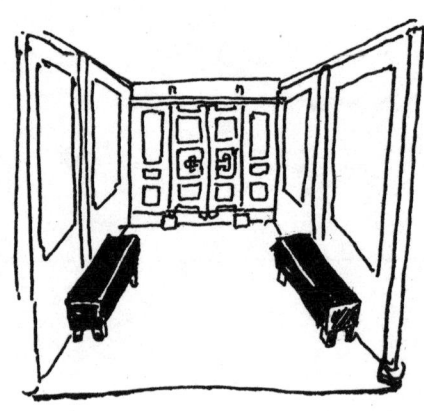

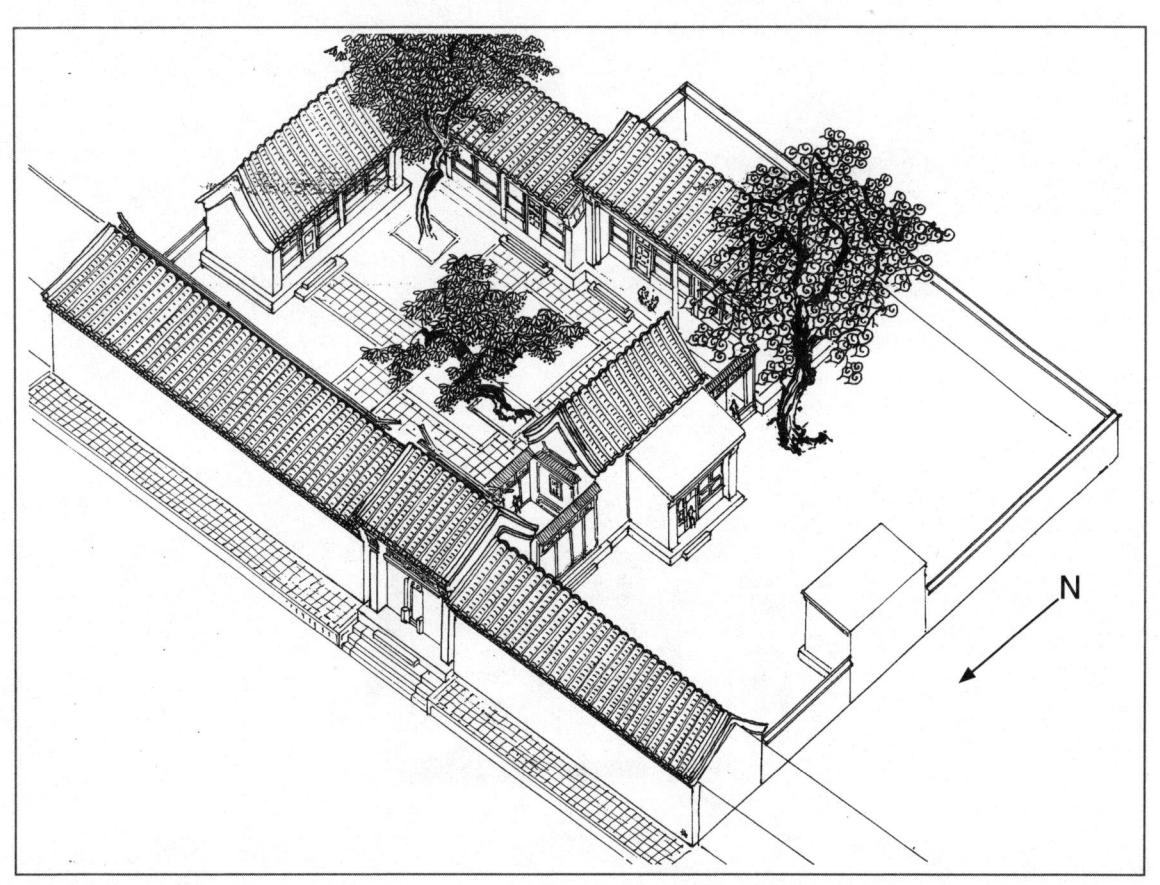

(2003年5月28日绘)

香河中医置京产

（崇文区花市上二条37号）

张宅，房主为香河人，祖上世代行医，做过太医，此院是其爷爷在京买的产业。此宅坐北朝南，门楼为清水脊，另四间倒座房为合瓦，北房为带地下室的洋房。台阶上为整扇的玻璃门和窗，房顶原有女儿墙。从东侧通道上五层台阶进小门转入后院，后院有栏杆护着通向地下室的梯道。后院最西为洗澡间，北房最西为厨房，其东为餐厅，再东为工人住房。

A Country Doctor's Beijing Mansion

Location: No. 37 Shang'ertiao, Huashi, Chongwen District

This is a mansion of the Zhang family, who came from Xianghe County, and have been doctors for generations. This mansion was bought by the grandfather in Beijing. It faces south. Its gatehouse features plain ridge and the four rooms opposite to the main room have closed tiles. The northern house is of foreign style with a basement. The west end of the rear building is a bath house. The kitchen is in the west end of the main house and the dining room next to it. The living quarters of the workers is to the east of the dining room.

(2003年5月30日绘)

小巧玲珑寸土金

（崇文区前门外大江胡同21号）

前门外，寸土寸金，房屋布置密集，此院落是大江胡同、小江胡同内经常见到的建筑，外观为居民院，实为小作坊，或是某种商品批发、做大买卖的院落。

此院一进门向左转，还能见到东房房山与门北墙间横着一块原来是字号的匾板。

Where Land is the Price of Gold

Location:No. 21 Dajiang Hutong, Outside Qianmen Gate, Chongwen District
Houses are densely packed outside Qianmen Gate. Courtyards of this kind are often seen in the Dajiang Hutong and Xiaojiang Hutong. They look like residential courtyards from outside but are in fact small workshops or wholesale distributors of some kind or deal in some business.
 A business plaque can be seen if one turns left after entering the courtyard.

(2002年8月17日绘)

魏忠贤宅伴冰窖

(西城区北海东门园景胡同4号~14号)

这个院落据说是明朝太监魏忠贤的宅子，从挑檐看风格一致，清水脊的做法也差不多。

此宅之前与陟山门街5号御使衙门相连，这院的西墙外就是古冰窖，与北海、景山等景色连成一片。

A Eunuch's House near an Ice House

Location:No. 4-No.14, Yuanjing Hutong, outside Beihai East Gate, Xicheng District

These courtyards are said to have been the residence of Wei Zhongxian, a eunuch of the Ming Dynasty (1368-1644).

In the past, it was connected with the Imperial Magistrates Court, or Yamen, at No. 5 Zhishanmenjie. Outside the west wall of this courtyard is an ancient ice house. It is close to scenic Beihai and Jingshan.

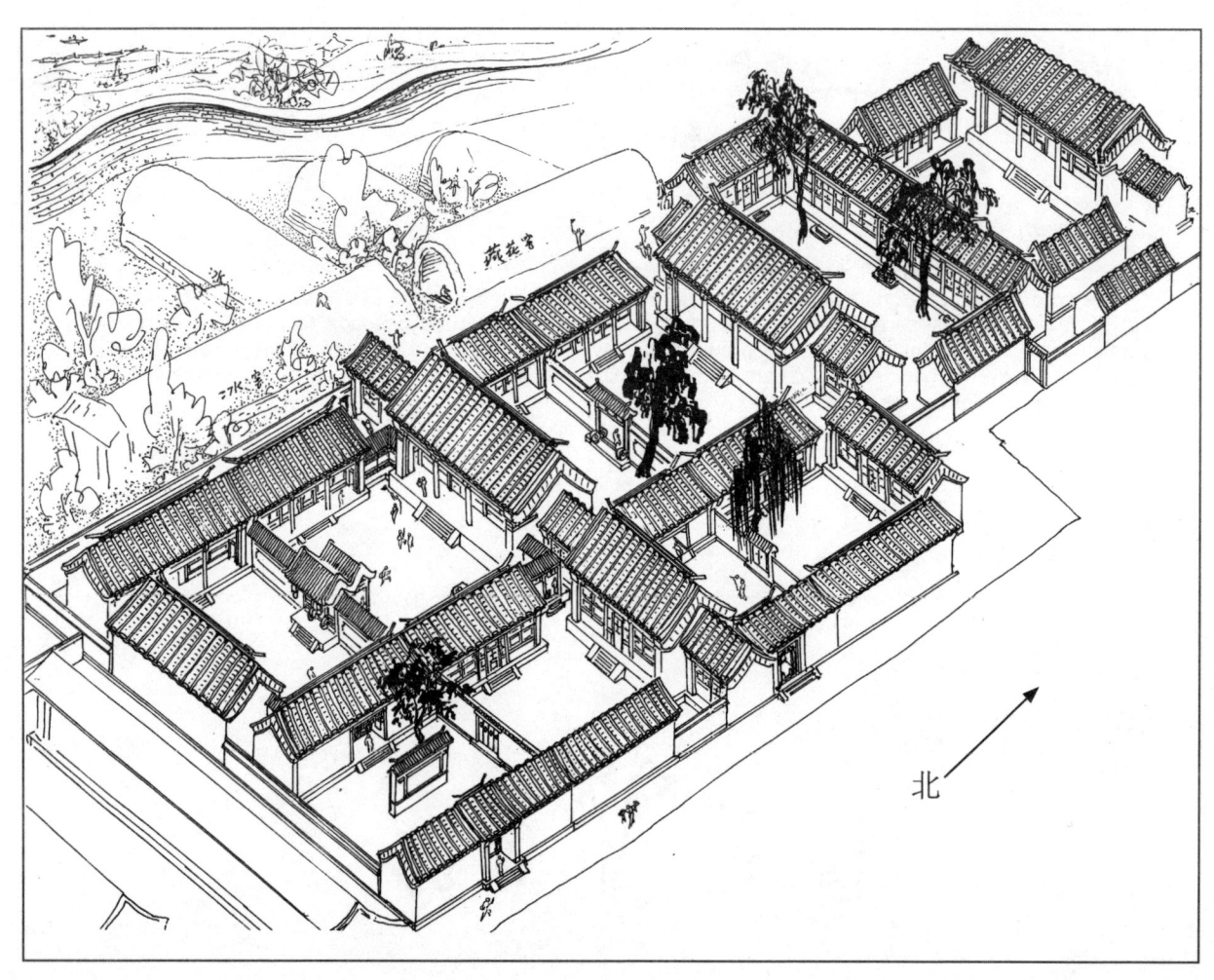

(2003年6月1日绘)

影壁横档外客院

（东城区横街28号）

此院坐东朝西，门楼为高大如意门，额为栏板式，下为三角形纹饰，门簪为阳纹篆字。此院为并连四合院，进院后，一东西向的大影壁将第一层院与通道隔开。迎大门沿通道在二进院门口是一垂花门，北面沿正房檐下有一小花门，里院为完整的四合院，两院间为勾连搭东西房，大门之南尚有两间车房，小院内还有两间平房。

A Screen to Hide the Guest Courtyard

Location:No. 28 Hengjie Street, Dongcheng District
The gate of this mansion faces west. The gatehouse is a high Ruyi Gate. It consists of two courtyards. A big screen wall separates the first courtyard from the connecting passage to the inner courtyard, which is a complete quadrangle. There buildings between the east and west courtyards are built back-to-back. There is a garage for two cars to the south of the main gate and there are two rooms with a flat roof in the smaller courtyard behind.

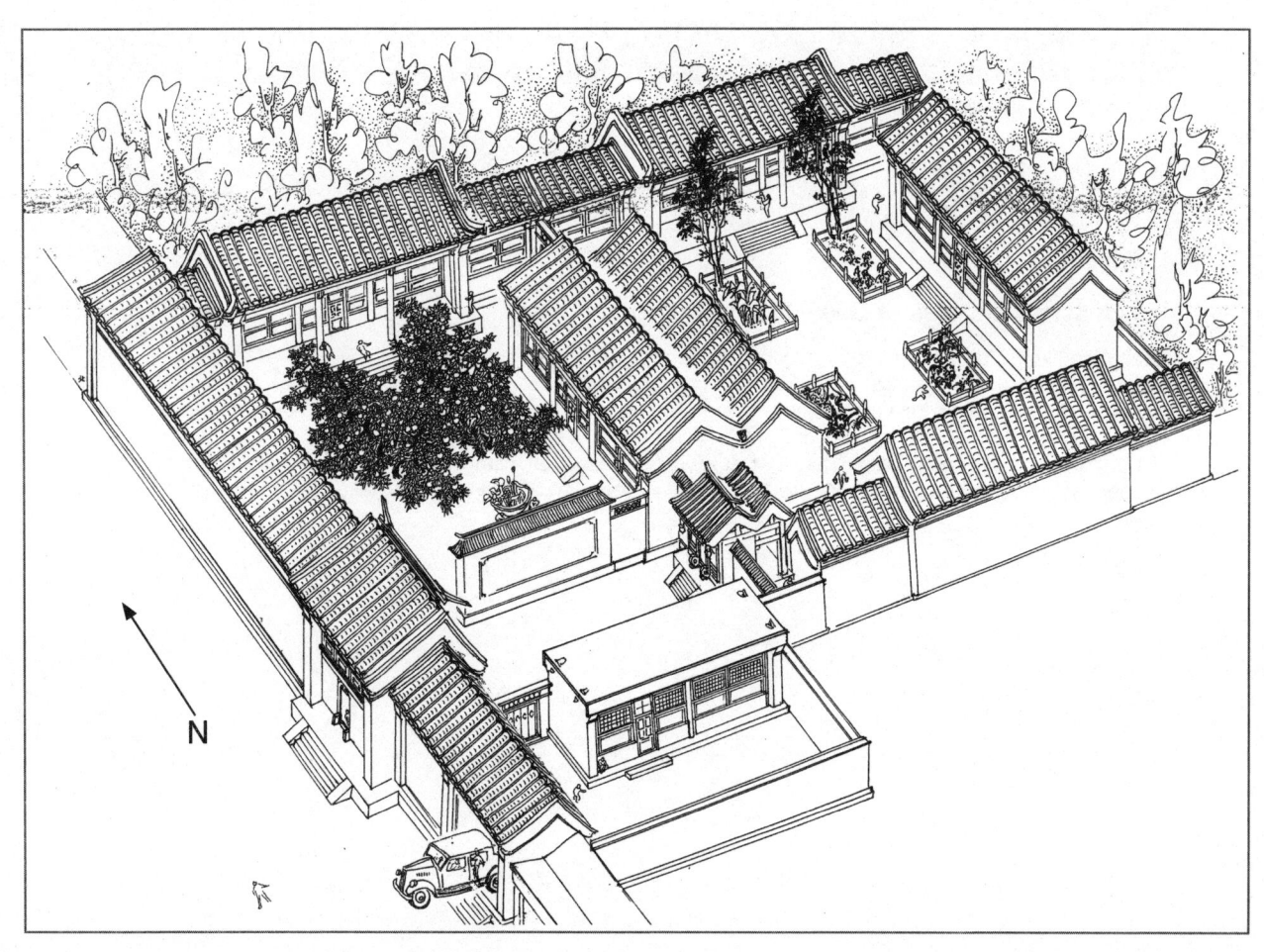

(2003年6月13日绘)

影壁还能做耳房

（东城区朝阳门内北小街33号）

据老居民讲，此院为管理禄米、海运、东门三个仓的官员之家，人称"仓高家"，原来从东四七条到东四六条之间的这一片院落全是高家的。现存影壁，四合院只是宅院的一部分，主要建筑在西边，那里原有高大的假山、花园，还有鹿苑。

此宅坐西朝东，居民说门楼原为如意门楼，现存的影壁在北京民居中是较特殊的一例，其顶为精美砖雕栏板式，额为单轴辘钱花瓦，两边有四方砖雕花饰，正中为大福字。此影壁最特殊的是其背后为一个两间平房与影壁连为一整体，此房为守卫人员的值房，影壁的西侧尚留有游廊的遗迹。进二门过厅，南房为一凉亭。

Spirit Screen Doubles as Guard Room Wall

Location:No. 33 Beixiaojie Street, Chaoyangmennei, Dongcheng District

According to the old residents, this mansion belonged to an official in charge of the three great storehouses Lumicang, Haiyuncang and Dongmencang. The existing screen wall and quadrangle are only part of the mansion. The major buildings are found in the west.

The mansion gate faces east. The sprit screen opposite the main gate is unusual among those in the residential houses in Beijing. There are two guard rooms behind the screen wall.

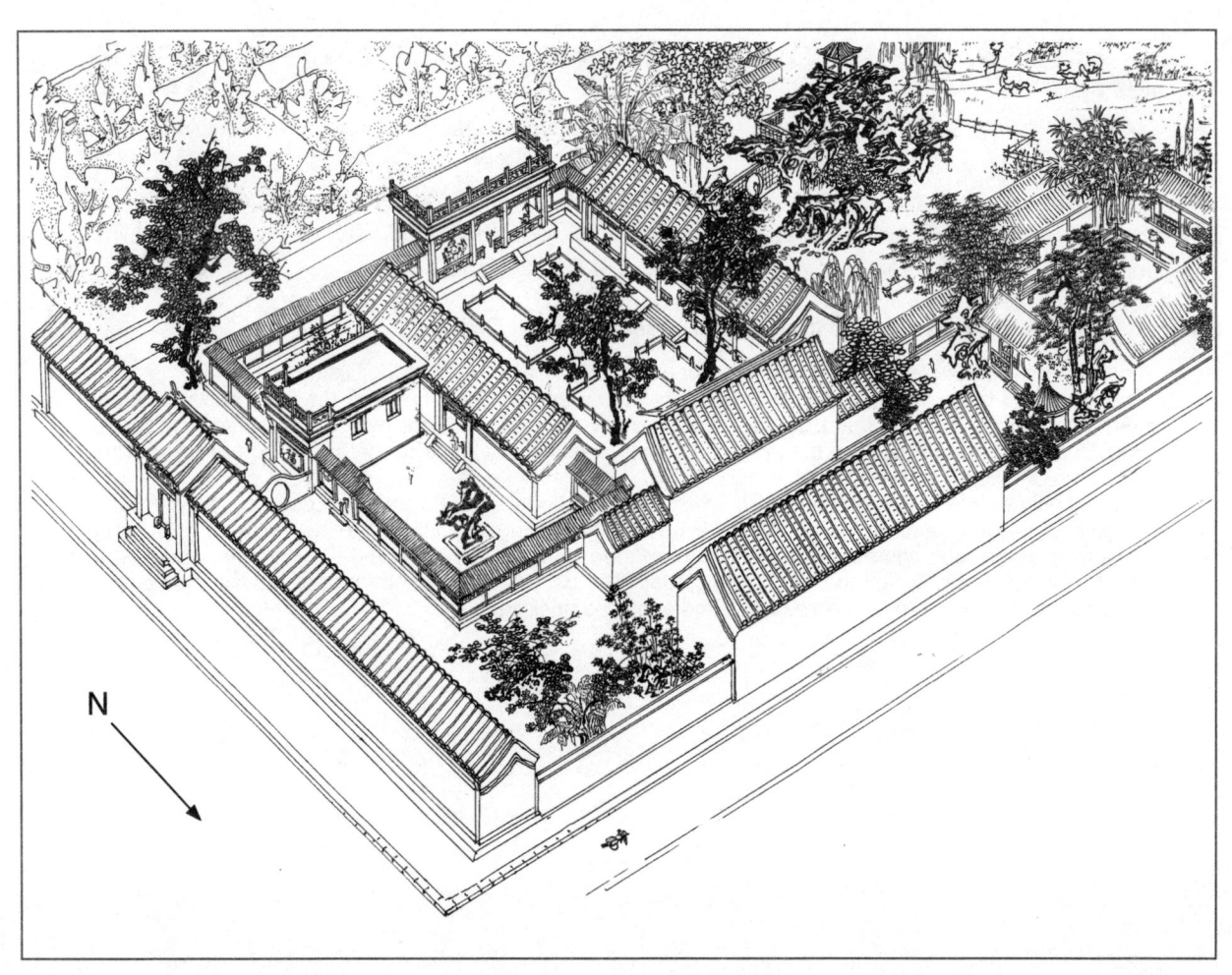

(2003年6月19日绘)

慈禧赏赐重建宅

（东城区大菊胡同29号、东直门内大街194号）

房主人是满族，祖上是武官，正红旗。其祖爷被八国联军杀害在南苑，西太后回京后给了一笔抚恤金，重修了此院。

此院坐北朝南，如意门开在东南角。从影壁前左转，进绿色四扇屏门，三间倒座房当为办公用。进入二门，迎面三间清水脊带拍子的北房为客厅，东、西各有两间小平房。东侧廊子转弯由小廊进入第三进院，此院为主人居室。向东进月亮门的侧院为子女们的住房，再东侧有小门可进入花园（此图将花园画小了）。花园中有五间北房，从其两侧有路可通向后院。后院有后门可通东直门内大街，门可进大车。此院为佣人院，院中放车马，东墙边上有马厩。全院的房都是清水脊，并有精美砖雕尚存。

A House Rebuilt with Money from the Empress Dowager Cixi

Location: No. 29 Daju Hutong and No. 194 Dongzhimennei Dajie, Dongcheng District

The master of this mansion is Manchu. His ancestors were military officials of the Plain Red Banner. A great-grandfather was killed by the allied expeditionary force of the eight western powers at Nanyuan. The Empress Dowager Cixi gave the family a pension in compensation after her returning to Beijing. This was used for rebuilding this mansion.

The mansion's main gate faces south, with the Ruyi Gate at the southeast corner. Three rooms alongside the four-panel screen door were used for handling official business. The master's living quarters is in the next courtyard. Children's rooms are through the moon gate in the side yard to the east, further to east of which there is also a garden. The backyard was used for servants. All the houses in the mansion have roofs with plain ridges and exquisite brick carving.

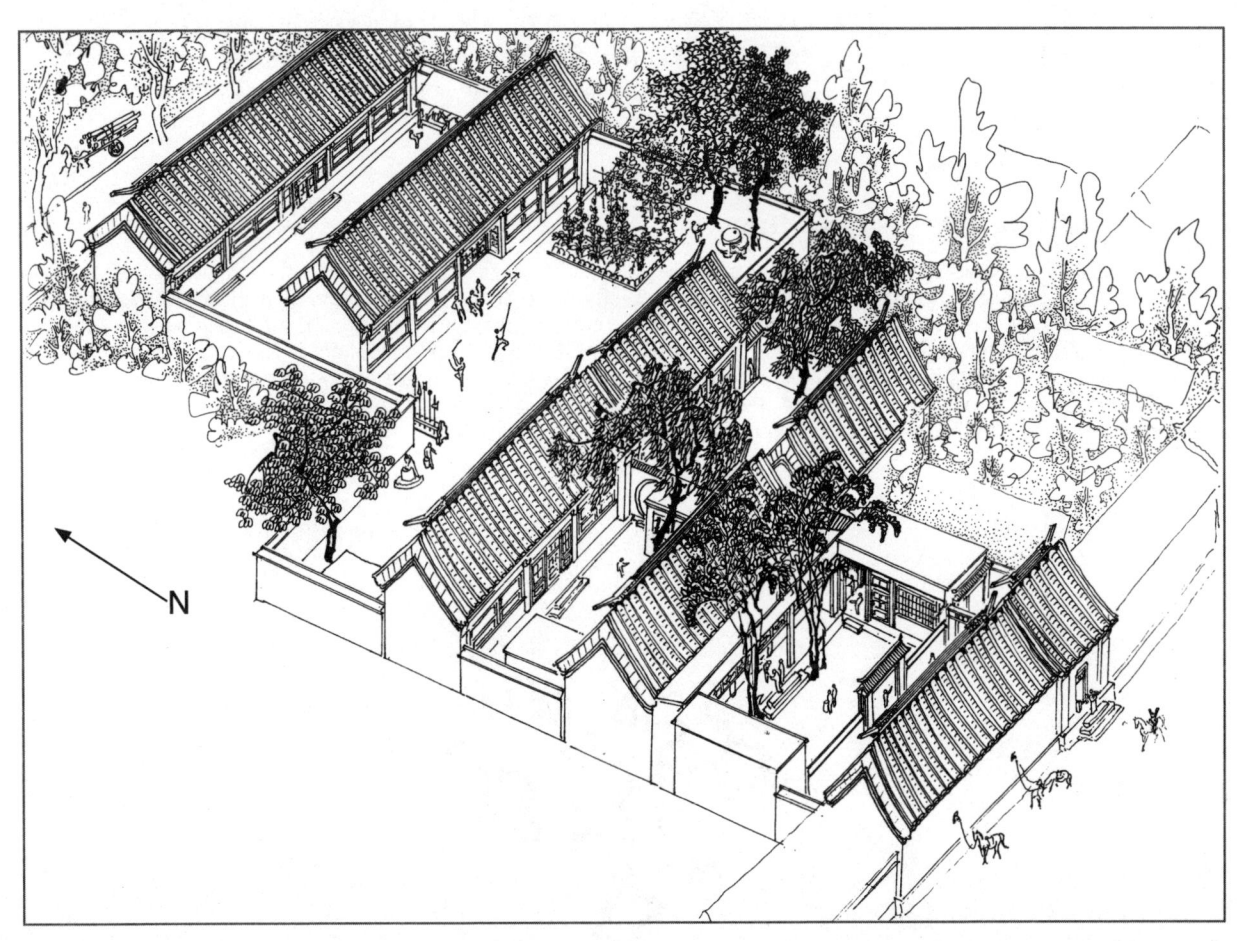

(2003年6月29日绘)

不吉门位巧安门

（西城区武定胡同59号）

此院坐北朝南，其地界为一凸字形，吉位东南角为别人的院，从胡同到里院只有窄窄的一条通道，因此只能因地制宜巧变化，将第一道大门做成很高的木栅栏门，建于通道正中，留一空间，有了一个停顿；将第二道门建在东南角，归入吉位，二门为清水脊广亮大门；第三道门为过厅，由此进入方正的四合院。此四合院南房中间为过厅，两边为带座的廊子，南半间为小房，西房三间中间有一凸出的平廊。正房五间，是前出廊子后出厦的大房。后院为花园。

Clever Placing of an Auspicious Gate

Location:No. 59 Wuding Hutong, Xicheng District

This mansion faces south and sits on an irregular shaped plot, which is narrow in front and broader behind. Only a narrow passage leads to the inner courtyard from the hutong, so the mansion is designed to fit the actual conditions. The first gate is simply a high wooden grill gate. The second gate is positioned at the propitious southeast corner. The main courtyard is entered through the third gate, set in the middle of the south building of the courtyard, three-bay eastern and western wings and a five-bay main wing. The backyard is a garden.

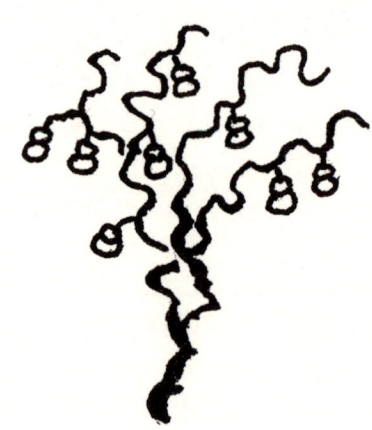

(2003年7月8日绘)

品位不高乱安置

（西城区鲜明胡同7号）

此宅地界不甚好，但比武定胡同 59 号强。若将东房和西院的北房移到两北房之间，即可形成一个好四合院；若再将南房和西房移到垂花门位，在东边建二门或在这片南房的中间建一过厅做二门，即可留出南院和西院为花园，再用抄手游廊将两进四合院连接，将是一座完美的四合院。

A Messed up Layout due to Lack of Refinement

Location: No. 7 Xianming Hutong, Xicheng District

The layout of this mansion is not reasonable. It would have been much better for some adjustments, as seen in the smaller sketch, i.e. moving the eastern wing northward to the second courtyard, and rotating the northern house in the western courtyard to face the courtyard between the two northern houses, would form a very proper inner courtyard. Then moving the south wing and western house to where the Second, *Chuihua* Gate stands, one could leave space for a southern yard and western yard to turn into gardens.

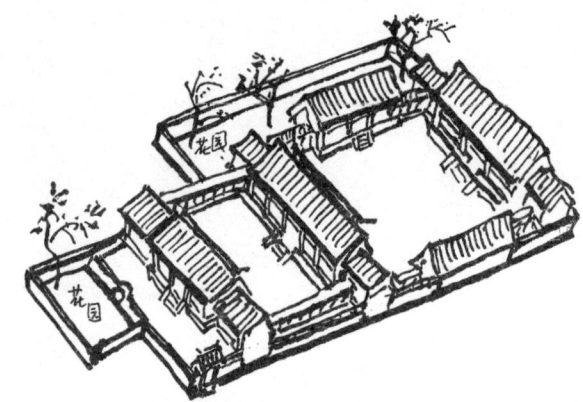

只将原有房屋变动一下，即成一美好的宅院

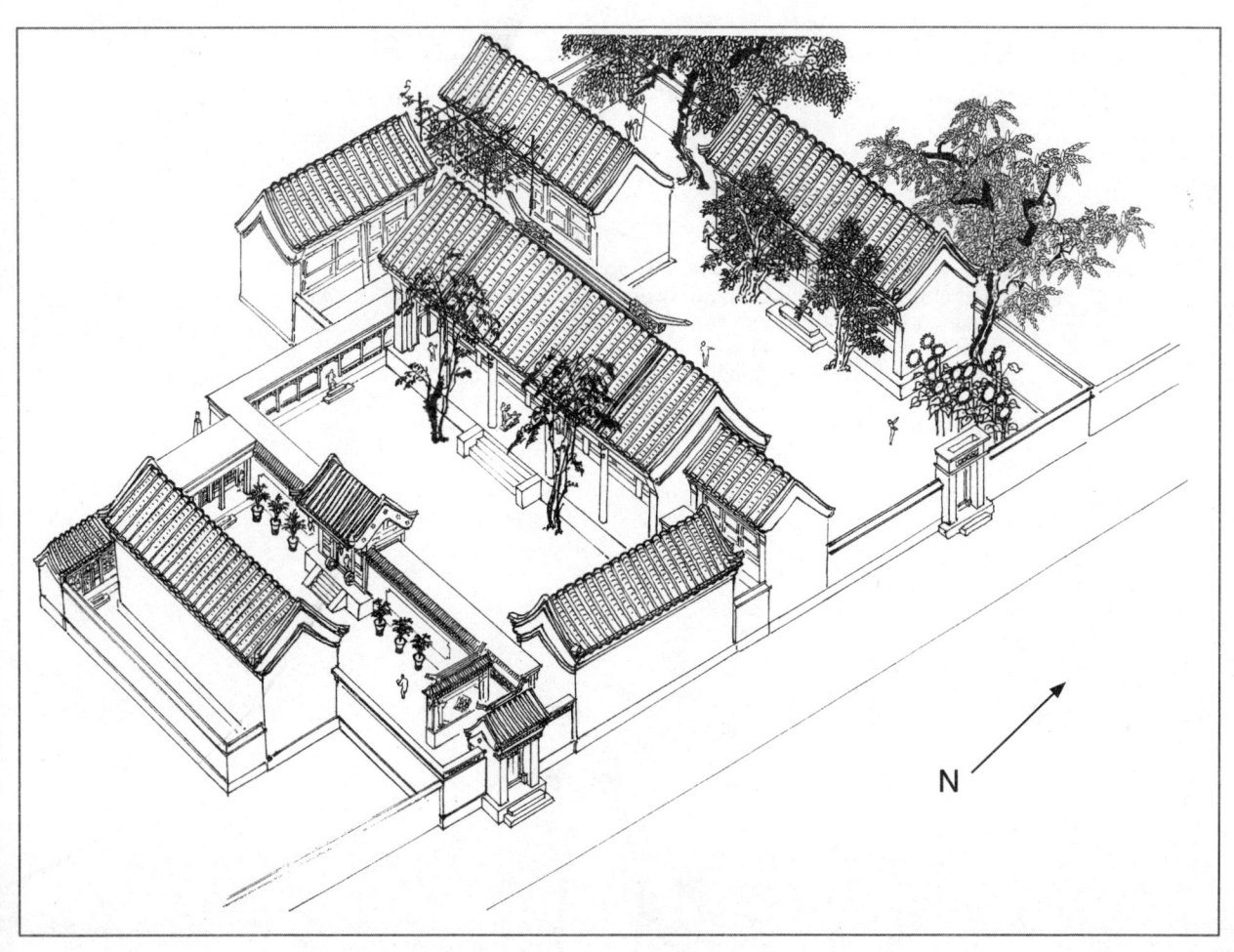

(2003年7月10日绘)

喜静避客精巧院

（西城区鲜明胡同4号、6号）

鲜明胡同为南北向胡同。房主将宅院西南角开一车门，留一东西向的通道，在东南方位开一精美砖雕的如意门。从如意门进院，迎门一砖雕影壁，右一屏门通东院，左一月洞门通内院。此院为一完整二进四合院，北房为三正两耳房，北房左右山墙前各有一红色的二扇小门，西可通临街小院到茅房，东可通东边的书斋小院。东院北房三间为合瓦，另有东、西各三间平房，院中有枣树、核桃和柿子树（早合适之意）及藤萝。此院凉爽幽静，真是读书的好去处，且有街门可单独出入。

A Serene Inner Courtyard to Hide from Guests

Location: Nos. 4 and 6 Xianming Hutong, Xicheng District

The Xianming Hutong runs north and south. A passageway from the street leads to a Ruyi Gate with exquisite brick carving at the southeast corner, through which, one can see a screen wall with brick carving. A screen door on the right side leads to the eastern courtyard and a moon gate to the two inner courtyards. The north wing has three main rooms and two wing rooms. There are two small red two-panel gates on the left and right sides of the northern house, one leading to the small yard adjacent to the street with the toilet, and one to the study in the east. Many trees and Chinese wisteria are found in the cool and serene eastern courtyard, a good place for reading.

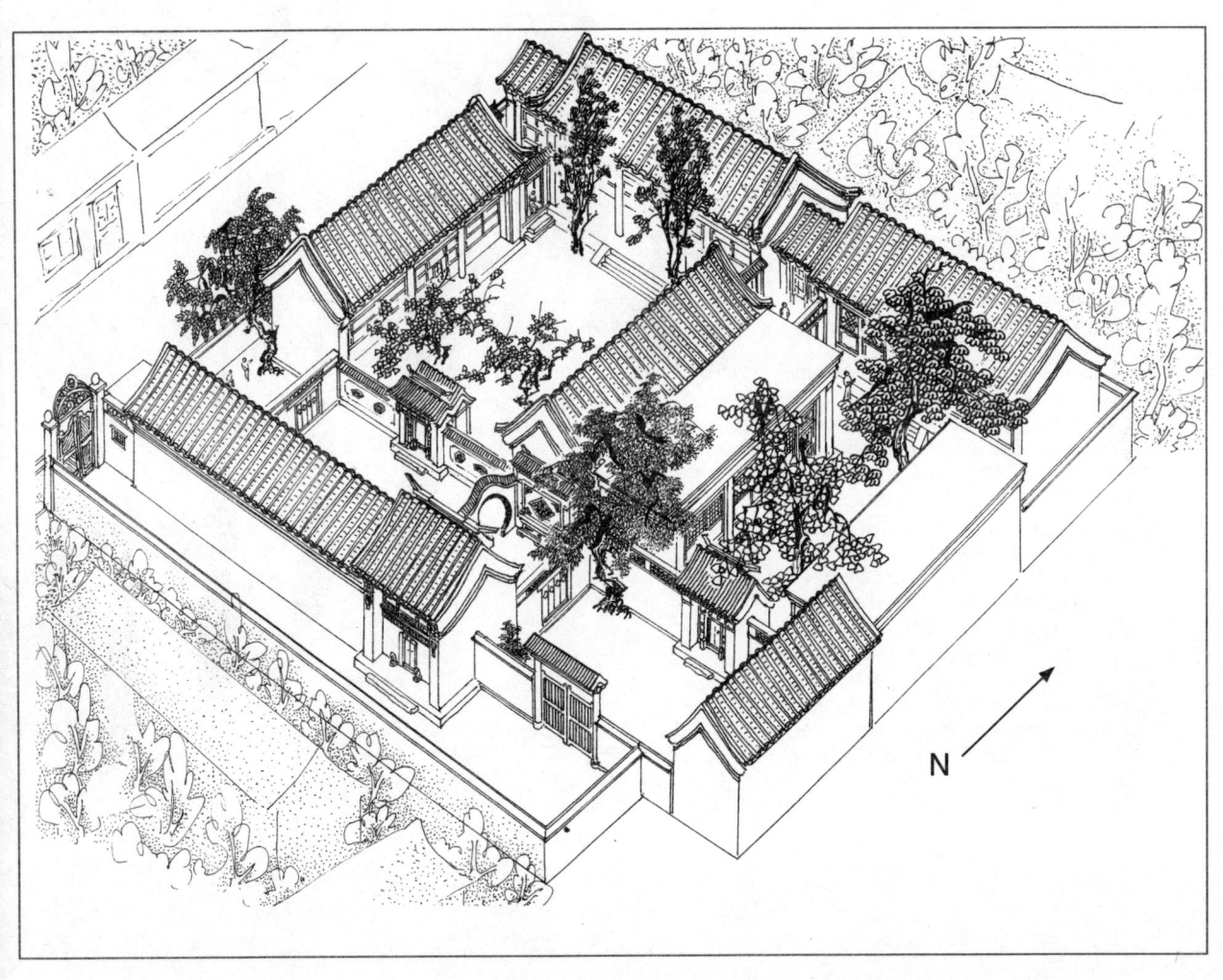

(2003年7月13日绘)

新宅院里庆周岁

（东城区东总布胡同10号）

此宅坐南朝北，据说是同仁堂乐松山儿子出生的住宅。这是清末民初北京四合院结合道济医院、协和医院等西式宅院变化出来的一种典型实例，是北京民居中西建筑风格合璧的典型。此院 2003 年 8 月已拆。

A Birth Celebrated in a New Courtyard

Location:No. 10 East Zongbu Hutong, Dongcheng District

With its main gate facing north, this mansion is said to be the birth place where that scion of the house of Tongrentang, Yue Songshan was born. It is a typical example of how the houses in Beijing tried to combine Chinese and Western styles in Beijing in the late Qing Dynasty (1644–1911) and the early Republican period (1912–1949). This was due in part to the influence of the western style of the buildings of Dow Hospital and Peking Union Medical College Hospital.

严谨舒畅三合院

(东城区八宝坑胡同63号)

此院结构严谨，小巧、舒适，大门和二门之间有一小院，两间平房即严谨又方便守卫，是一个极好的过渡之笔。正房两边有两组屏门将中院划为整齐的方院，东、西小院，更为清幽之所。

A Precise Three-wing Courtyard

Location:No. 63 Babaokeng Hutong, Dongcheng District
This courtyard is precise in structure, neat and comfortable. There is a small courtyard between the main gate and the secondary gate. The two-bay building inside the gate is both precise and convenient for guarding purposes. Two sets of screen doors on either sides of the main yard create a middle courtyard in a neat square and two small yards in the east and west respectively, making them more secluded.

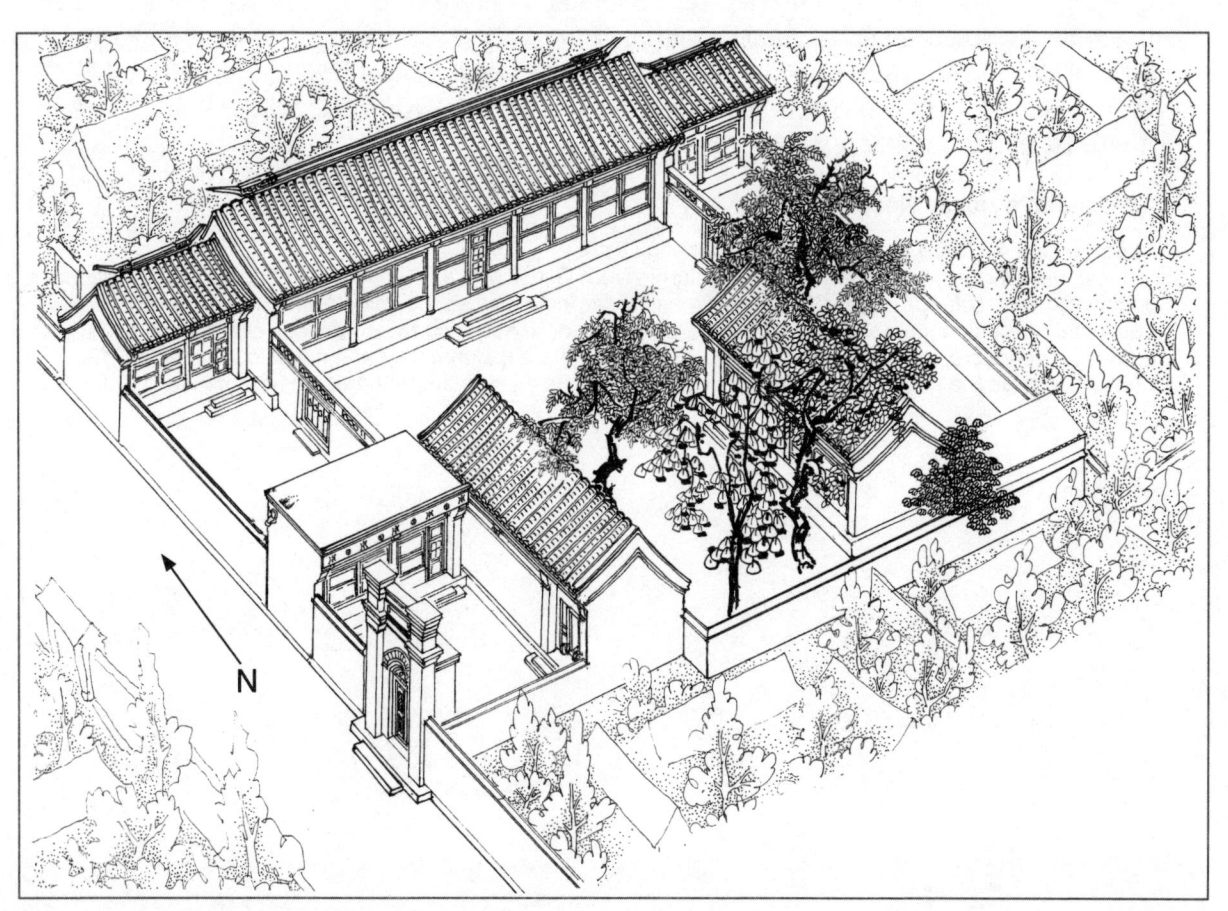

(2003年9月7日绘)

增设三门军客多

(东城区北新桥头条59号)

此处为100年前甘肃人卢陆民中将自己设计的私家宅院。此院为金柱大门，三进院落，中院与后院有抄手游廊相连。此院独特之处是一进院的正房南面不开门不留窗，使其成为南房，使中院成为一完整的有东西南北房的四合院。外院倒座房与西房自成一院。军人之友，男人为多，外院与内宅严格分开是主人特意设计的独特之笔。再有，在进入二门后南房为接待更高一级的军人宾客或女宾之客房，还有第三道门和影壁保持私密，三道门之内才是真正的内宅。

A General's House Needs much Privacy

Location:No. 59 Beixinqiao, Toutiao, Dongcheng District

This is the private mansion of General Lu Lumin from Gansu which he designed himself. With a main Jinzhu (golden-column) gate, this mansion has three courtyards; the middle one and inner one are connected through a gallery. Uniquely, there is no door or window on the south wall of the main house in the first courtyard, making the middle courtyard a complete quadrangle with houses on four sides. The house alongside the main gate in the outer courtyard forms a courtyard with the western house.

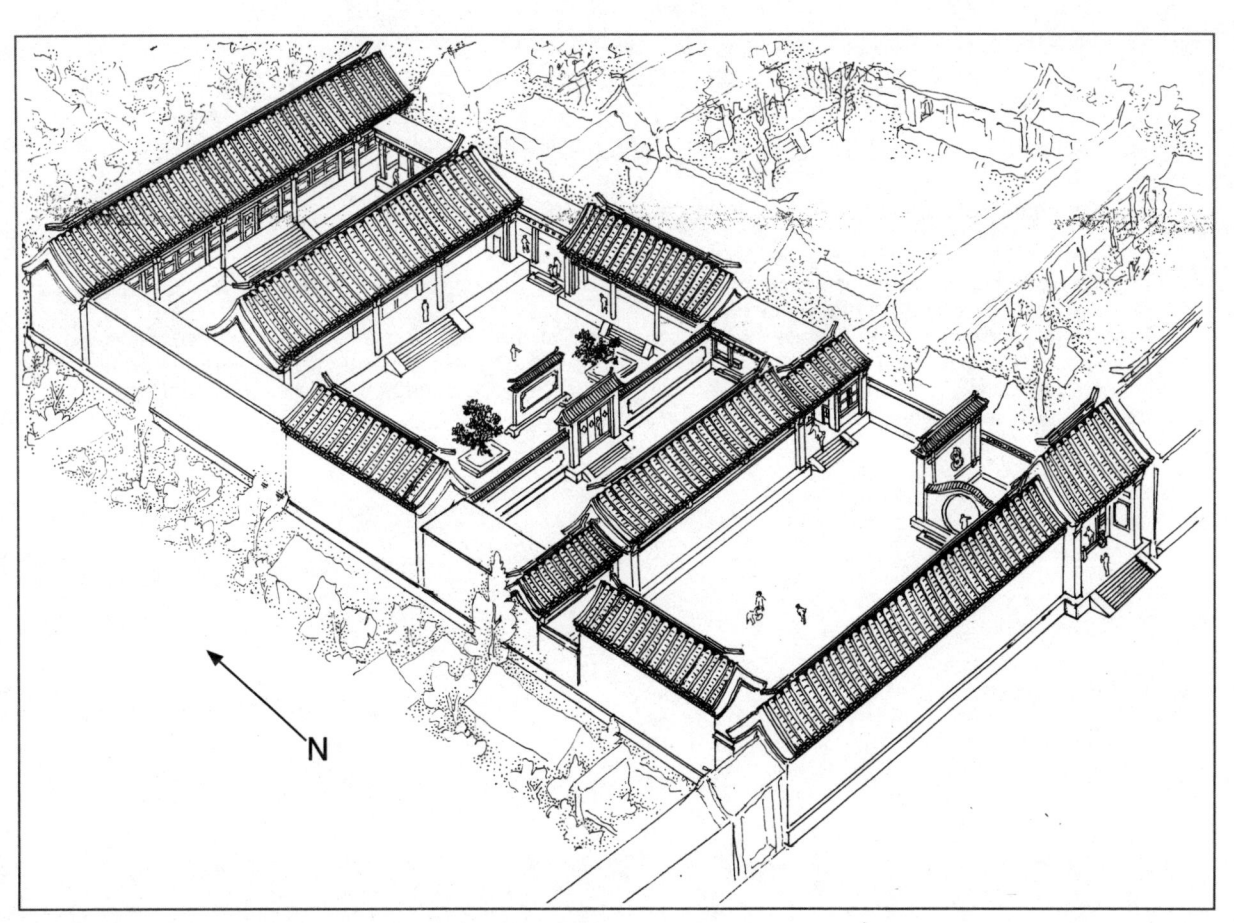

(2003年9月13日绘)

垂花门退待高宾

（东城区皇城内北河沿14号）

原皇城内有一条玉河，此宅坐南朝北，《加摹乾隆京城全图》内即有此院之图。

1949年任弼时曾住此院。

此院为四进，很有特色，其垂花门放在二进院之后，如此二门（内宅）之外又有了比较宽广的空间，为外来客人留有更充分的活动空间，也可使来客分为四至五个层次的亲疏等级来接待。内宅有廊子与东院相通，下人由西小门进出，可方便进出服务，后院也可方便利用空间。此院设计合理，使用舒适。

The Chuihua Gate Set Back to Leave More Space for Guests

Location:No. 14 Beiheyan, Huangchengnei, Dongcheng District
Its gate facing north, this mansion can be found in a map of Beijing made in the reign of Qianlong.
Ren Bishi ever lived in this mansion in 1949.

It has four courtyards. The Chuihua second gate is set at the back of the second courtyard, leaving more space for guests who could be received at four or five different degrees of familiarity. A corridor connects the inner courtyard with the eastern courtyard. The back courtyard also has abundant space. This mansion is reasonable in design and comfortable to use.

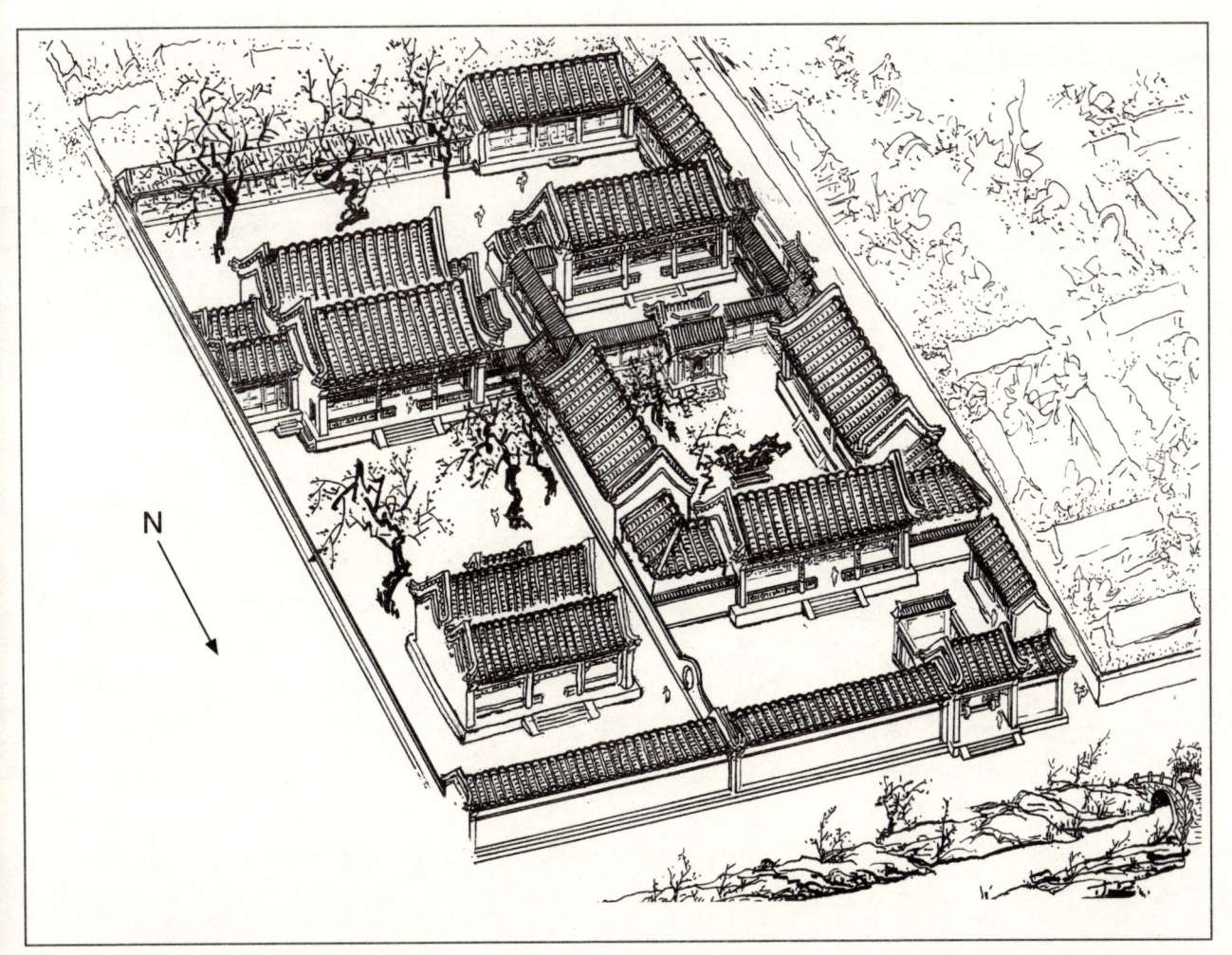

(2003年6月16日绘)

休闲听戏自家乐

（东城区本司胡同17号）

有人说这儿可能是末代皇帝溥仪的夫人李淑贤的故宅。东院之悬山顶、卷棚勾连搭的大花厅是北京民居中少见的保存完好的实物，广亮大门内的条石路也是少见的、完好的甬道。

东院的东墙边上原来有戏楼，有廊子相通，原有假山，这里是花园……其西有一敞轩。

Leisure listen their music

Location:No. 17 Bensi Hutong, Dongcheng District

Some say this is the former residence of Li Shuxian, wife of Pu Yi, last emperor of the Qing Dynasty (1644–1911). The parlor in the eastern courtyard featuring the overhanging gable roof and round ridge is well-preserved and rarely seen in the residential houses in Beijing. The complete slab-stone path inside the *Guangliang* gate is also rarely seen.

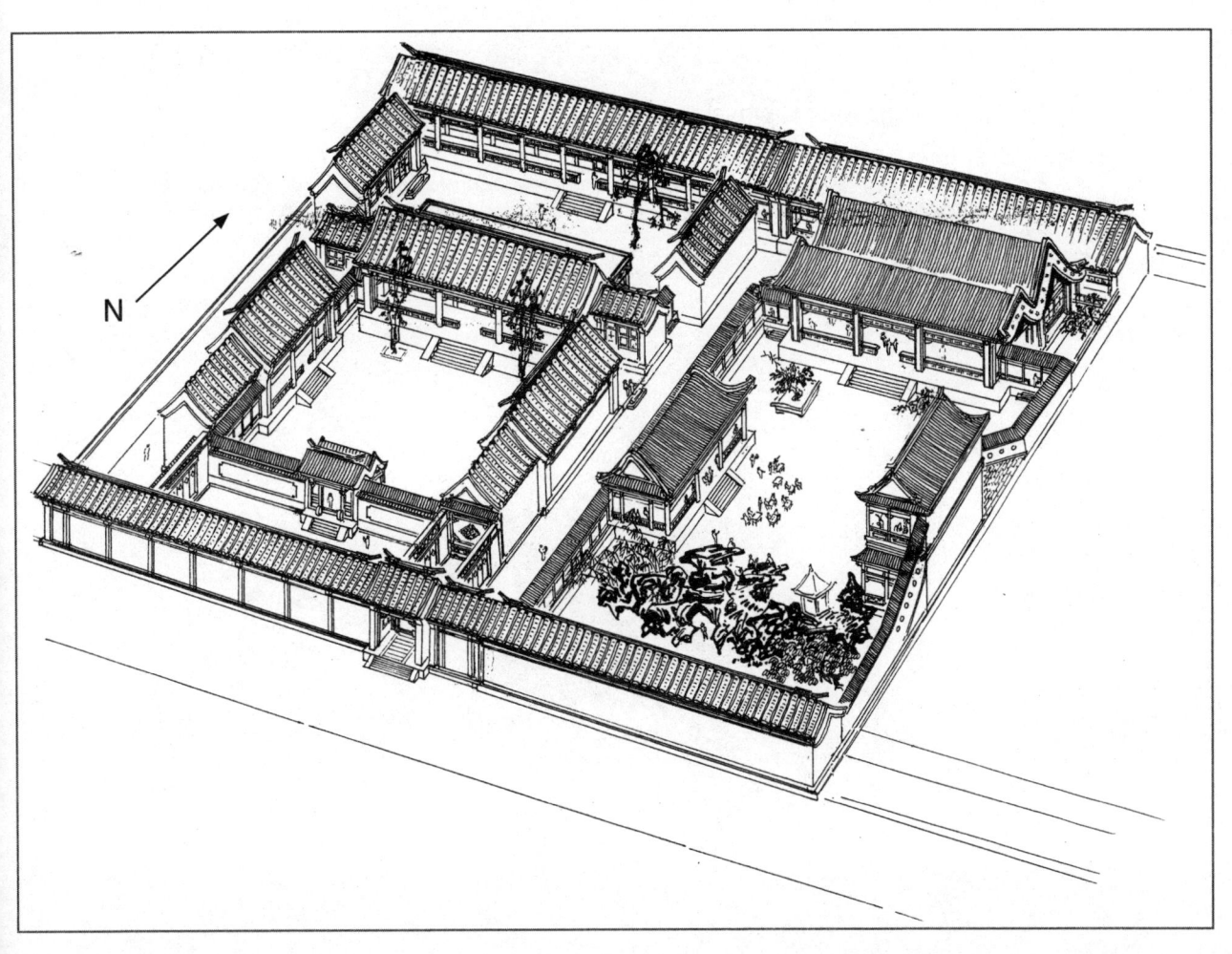

(2003年9月17日绘)

花卉满院为谁开

（东城区本司胡同27号）

此院坐北朝南，进门下六层台阶，才至垂花门，院内抄手游廊为平廊，后院花卉满园，美极了。

A Flower Garden in the Rear Courtyard

Location:No. 27 Bensi Hutong, Dongcheng District
This mansion's main gate faces south. Entering the main gate, one goes down six steps to reach the Chuihua second gate. There are corridors linking the courtyards. The back courtyard is a garden filled with flowers.

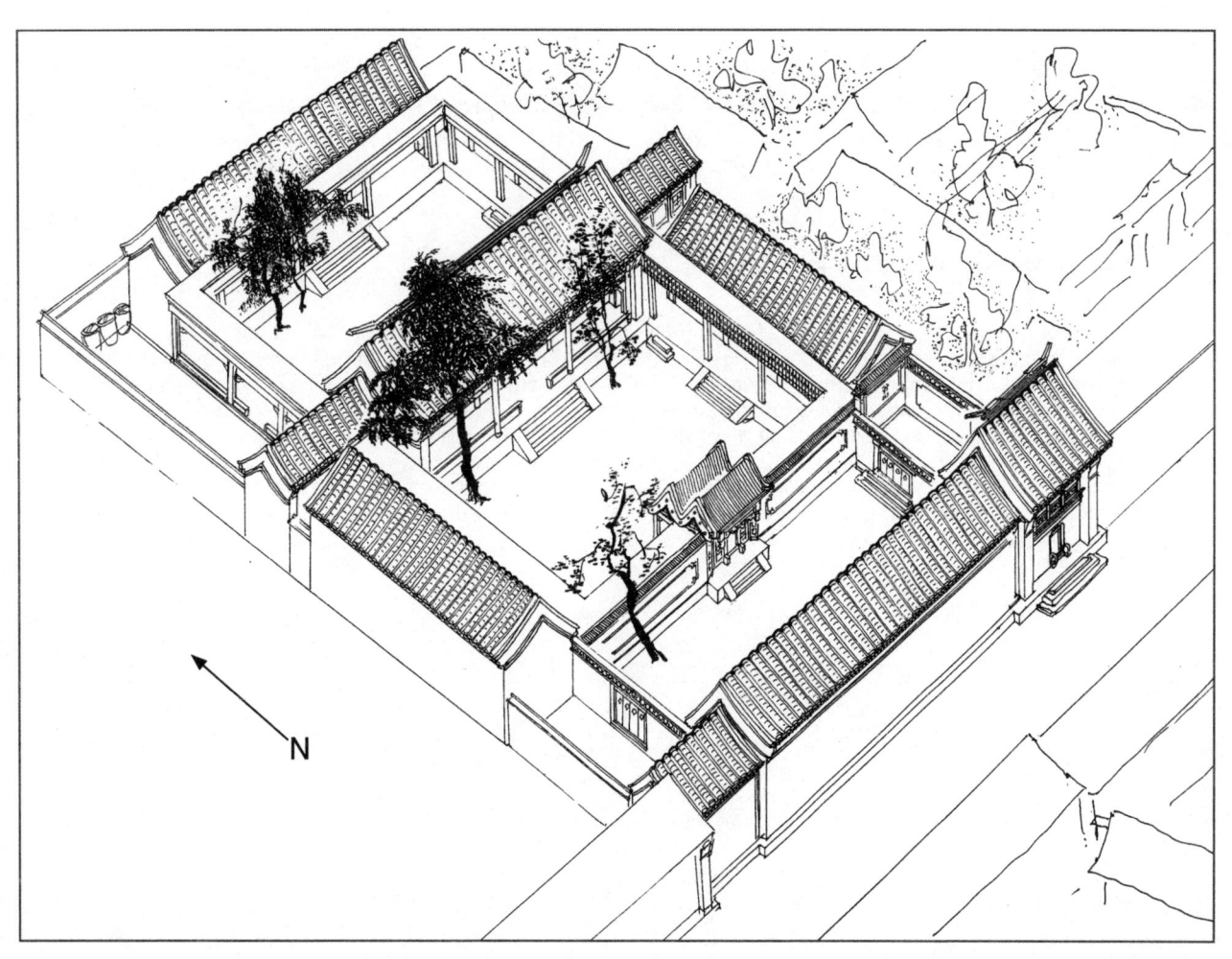

(2004年1月27日绘)

和睦兄弟廊相联

(西城区东养马营胡同17号、15号)

这是雍正年间一高官建的住宅，距今已300余年。西院是有官职的兄宅，东院是无官职的弟宅，两院有穿廊连接。两宅坐北朝南，西口有木栅栏的胡同大门。西院为广亮大门，磨砖对缝的影壁，东、西都有屏门；第一进院除倒座房外，只有西房没有东房；二门为垂花门，二进院为三正两耳的正房和三间的东、西厢房，四周有抄手游廊，画有二十四孝等故事的彩画。从垂花门向东可通向东院，西北角有花园。东院为砖雕如意门楼。

Two Brothers Live together in Harmony

Location:Nos. 17 and 15 Dongyangmaying Hutong, Xicheng District

This is a mansion built by a high-ranking official during the Qing Yongzheng Period, with a history of over 300 years. The western part belonged to the elder brother with official position and the eastern part to the younger without official position. The two sides are connected with a covered corridor. The mansion faces south, with a wood fence gate opening onto the hutong in the west. Inside the forecourt of the western section, there is only a western wing building with no corresponding eastern wing. There is a three-bay main house with two wing rooms and three-bay wing houses in the east and west respectively in the second courtyard. Covered corridors surround them, and these are painted with depicting the 24 Filial Exemplars. The Chuihua gate can also lead to the eastern part. There is a garden at the northwest corner.

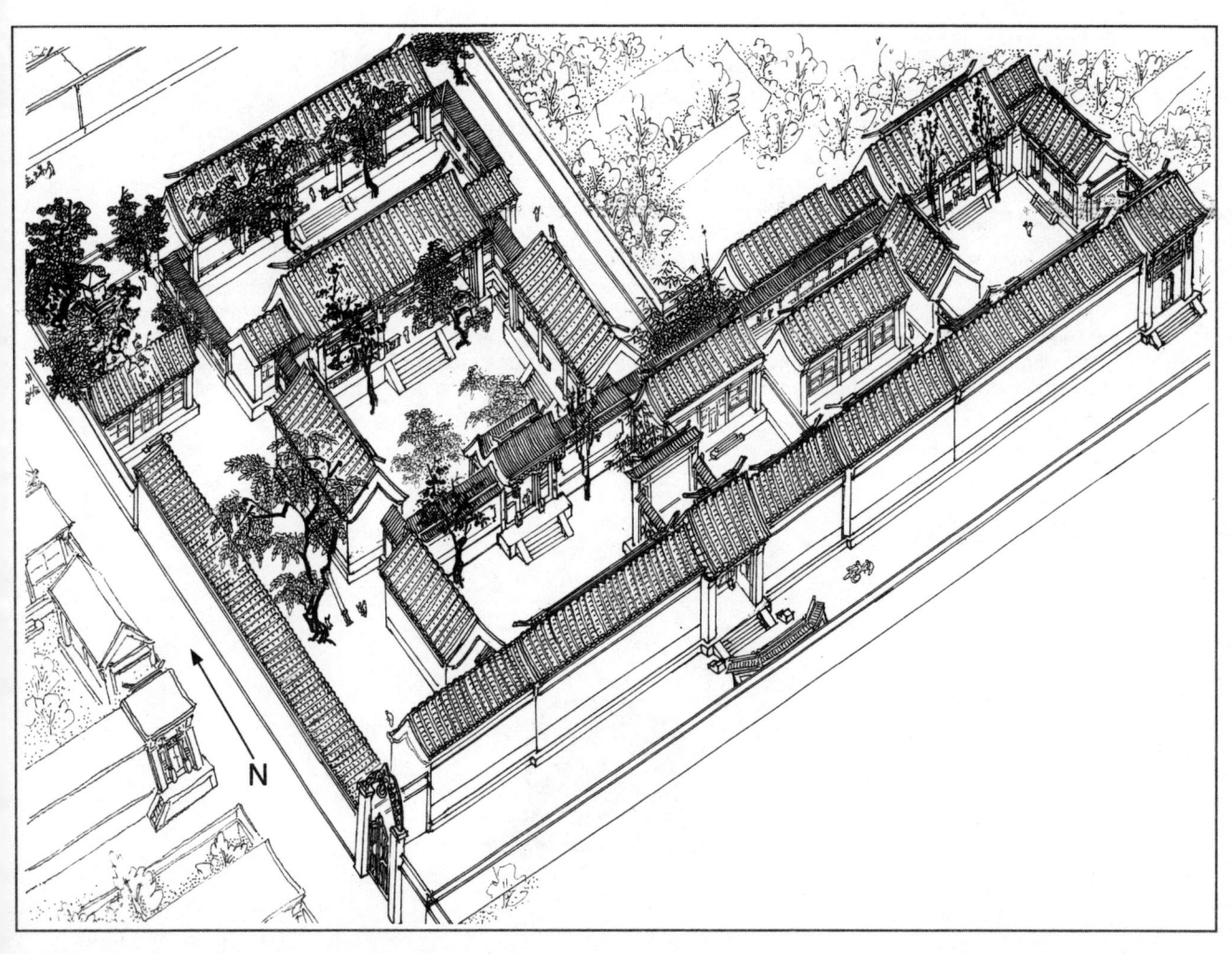

(2003年8月30日绘)

孝悌楷模今尚在

（东城区九道湾东巷7号）

九道湾东巷7号韩家。每个孩子到了高考时，其父都在里院专门拨一间房供其读书，因此韩家兄妹们都大学毕业，成为国家栋梁。

为了怀念父亲，弟兄们决定合资将祖屋按父亲设计的原样修建，感谢父亲及祖屋对他们的培养，并誓言"永不分家，共建共利"。

A Model Filial Family

Location:No. 7 Dongxiang, Jiudaowan, Dongcheng District
This is the Han's mansion. When ever a child was preparing for the college entrance examination, father would especially designate a room in the inner courtyard for the child to study. Hence, they all passed the exam and graduated from university.
To commemorate their father, they decided to pool some money to rebuild their ancestral shrine room according to the design of their father. They vowed to live together and never break up the family.

(2007年11月22日绘)

明亮南屋南有窗

（东城区大菊胡同34号）

此两院20世纪初为大军阀张作霖的秘书的住宅，两院有门相通。大菊胡同的院为主院，坐南朝北，二进，进二门有高大的南为上的三正两耳的正房。虽为南房，在后罩房前有一小院，正房又有三层高大的后窗，因此和北房一样充满阳光。此院后罩房、正房、倒座房、门楼的房脊都已变换，门楼西侧小房是卷棚脊，而东西厢房都是完好的清水脊。

A Bright Southern Wing with Big Windows

Location:No. 34 Daju Hutong, Dongcheng District
This was the former residence of the secretary of Warlord Zhang Zuolin in early 20th century. Its two courtyards are connected through a gate.
The north–facing gate on Daju Hutong is the main one. It has two courtyards. The three-bay main house with two wing rooms is found on the south side of the chuihua second gate. There is a small yard south of this, This main wing has three high and large south-facing windows, thus is filled with sunshine just like one facing south.

(2003年12月13日绘)

东直门街此宅高

(东城区东直门内大街192号)

洋式院门为此宅后门,前门在大菊胡同,为广亮大门。

此宅分东西两路,东路为四进的住宅,这东路二门为垂花门,二进三进为起脊合瓦标准四合院,并有抄手游廊将两院连接,三进院北房为非常高大的清水脊前出廊后出厦的五间正房。西路是花园。最北是高大的卷棚脊正房,面对花园对面的三间花厅,花园的西北角有一屏门可通向西边的小院,有通道向北经过厅可达贯通东西路的后罩房。东西北角有一大单门可通东直门内大街。

Front and Back Entrances Span the Block

Location:No. 192 Dongzhimennei Dajie, Dongcheng District

The back gate of this mansion is of foreign style and the Guangliang Gate (not shown) is its front gate, located on Daju Hutong to the south.

This mansion is divided into the eastern and western parts. The eastern part has four courtyards. The second and third courtyards are standard courtyards with ridge and closed tiles on the roof; they are also connected by a corridor. The central building is an extremely high five-bay main house with front and back corridors. The western part is a garden. A high main house with round ridge roof is found at the southernmost end of the garden. A screen gate at the northwest corner of the garden leads to a small yard further west.

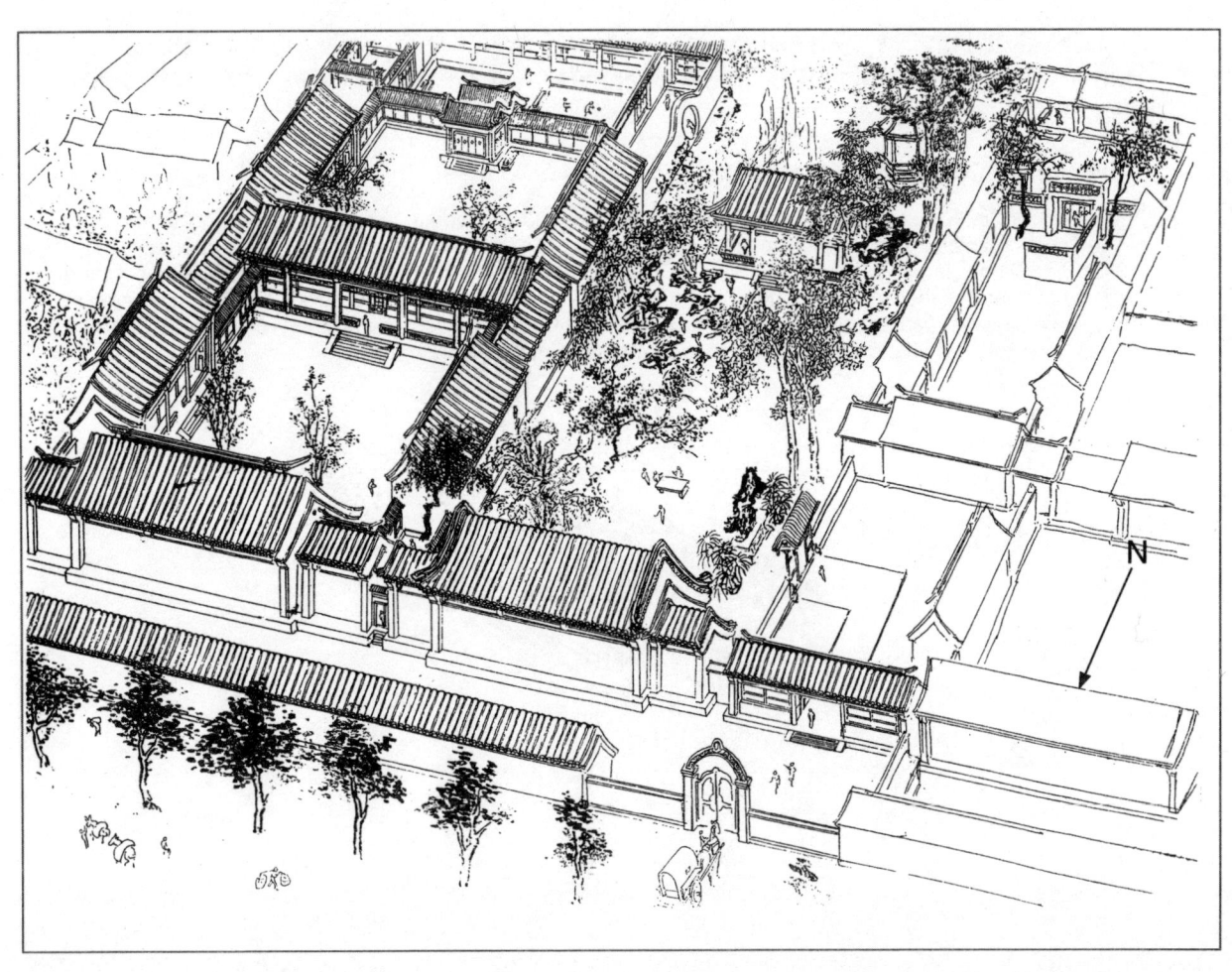

(2004年1月17日绘)

丁家大院多层次

(东城区南池子大街32号普渡寺西巷5号、7号、9号、11号)

　　丁家大院建于清末民初,丁家系商人。南池子大街32号为前门,是正院,普渡寺西巷11号为并连之院。东南角有浴室和厕所、后门,后门外另建三个伙计们自住的小院(现普渡寺西巷5号、7号、9号)。整个院落主次有序,完整舒适。

Ding Family Compound with Multiple Courtyards

Location: No. 32 Nanchizi Dajie and No.5, No.7, No.9 and NO.11 Pudusi Xixiang, Dongcheng District
　　The Ding's Mansion was built in the late Qing Dynasty (1644–1911) and early Republican period (1912–1949). The Ding's family did business. The main courtyard is located at No. 32 Nanchizi Dajie, connected with a courtyard at the No. 11 Pudusi Xixiang. There is bathroom, toilet and back door at the southeast corner. Three small yards for servants are found behind the back door (the present-day Nos. 5, 7 and 9 Pudusi Xixiang). The whole mansion is in good order, complete and comfortable.

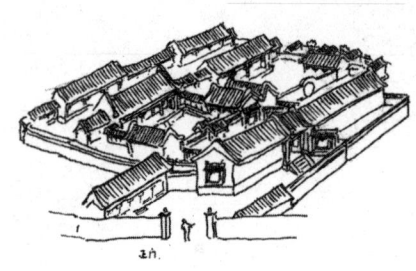

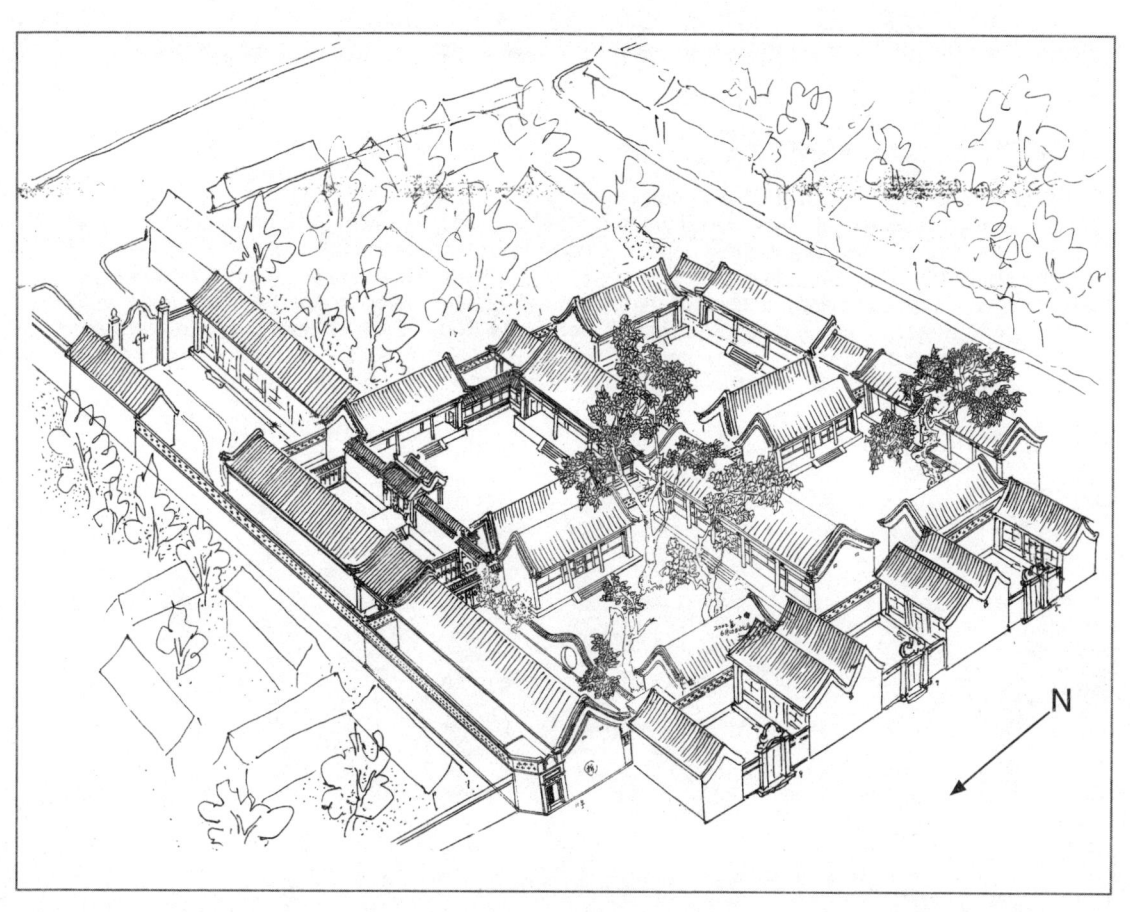

(2002年6月12日——2004年4月12日绘)

「二门后退前庭宽」

（东城区骑河楼街福禄巷4号）

此院20世纪30年代前是一王府，后被蒙疆司令李守信购得，后将此院赠与郑介仁同志。郑参加革命后，此院成为中共华北局城工部之地下工作站，负责人为郑介仁、崔月犁同志。曾以"中西医院"之名义，进行地下工作，直至解放。

A Gift Turned into a Hospital

Location:No. 4 Fuluxiang, Qiheloujie Street, Dongcheng District
This was once a traditional Chinese and western medicine hospital, with clinic and sickbeds. During the period of the war of resistance against Japanese aggression, resistance fighters hid a radio transmitter-receiver here. The Japanese invaders built an observation tower in a courtyard to the west to keep watch on activities in this compound and made raids and searches. This compound had originally belonged to Mongolian General Demchugdongrub (Prince De). Since Prince De had been cured of an illness by a doctor Zheng, he made the doctor a present of this mansion. Thus, doctor Zheng became the master of the mansion. Prince De's also exerted some influence to protect the hospital.

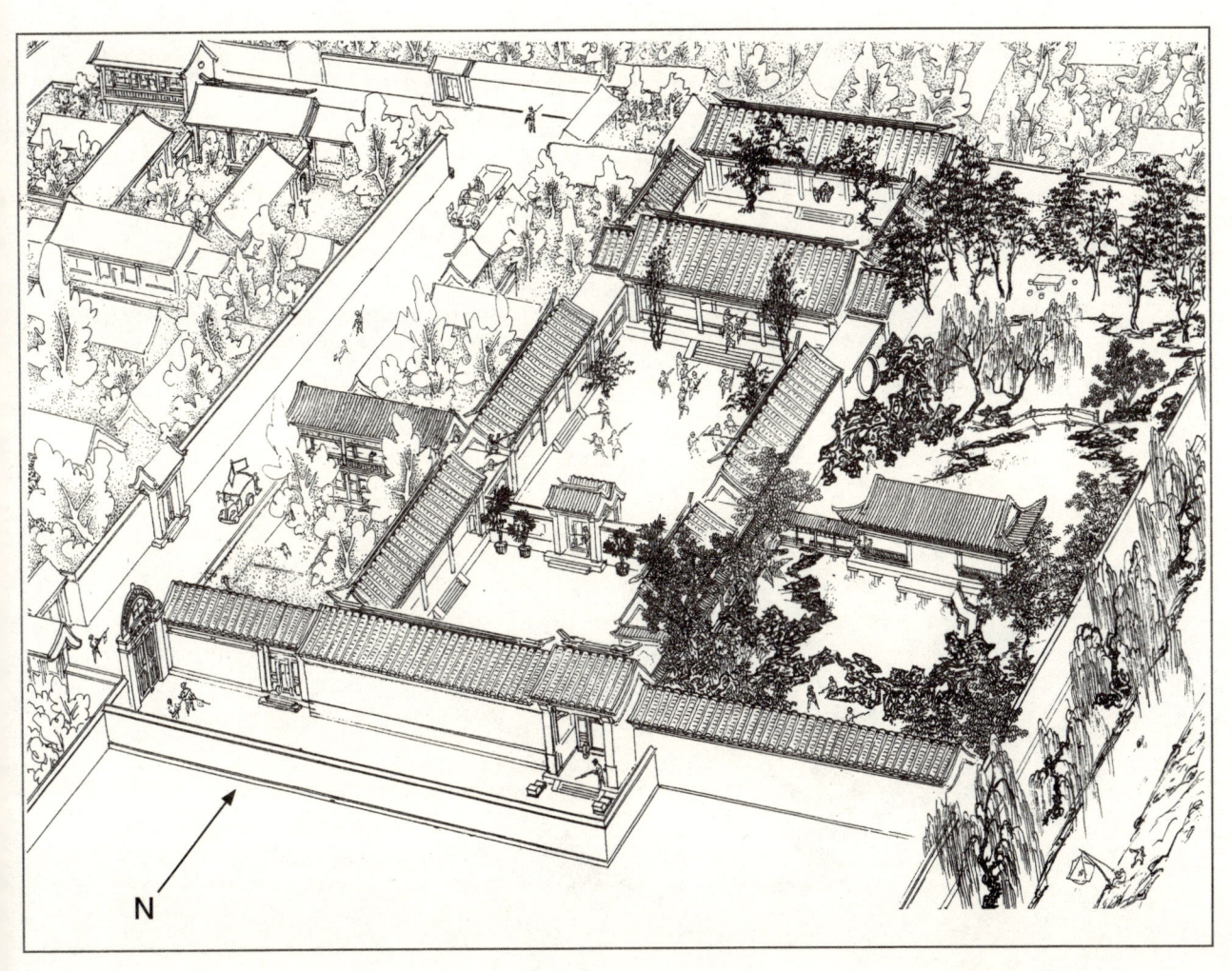

(2004年5月26日绘)

| 冬雪春风度闲日 |

（东城区美术馆后街22号（之一））

"美术馆后街22号……全院两进1000余平方米……1950年经梅兰芳的家人介绍，赵紫宸先生以100多匹布的价格从一赵姓中医手中购得此宅，一直住到1979年他91岁高龄逝世。"

"美术馆后街被称为家庭博物馆和玫瑰园，是说它的文化含量和美丽景致。"

（摘自2004年10月《文明·北京时间》总第十七期32页）

注：赵紫宸：燕京大学教授，曾任宗教学院院长，全国政协委员。

A House Purchased with Bolts of Cloth

Location:No. 22 Meishuguan Houjie, Dongcheng District (Part I)
This mansion has two courtyards, covering an area of over 1,000 square meters. It is said that in 1950, through an introduction by Peking Opera star Mei Lanfang, Mr. Zhao Zichen bought this mansion from a herbalist doctor surnamed Zhao at a price of over 100 bolts of cloth. Zhao Zichen lived there until 1979 when he died at the age of 91.

(2004年7月20日绘)

夏雨秋霜美景寒

（东城区美术馆后街22号（之二））

　　1998-2000年在这里展开了首次"北京四合院保卫战"，舒乙等众多文人专家呼吁保护此院。赵景心（赵紫宸先生的儿子）夫妇，二位80多岁的老人拿起法律武器保卫此院。第一稿是据陈翰博士的照片画成。近日，蒙赵老指出一稿之误，又画此图。从陈的照片中可以看出，此院四季各有美色，所以第二稿画夏秋之景。遗憾的是，我尽全力也未必能画出此院色彩斑斓、幽静舒适的感觉。

A Battle to Preserve an Old Courtyard

Location:No. 22 Meishuguan Houjie, Dongcheng District (Part II)
　　Later a "Beijing Courtyard War" was waged over the mansion from 1998 to 2000. Many scholars and experts including Shu Yi called for protecting this mansion. Zhao Jingxin (son of Mr. Zhao Zichen) and his wife, then both over 80 years old, tried to protect this mansion through litigation.

(2004年11月11日绘)

统一规划居易里

(东城区麻线胡同10～22号)

"里文化"是北京民居文化的一大变奏曲,这里有很多内容还未挖掘。

在北京民居文化中的"里"文化,如西四的"义达里",鼓楼前的"辛安里"等,有的是由一户出资,有计划地统一建筑风格和相同的格局的建筑群;亦有不同用途不同格局,但有一条共用大道组成多变而统一的建筑群。

此"居易里"应是清末民初之建筑,"居易"取材于历史故事:白居易十五岁入长安,顾况在宴会上出一上联"花折一枝春日暖",白居易对出下联"风吹白草野田香",惊四座,顾曰:"汝在长安可居易也。"此宅七个院落各不相同,靠北的四个院应是主人之居,建筑富于变化,颇有情趣。

A *Li* Courtyard Group

Location:No.10–No.22 Maxian Hutong, Dongcheng District

The "li" is a group of buildings built on either side of a gated alley. Li culture was an important variation on the courtyard houses in Beijing. Take the "Yidali" at Xisi or "Xin'anli" in front of the Drum Tower for example. Some Li are building complexes with the same style and pattern, developed by one household. Some are complexes varying in style and purpose, but have one common access.

This is "Juyili", built in the late Qing Dynasty (1644–1911) and early Republican period (1912–1949). It has seven different courtyards. The four to the north are the owner's residence. The buildings are interesting and rich in variation.

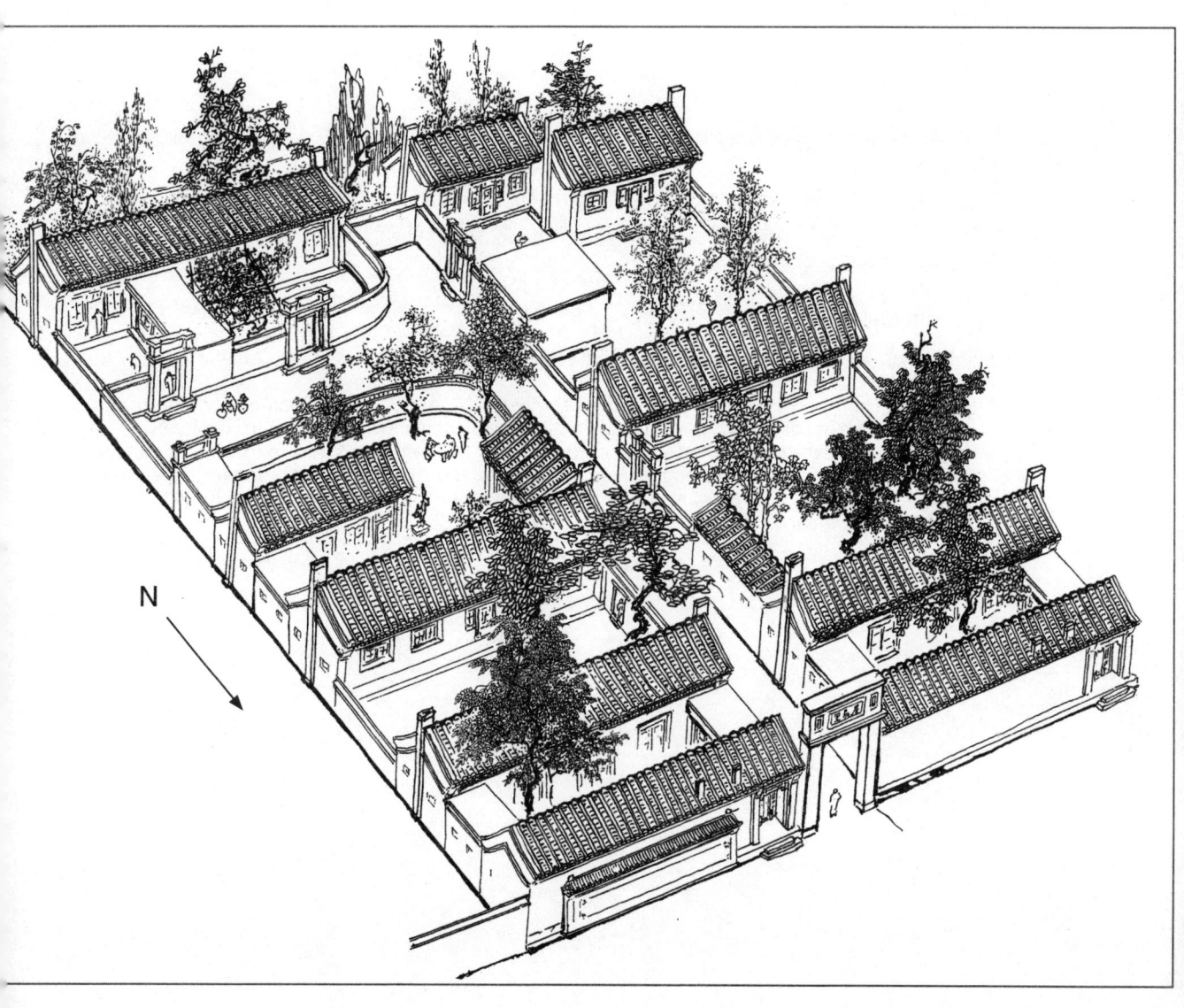

(2005年11月13日绘)

> 夹缝小门做二门

（西城区府右街罗贤胡同19～23号）

这是一个藏有壁画的"里文化"实例。

梁宅，清末自家建造，通道东、西、北几个院落都是梁家祖宅。梁敬行先生的父辈按兄东、弟西分住，梁父继承了西院。

北房磨砖对缝，柁檩粗大，门窗砖地及顶篷都是原来的，保存完好，这在北京现存民居中已不多见。难得的是，廊子两边廊墙上有保存完好的两幅壁画，壁画上方有与其对应的两条砖雕对联，东为"春前有雨花开早"，西为"秋后无霜叶灰尽"。

A House with Murals

Location:Nos. 19–23 Luoxian Hutong, Fuyoujie Street, Xicheng District
This is an example of a Li with murals.
The Liang's Mansion was built in the late Qing Dynasty (1644–1911). The eastern, western and northern courtyards are ancestral houses of Liang Family. The sketch shows the western courtyard.
The northern house features polished–brick exterior walls and large and thick girders and purlins. The door, window and brick floor are original and well–preserved, which is rarely seen in the existing residential houses in Beijing. There are also two murals on the walls of the covered corridor with a pair of couplets carved above each.

(2005年6月5日绘)

通州漕运积仓廒
（通州粮仓）

应通州政协杜主席之邀，为其"古韵通州"画插图，见到通州八十高龄的王文续先生等写的有关通州古文化的记叙之文，深感通州的抢救文化工作着实令人钦佩。

王老文中详细介绍了运河漕渠、仓厂、衙署、验收等，写得十分清楚。在北京还能见到一些仓房，但其结构已无人知道。

Store Houses for Grain Shipped up the Canal

Location: Tongzhou Granary
Some ancient storehouses can still be seen in Beijing, but their structure is unknown.
Tongzhou (meaning Trans-ship prefecture) is the north end of the 1700 k.m. long Grand Canal built in the Sui Dynasty (589-617). Grain shipped up from south China was often stored in granaries before being trans-shipped to Beijing up the Tonghui Canal built in the Yuan Dynasty (1279-1368). During much of the Ming and Qing dynasties the Tonghui Canal water level was too low, so most grain had again to be stored in Tongzhou before being transported to Beijing by land. A few grain stores of similar design still exist in Beijing itself at Nanxincang.

(2004年11月25日绘)

羊市口街羊肉铺

（崇文区北羊市口街47号）

原是羊肉铺，现房主于50年前购买。

这地区回民多，我年轻时即看到，他们往往赶着几只羊，进入小胡同里羊肉铺后面的小院中。街道上卖着"羊霜肠"，楼上阳台主人与伙计在忙碌，女主人在哄孩子。

A Mutton Shop on Mutton Lane

Location:No. 47 Beiyangshikou Street, Chongwen District
This was originally a mutton shop. The current owner bought it 50 years ago.
There are many Hui Muslims in this area. When I was young, I often saw several sheep being driven into the small courtyard behind the mutton shop. The sheep intestines filled with blood were sold in the shop on the street front. On the roof, the boss and helpers would be busy while the mistress was taking care of the children.

(2003年12月4日绘)

二条口外铺面楼

（东城区东四北大街492号）

东四北大街 492 号的铺面房，估计是布铺一类。此店高大，房舍整齐，紧临东四二条西口，路南再过去 20 米就到东四十字路口，第三进房南墙有二折短梯可上楼，此房的雨水从南边走。

A Shop Near Dongsi

Location:No. 492 Dongsibeidajie, Dongcheng District
This house with store front rooms is orderly, high and large. It is located at the west end of Dongsi Ertiao Street. Dongsi intersection is just 20 meters southward from there. A pair of steps lead to the upstairs along the southern wall of the house in the third row. The rainwater on the roof of this house drains down from the south gutter.

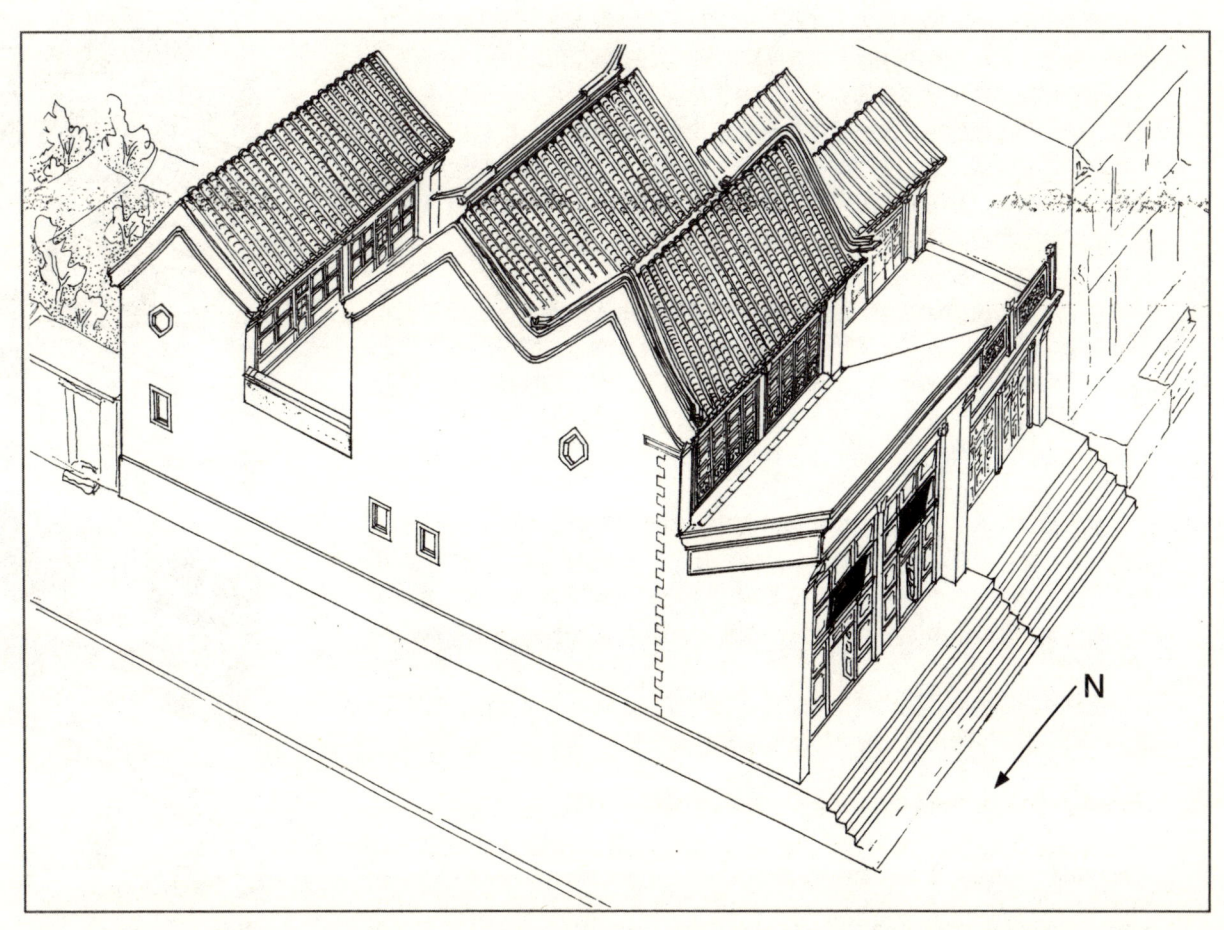

(2003年12月22日绘)

通州"水会"忙灭火

（清末救火队）

应通州政协杜主席之邀，为通州作画。他们邀请很多老北京人挖掘遗失的北京文化，老人们给我讲解了北京早期民间自发的消防组织——"水会"。

晚清时期，老北京繁华的商业区，商铺林立，民房密集。因其建筑大多是砖木结构和纸糊门窗，故经常发生火灾。由大户商家牵头，串联附近的中小商户共同协商成立自己的消防组织——"水会"，选出会首，制定防火公约。户按铺面大小分等级出资筹备经费，每月还须按等级交纳一定数目的会费。组织分工严密，有带红袖标挥旗观察的叫文善，有敲锣报警指挥的叫武善，有救火送水的叫助善。水会的灭火工具以水车为主，此外还有水龙带、唧筒、挠钩、梯子、水桶和灯笼等。起初水车并无车轮，由人抬着走，后经改进才安上铁轮。水车为长方形大木柜，外包铁皮，内设水槽，水槽两边各有几个如同压水机样子的压水装置。水车做工精细，车身四周安有铁环，便于用手拉车。车内可装水1立方米，由4人共同操作，反复提起压下左右杠杆，形成一定压力，将水唧起，再通过车中间的出水口经水龙带射向火场，射程可达15米。

在北京历史上，以前门大栅栏地区为中心的城南水会最多。如同仁堂独资兴办的"普善水会"就是成立最早、设备最好、实力最强的"水会"。其组织庞大，管理严格，水车的压水装置也多，喷出的水柱又粗又高，灭火威力很大。当时的京城，凡商铺多而集中的地区都有水会，连40里开外的通州也有好几家"水会"。

我单位的厂房原是同仁堂乐老板母亲的宅院，后院有一个小楼，听说就是当时的"水会"所在地，院中的地下还有一大水窖。

Fire-fighting in the Late Qing Dynasty (1644-1911)

In the late Qing Dynasty (1644–1911), shops stood in great numbers and residential houses were densely packed in the prosperous commercial areas in Beijing. The buildings were mostly built of bricks and wood, with paper-pasted windows and doors, so there was often fire. The large commercial households led the medium and small-sized commercial households to establish their own fire-fighting organization—the Water Association.

Historically, the south region of Beijing centering on Dashilan near Qianmen had the most water associations. For example, the "Public Benevolence Water Association" solely sponsored by Tongrentang was one of the earliest with the best equipment and most effective.

正对二条风水楼

（东城区东四北大街499号）

　　东四北大街499号铺面房是一座中为本、西为面的中西结合铺面房。后院尚存中式旧窗，西式房顶又增盖一中式建筑。

Chinese-Western Fusion Roof

Location:No. 499 Dongsi Beidajie, Dongcheng District
This house with store front rooms combines Chinese and western styles. There are still Chinese-style windows at the backyard. An additional Chinese-style structure was built on top of the western-style roof.

(2006年6月15日绘)

东四四条美阳台

（东城区东四四条86号）

初见此楼，尤其是小阳台，好像在美国西部电影里所见的小镇。再看其大门，又是典型的中国式的蛮子门，真是别有风味。

A Weranda above a Festoon Gate

Location:No. 86 Dongsi Sitiao, Dongcheng District
When you see this building, in particular its small balcony, you may imagine you are in a small town in an American western. But its gate is typical Chinese-style Manzi Gate.

(2006年5月19日绘)

| 临街筒瓦何讲究 |

（东城区东四北大街424号）

从东四北大街临街为楼的铺面房，可以看出一个规律：临街楼房商铺的屋顶都是筒瓦，都是卷棚，后面的房顶可以是清水脊，也可以是合瓦顶。

Roof Styles of Shops

Location:No. 424 Dongsi Beidajie, Dongcheng District
The houses with store front rooms along the Dongsi Beidajie Street reveal a rule: all the stores have the round ridge roofs with semi-cylindrical tiles, while the residential buildings behind have plain ridge or closed-tile roof.

(2006年5月24日绘)

孝和艺辉敬真主

(崇文区豆腐巷7号)

此院是京剧艺术大师马连良先生1920—1940年步入辉煌时期的住宅，是由豆腐巷一个二进五开间的小四合院与巾帽胡同一个南北狭长的小院组合而成。

院门开在东南角，门楼顶为清水脊，全院其余房顶都是合瓦。迎门有大鱼缸，影壁上有两个凸起的圆形阿拉伯文字。倒座房第一间为门房，另三间为客厅。二门为木门，木栅栏墙。

进入二门，西房的第一间为礼拜房，从影壁上的阿拉伯文及礼拜房来看，马先生当时是虔诚的伊斯兰教徒；第二间是马先生三儿子马崇礼的房间；第三间是马先生的弟子，后来一直为他拉胡琴的李慕良的居室。正房为马先生父母的居室及其他子女的居室。

西院小四合正房为马连良夫妇的居室，南房为其活动室，北面的房为厨房、工人宿舍、储煤室、仓库、戏衣库房等。

A Devout Muslim Artist's Home

Location: No. 7 Doufuxiang, Chongwen District

This mansion was the former residence of Beijing Opera Master Mr. Ma Lianliang during his golden period from 1920 to 1940. It comprises of a small courtyard with two rows of five-bay buildings on Doufuxiang (alley) and a long, narrow north-south courtyard on Jinmao Hutong.

The main gate is set at the southeast corner. The gatehouse has a plain ridge and other houses feature closed-tile roof. There is a large ceramic fish bowl just inside the main gate and two convex Arabic inscriptions on the spirit screen wall. The first room of the house abutting the main gate is the gate keepers room and the other three serve as the reception rooms. The second gate is made of wood with wood-fence wall.

Mr. Ma and his wife lived in the main house in the western courtyard. The southern wing served as the activity room. The northern courtyard includes kitchen, dormitories for workers, coal room, storehouse and storage for costumes.

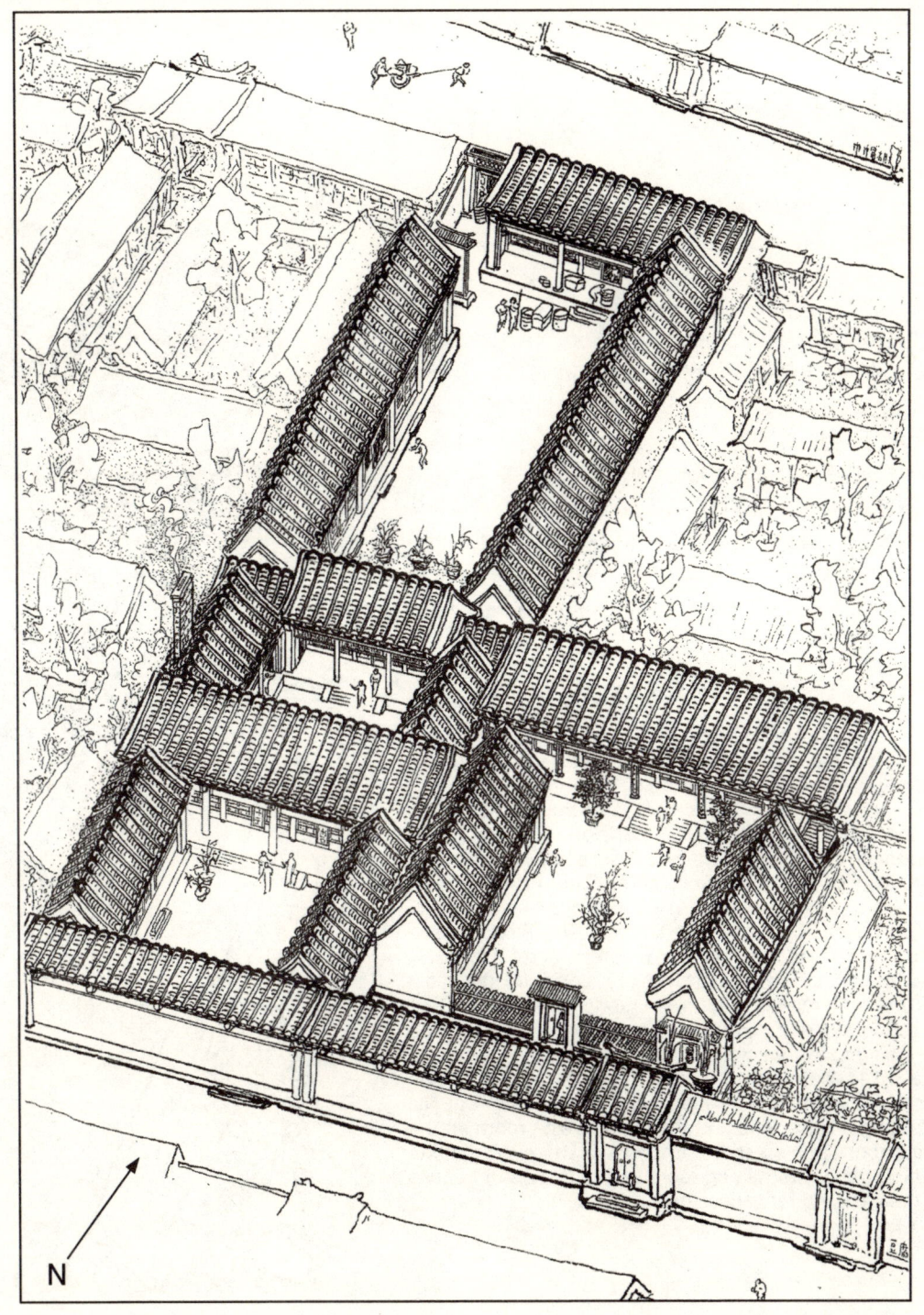

(2006年8月25日绘)

马连良大师故居

(西城区南宽街13号)

此院落是我最敬佩的京剧艺术大师——马连良先生20世纪40年代的住宅。我据马先生之孙马龙先生所绘之平面图追绘。

此院是马连良事业最盛旺时的住宅,处在南北胡同中,外门坐西朝东,门内有汽车库,宅院大门为卷棚脊广亮大门,迎门雕砖影壁,东西屏门。东屏门内可通东院厨房、洗衣房,工人院在西屏门内。倒座房五间为外客厅。进垂花门抄手游廊,东厢房为餐厅,西厢房为西客厅,正房三间为正会客厅,西耳房为马连良夫妇的卧室,东耳房为其子马崇恩的居室。西客厅后面花园边有廊,是马连良与孩子休息之所,花园西墙有一排果木树。后院第一进十一间房,中间是通道,最东间为粮库,其余都是家属住房。最后一进院,后门边两间是门房,往东是戏衣房、库房、厕所、洗涤间。

The Home of an Opera Master

Location:No. 13 Nankuanjie Street, Xicheng District
This mansion was the former residence of Beijing Opera Master Mr. Ma Lianliang in 1940s.

Its street gate faces east, and there is a garage inside. The main gate of the mansion is a Guangliang Gate with round ridge. There is a screen wall with brick carving and east and west screen doors just inside the main gate. The eastern screen door leads to the eastern side courtyard with kitchen, washhouse while staff rooms are beyond the western screen door of the forecourt. The five-bay house alongside the main gate are the reception rooms. Entering the chuihuamen second gate, one can find the eastern wing room used as dining room, western wing room as the living room, the three-bay main house as the formal reception room, its western side room being the bedroom of Ma Lianliang and his wife and the eastern side room as the living room of his son Ma Chong'en. There is a garden behind the western living room and two rows of houses in the backyard for various uses.

风水不吉连遭难

(西城区复兴门内大街54号)

此宅院为坐南朝北的院落，大门应在西北角，但此院门在东北角，位不吉，若将院内的通道一直延伸到南墙，由东南再进入里院也可以，但没做此改正，进大门即算入宅。按北京民俗，此为不吉。

An Unpropitious Gate

Location:No. 54 Fuxingmennei Dajie, Xicheng District
This mansion faces north, with the main gate at the northeast corner instead of the northwest corner which is a propitious position. A passage could have led directly from this gate to the southern wall where another gate might have be built, or the main gate could have been placed in the southwest, but it wasn't. According to the folk custom of Beijing, this is not propitious.

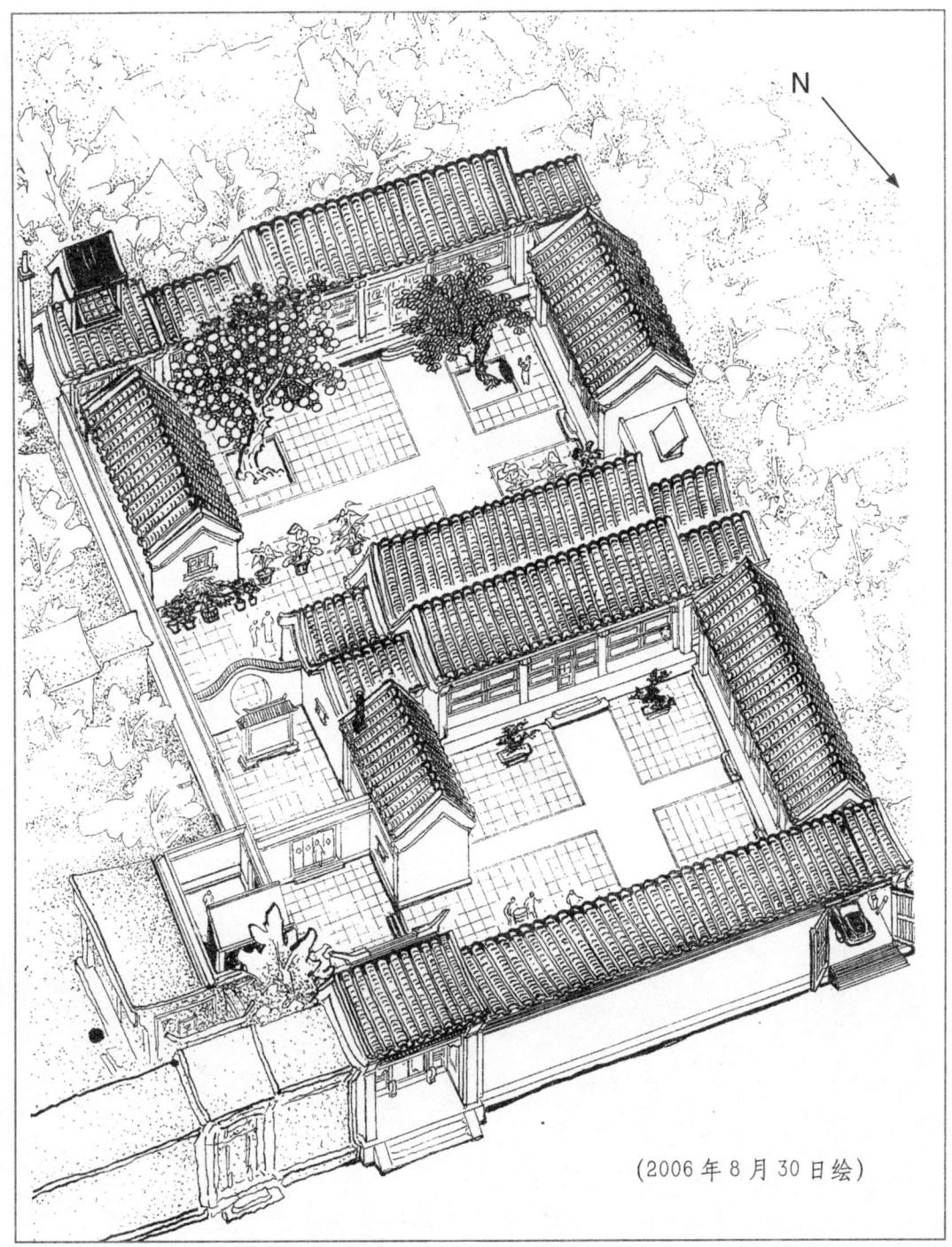

(2006年8月30日绘)

胡同之神我单府

（东城区新太仓胡同42号）

原"新太仓"的正中心有座仓神庙。1966年以前这里是尼姑庙（广音寺）。由庙往南，路东第一家是我的府学胡同小学（三区一中心小学）、1952年毕业的六丁班同学王谭的家；第二家是"益识学校"校长张岐山家；第三家是粮店，新太仓胡同42号，六丁班同学李维国住在后院。

Neighborhood of Old School Mates

Location: No. 42 Xintaicang Hutong, Dongcheng District
There was a Temple to the Granary's Deity at the center of the original Xintaicang. It was a nunnery (Guangyinsi Temple) before 1966. Two of my schoolmates in Fuxue Hutong Primary School, i.e. Wan Tan and Li Weiguo lived respectively in the first house and behind the third house (a grain shop) to the south of the temple on the east side of the road. President Zhang Qishan of "Yishi School" lived in the second house there.

(2008年7月25日绘)

通州贡院小而全

(通州贡院)

幸亏通州政协王文续老人，将此院说得清清楚楚，使我解开了贡院之谜，据此画出了当年通州的贡院考试情景。

Tongzhou Examination Halls

This picture shows the scene of the civil service examination halls of the day.

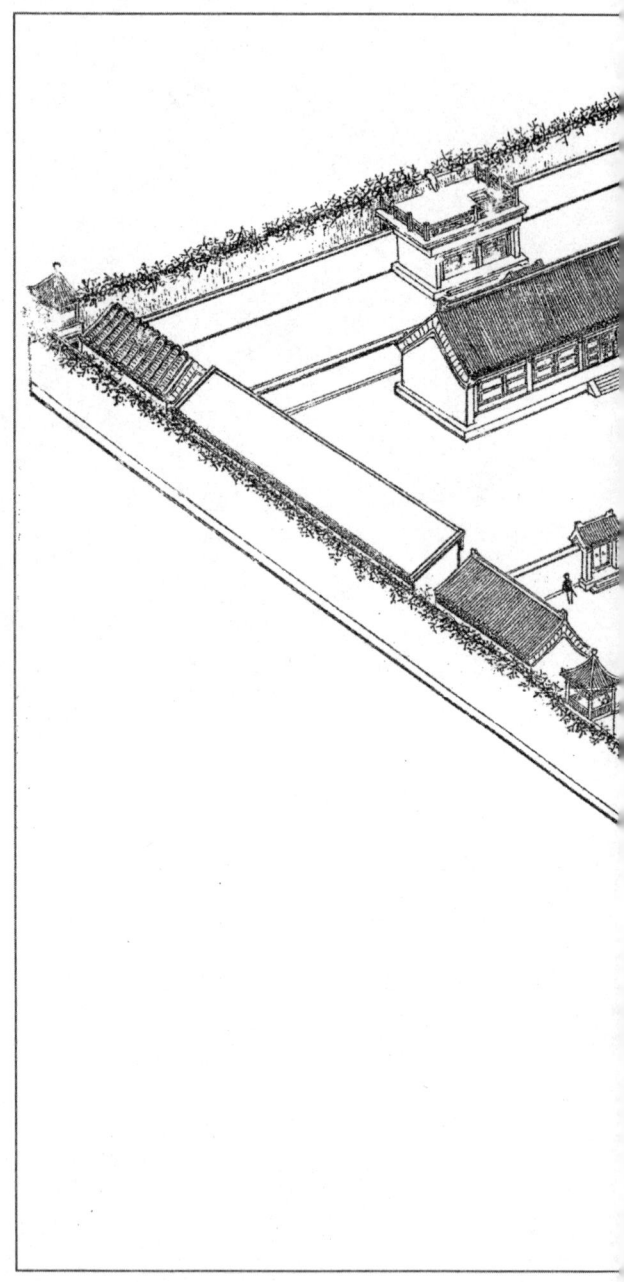

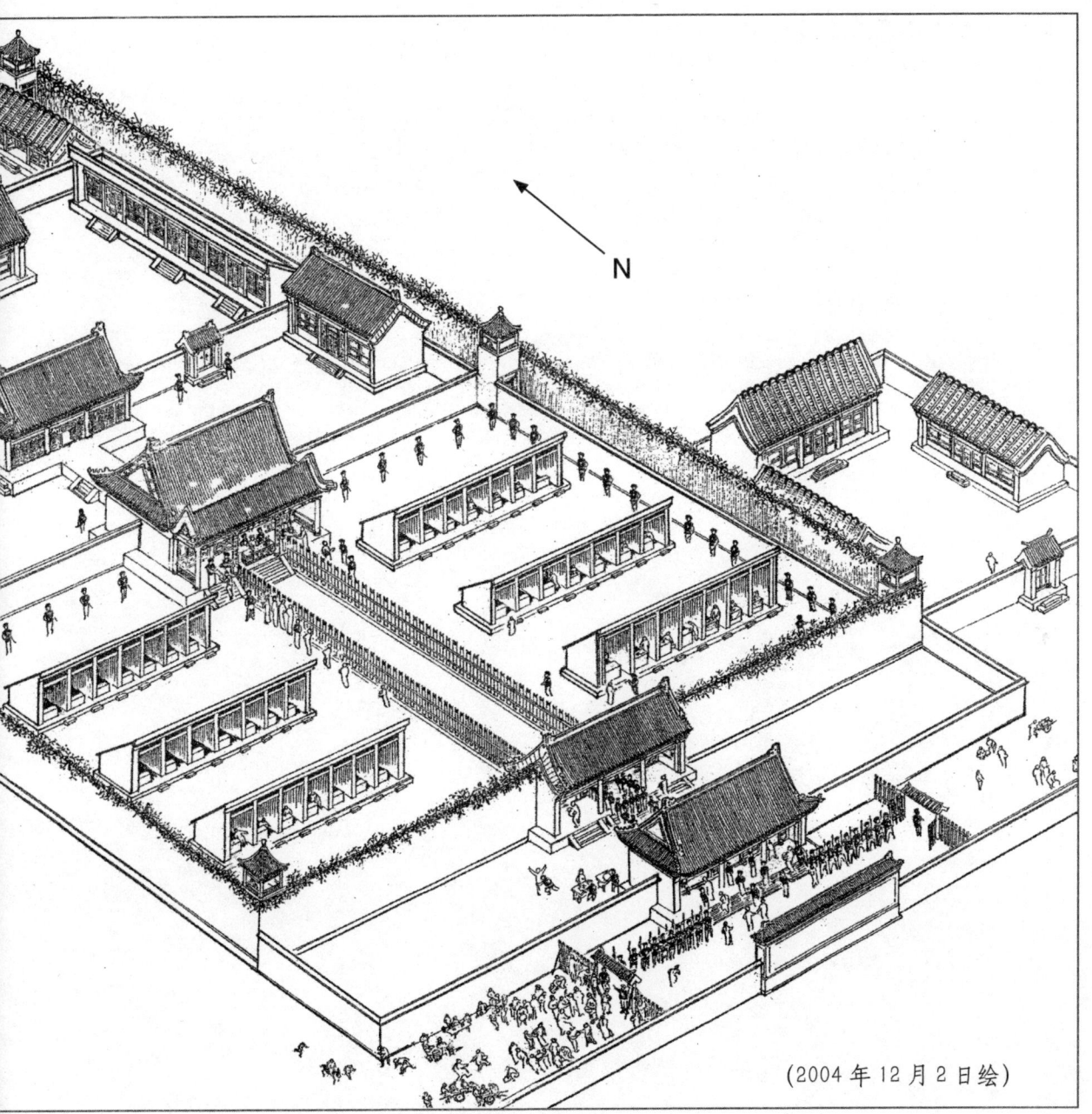

(2004年12月2日绘)

李万春武圣故居

（宣武区菜市口北大吉巷22号、21号）

　　这个院落原是京剧大师余叔岩的房产，1924年李万春父给付4500银元购置，后改建装修，门外山墙戗檐上的带作者印章的精美砖雕、影壁及二门，这些在北京是独具一格的。最精美的是廊门上的砖雕，十分讲究。

　　此院坐南朝北，以南为上，正房为李万春父母居住，由西廊门进入西小院，此三间西式房为李万春夫妇住。

　　院对面的21号是创建于1938年的鸣春社，南屋为宿舍，两间西房为厨房，北房是李万春为弟子们说戏的地方。

Opera Master and Opera Troupe

Location:No.21 and No.22 Beidaji Xiang, Caishikou, Xuanwu District

This mansion originally belonged to Beijing Opera Master Yu Shuyan. In 1924, Li Wanchun's father bought it at a price of 4,500 silver dollars. It was rebuilt and decorated later. There was exquisite brick carving with the seal of the carver on the eaves of the external wall, spirit screen wall and the decorative chuihuamen second gate in a class by itself. The brick carving on the corridor gate is most exquisite.

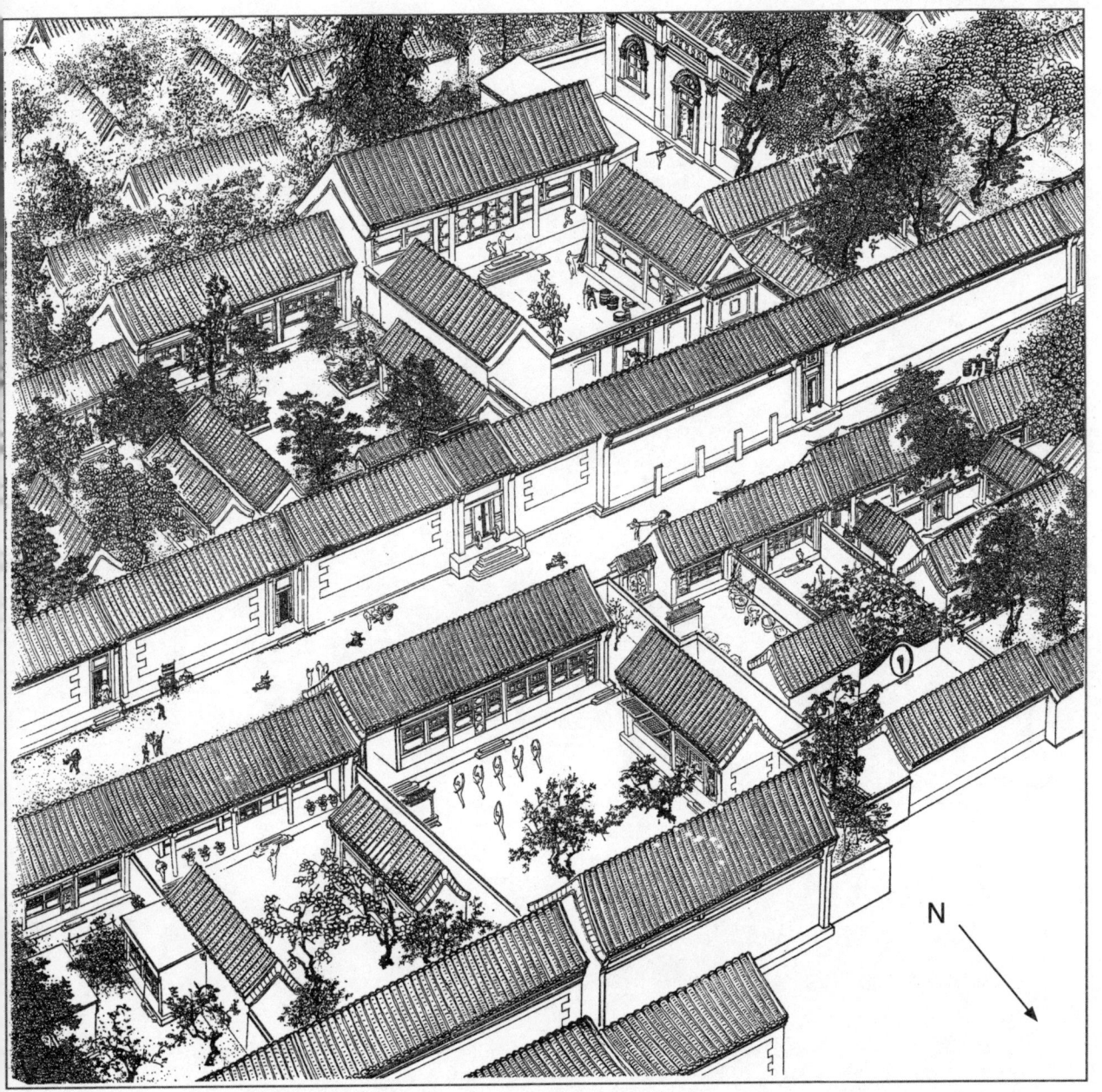

(2004年7月22日绘)

185

东四四条绵宜宅

（东城区东四四条1号、3号、5号）

据说此院为光绪年间户部侍郎绵宜的住宅。其宅为四进，东院为花园，从其位于五条的后罩房可以看出，1号（左）、3号原为一宅。

进垂花门、抄手游廊通过厅就到主院，在二进院往西的廊子里，屏门上还有篆字遗存。进门后为此宅的佛堂，筒瓦，其后是洗衣房、厨房。

东四四条5号，同是四合院，因楚图南曾住过此院，因而保存得较好。从二进院到三进院的通道与其他院有差异，很有味道。

(2004年9月10日绘)

Home of a Vice Minister of Census

Location:No.1, No.3 and No.5 Dongsi Sitiao, Dongcheng District

This mansion is said to be the former residence of Mianyi, deputy minister of census during the Guangxu Period of the Qing Dynasty (1644–1911). It has four rows of houses and a garden in the eastern courtyard. From the rear building on Dongsi Wutiao, we can see that No. 1 and No. 3 had been part of one mansion in the past.

One can reach the main courtyard after entering the decorative Chuihua second gate and passing through the hall of the side corridor. Engraved inscriptions can still be seen in the corridor and the screen door leading to the west in the second courtyard. The Buddhist Hall with semi-cylindrical tiled roof is inside the screen door.

The No. 5 house is also a quadrangle. Since Chu Tu'nan once lived there, it has been well preserved. The passage linking the second and third courtyard differs from others, which is very interesting.

河沟交错三转桥

(崇文区三转桥地区)

古运河从通惠河到泡子河逆水向西,经玉河到达积水潭。此水从西北来,还有两条泻水道。一是从前门斜向到三里河、法华寺街,再到黄河沿(现在的新生巷),沿唐洗泊街到三转桥转西向南到龙潭湖。再一条水道,是从泡子河向南(元代此处在城外)。在南羊市口还有大石桥,在北羊市口也有向南的水道和桥可资佐证。此水在南羊市口分为两支:一向南经今北河漕、南河漕到三转桥,另一支经东河漕南下。

南羊市口南口,地势就属那里高,因此地有桥墩。

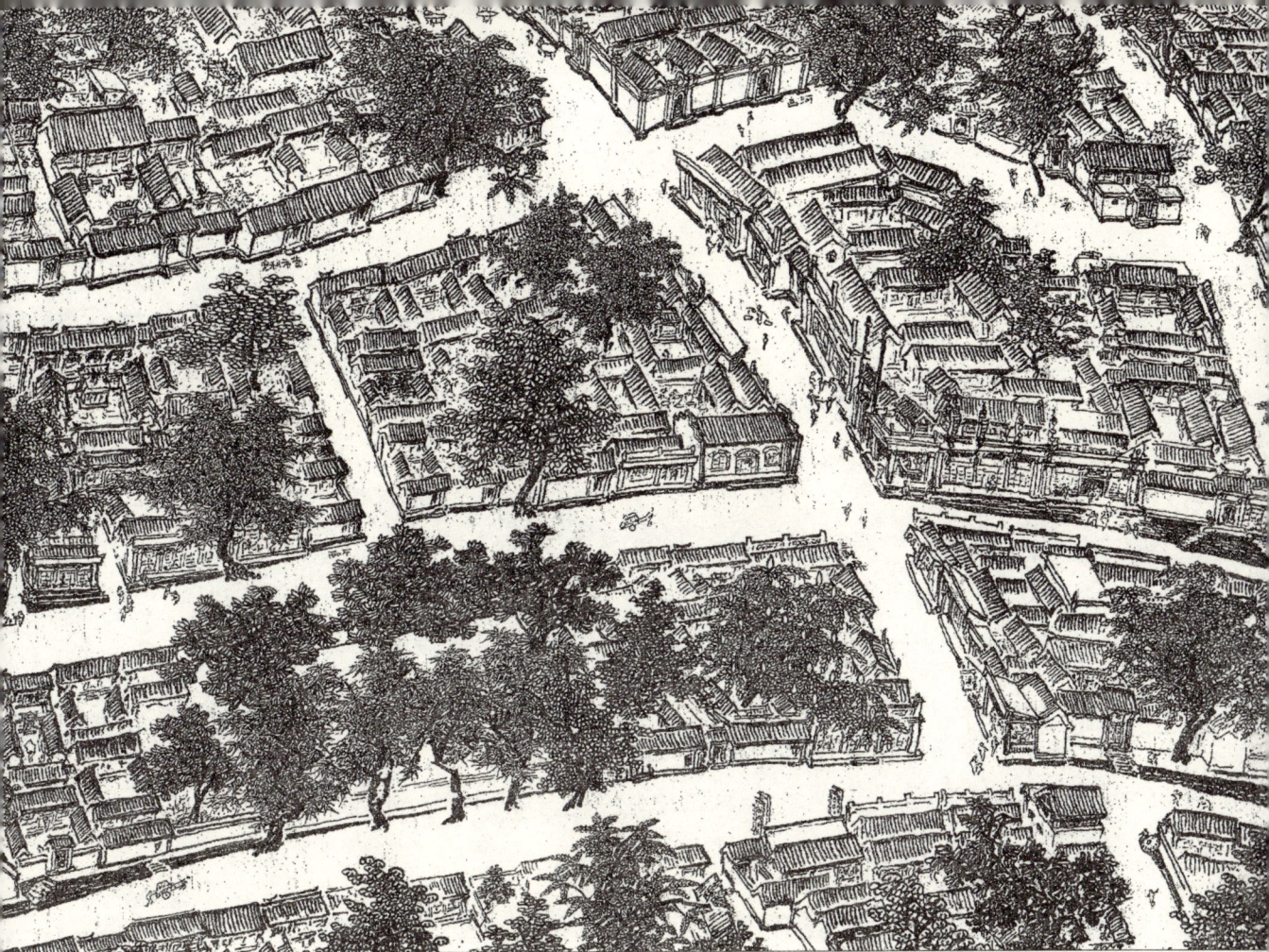

(2007年6月28日绘)

Where Old Canals Used to Run

Location: Sanzhuanqiao Area, Chongwen District

The ancient Tonghuihe canal runs westward and barges can go upstream along Tonghuihe River to the Paozihe River and reach Jishuitan via the Yuhe River. It has two flood diversion channels. One extends from Qianmen to Sanlihe and Fahuasi Street, and then to Huangheyan (the present-day Xinshengxiang) and then runs westward to Sanzhuanqiao via Tangxibo Street and then extends southwards to Longtanhu Lake. Another channel extends southward from Paozihe River. It falls into two branches at Nanyangshikou: one extends southwards to Sanzhuanqiao via the present-day Beihecao and Nanhecao; and the other runs southwards via the Donghecao.

The land at the south entrance of Nanyangshikou is high, so piers can be found there.

厂甸遗路房应保

（宣武区西河沿街222号）

正乙祠往西西河沿街222号是北京唯一由文物局为一个院落出具文件要求保护的宅院。我去一看，确实是十分精致的小院，院中两组流水的大盆景山水，水中有鱼，山上有树、有亭，全院花树满庭。224号，为马应龙的住宅。这一片，各个院落都各具特色。

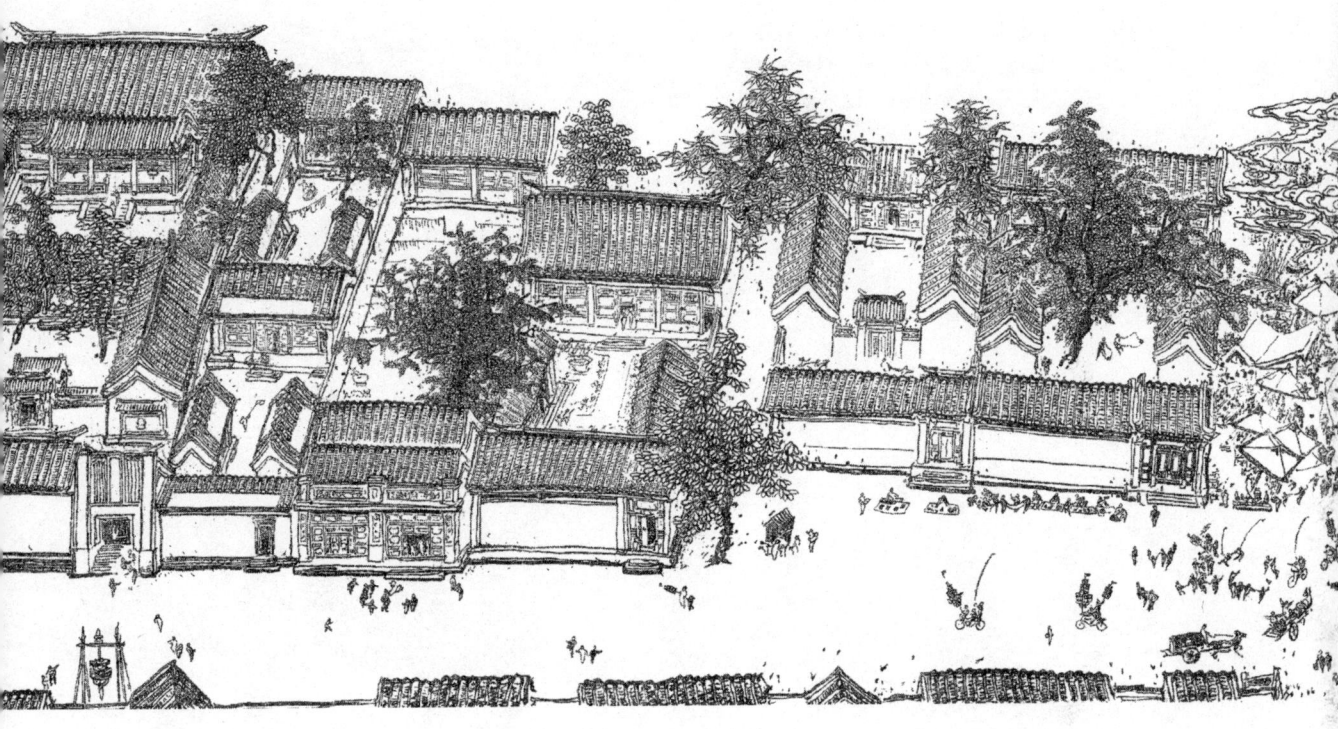

(2007年12月22日绘)

The Protected Courtyards at Changdian Region

Location: No. 222 Xiheyan Street, Xuanwu District

No. 222 Xiheyan Street to the west of Zhengyici Peking Opera Theatre is the only mansion for which the Cultural Relics Bureau filed a separate document to protect. Within the courtyards there are two groups of large rockeries with flowing water. On the rockeries are trees and pavilions. The whole mansion is filled with flowers and trees. No. 224 was the former residence of Ma Yinglong. The mansions in that area are unique.

可园保护需整体

(东城区可园)

可园，系清咸丰年间，直隶总督文煜宅之私家园林。可园分前园、后园两部分，原来从宅子东侧进入园中正房，为硬山合瓦五间大厅，往南沿厅前之路，林左有石桌可品茗、可书画琴棋；右行经小巧的石桥，左望一池清水，见"叩壁"山洞，出洞左侧有山，山上有六角攒尖凉亭，从假山后转出，经"通幽"山洞，右转登山，山上一敞轩屹立。由敞轩南望山沟里，另一幽深之处引人遐想。往东爬上山顶，回望身后之景，真有红楼中凸碧楼、凹晶馆之意境。从山顶向北眺望，沿来时上山之路，有一爬山廊可至此山。沿爬山廊一线，都有对应的建筑与可园之廊边建筑呼应，可知此东院一定是可园原有的一部分。

沿爬山廊向北，再过五间大厅，可以从东边进入后园。只见一组假山为屏，东面为爬山廊，后有水榭，最北是前廊后轩的正房。

Keyuan Garden, Dongcheng District

Keyuan Garden was a private garden of Wenyu, Viceroy of Zhili, during the Xianfeng Period of the Qing Dynasty (1644–1911). It is divided into front and back parts. One can reach the main house in the garden from the east side; it is a five-bay hall with closed-tile flush gable roof. There are rockeries in the garden. There is a climbing corridor is in the garden. Buildings of various kinds are found along the climbing corridor, echoing each other.

One can enter the back courtyard from the east after walking along the climbing corridor northward and passing through a five-bay hall. A group of rockeries form a screen. At the northernmost end is the main house with a corridor in the front and a veranda with windows in the back.

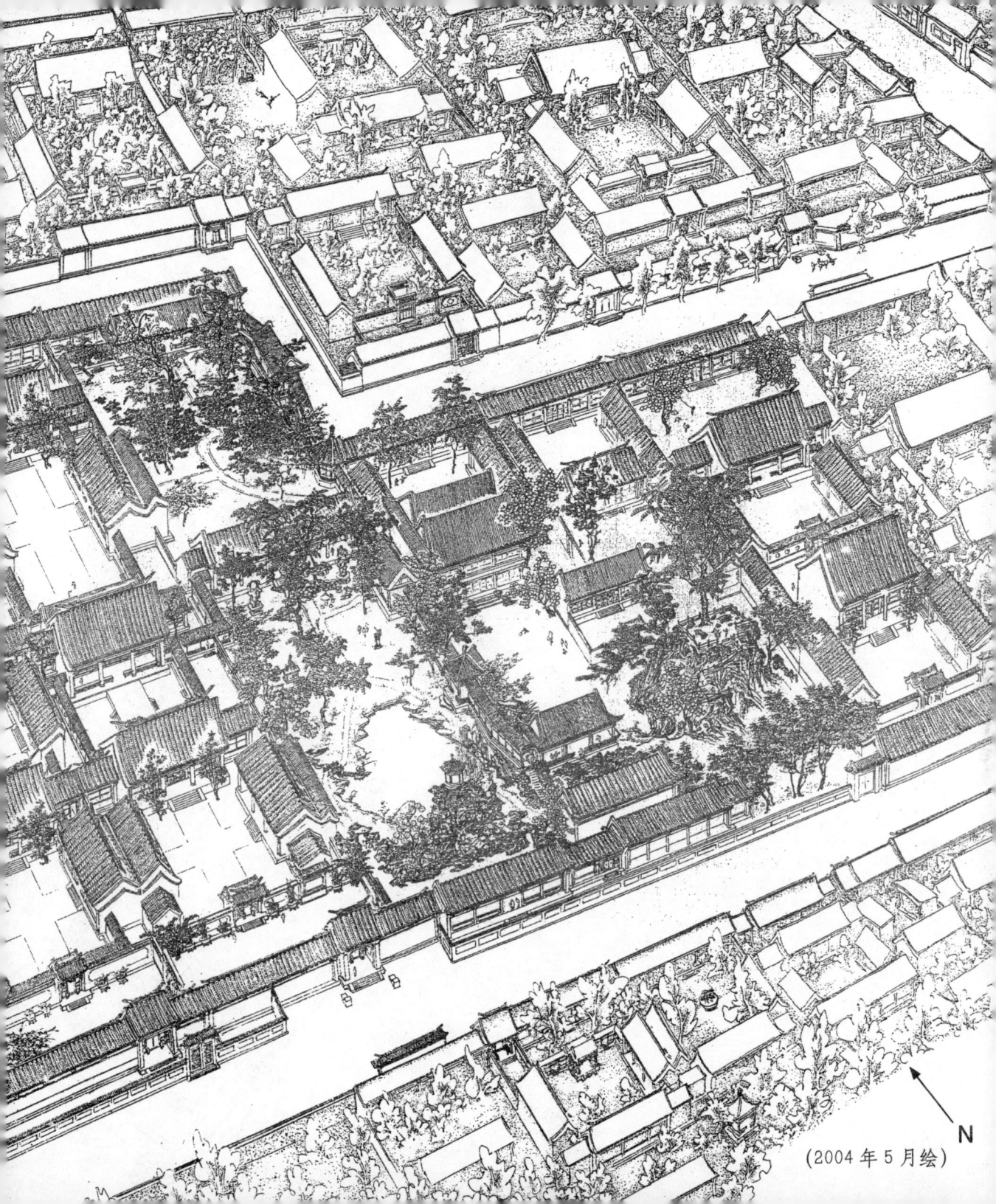
(2004年5月绘)

（通州）

明代朝廷一妃子给自己的家乡修建的寺庙。此庙给该村带来了福气。

Tongzhou Great Temple

According to Zhang Yuan, a painter and calligrapher, a big temple in his hometown has a beautiful legend:

A rich man in Shuangbutou Village in the Ming Dynasty (1368–1644) had a young servant girl in charge of herding ducks. She herded ducks in a pond in front of the house of the rich man every day. There was also a small temple by the pond. The girl often rested by the temple. She was kind-hearted. She said to the small temple which provided a good resting place for her that she would rebuild the temple if she got on in life.

Later, when the Ming Court was selecting candidates for imperial concubines in the area, the rich man's daughter was selected. The rich man sent the servant girl in charge of herding ducks to the capital in place his own daughter. Later, she got favor from the emperor and sent people to rebuild the temple. However, they made a mistake and built a temple in another village. Afterwards she found out, and they went to the right village and built the temple in front of the house of the rich man.

People said that it was that temple that brought good luck to that village.

（2006年2月绘）

文化大家冯公度

（西城区羊肉胡同73号）

冯恕，又名冯公度（1867—1948），实业家，书法家，收藏、鉴赏家，"毛公鼎"、"虢季子白盘"等均藏于他家，解放后献与国家，收藏于国家博物馆。

此宅原为清末状元陆润庠的状元府，陆于1915年故，冯公于1920年购得此宅。此宅位于西四历代帝王庙大影壁之南，此处开有后门，前门在羊肉胡同西段，广亮大门，到后门共七进院，东院南为花园，北为祠堂院。

Top Scholar's Home with a Family Shrine

Location: No. 73 Yangrou Hutong, Xicheng District

This mansion was originally the residence of Lu Runxiang, who won top place in the palace examinations at the end of the late Qing Dynasty (1644–1911). It is located to the south of the large screen wall of the Temple of Emperors at Xisi. Its back door is found there. Its main, Guangliang gate is set at the west section of Yangrou Hutong. There are seven rows of houses in the mansion. A garden is found to the south of the eastern courtyard and a family shrine to the north of it.

(2006年12月31日绘)

九爷府

（东城区朝阳门内大街137号）

孚郡王府，俗称九爷府，现在的南门开在朝阳门内大街137号。清雍正年间为怡亲王府，第二代怡亲王弘晓就住在这里。传到第六代载恒，因同治年间他是八个顾命大臣之一，被慈禧赐死、夺爵，王府也就易主，被转赐孚郡王奕譓，因而此府就名为孚郡王府。奕譓是道光的第九个儿子，因而此府又称九爷府。

此府在《加摹乾隆京城全图》内即有，与今基本上一致，尤其中路保存较好，是今天研究王府的主要宝库。

Ninth Prince's Palace

Location: No.137 Chaoyangmennei Dajie, Dongcheng District

It is the Palace of Prince Fu, commonly known as Palace of the Ninth Prince. This mansion can be found in a *Map of Beijing made in Emperor Qianlong reign*, in which it is represented basically the same as it is today. In particular, the central axis of the complex is well preserved. It is a major source for research on prince's palaces today.

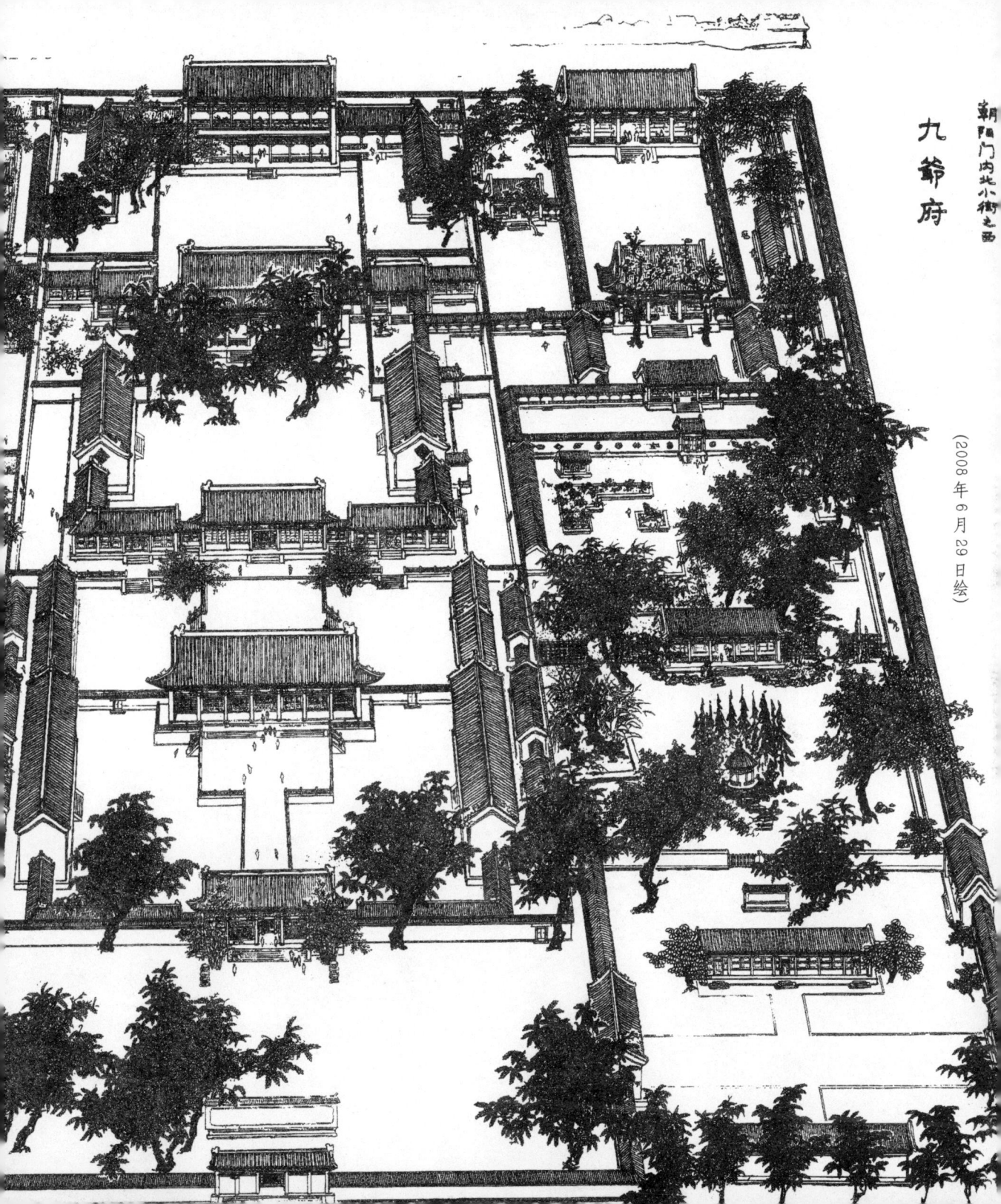

朝阳门内北小街之西 九爷府 （2008年6月29日绘）

题 记

　　作者希成，年逾七旬老者，且足跛，行路难。自幼喜画，执业牙雕，技艺精湛，曾获嘉奖。

　　新世纪初，北京腾飞。以危改之名，连街成片拆除旧房，殃及诸多民居宅院。推土机轰鸣喧嚣处，希成瘦弱残病身影常现；手执画板，奔走号呼，亦曾受人推搡驱赶，仍坚持不懈；为保护京城历史遗存，其诚心可见一斑。

　　吾曾劝慰：欲拆者，挡不住，拆矣；欲盖者，拦不了，盖也。然则，希成以白描绘画手法，绘成百余幅民居宅院遗容，毕竟保存了半世纪前京城民居宅院部分原貌，且真实而形象，此乃京城遗存之大幸，其社会价值之所在者也——以供决策者慎思，以供研究者探索，以供鉴赏者欣赏，以供怀旧者留恋……

　　吾与希成乃小学同窗，交往近六十年，谊重情长。考大学前，曾借居希成九道湾西巷11号小院北房西屋，苦读月余，倍受伯母关爱，而如愿考进北大中文系。当初院中小香椿和枣树，如今伟岸挺立，枝繁叶茂。伯母在天有灵，欣闻图册出版，其亦庶几无憾尔。

李维国
戊子夏至

后 记

这本书终于要出版了。

首先要感谢袁大威先生。早在2002年他与吴天明先生到王大鹏教授家，看到精致的房舍、扇、古典家具，极为赞赏，再看到我为此院画的复原图，更加赞美此院之完美，也为此院之现状而惋惜。从吴天明口中得知袁先生当时对我的画非常感兴趣，即有动员我将其出版之意。

2005年袁先生与我在他即将消失的自家小院里畅谈到深夜，天南地北离不开北京的胡同，离不开北京民俗，他又信誓旦旦表示一定帮助我将此书出版……我不敢相信，也不愿多想。

今年春袁大威先生又来电话，要商谈出书之事，我一直对能出书之事不敢期望，正巧我又要住院，于是推托。算准出院之日期，大威又来电说："出版社亦要来人商谈。"是日，他与出版社编辑张翔先生来，社长孟白先生亦亲自来谈。一谈非常投缘，马上进入实际操作，我还没反应过来，书真的要出版了。

感谢您，袁大威先生。

在这里更要感谢学苑出版社，社长孟白、编辑张翔及美编等先生。

在编辑出版过程中，从他们对《老北京民居宅院》一书的认真负责的态度中，看到他们总是从读者的角度着想，想到读者是否能读懂，看得明白，从而使我非常感动。每张图的各个细节，每篇文字、标点都反反复复多次查对，从不轻易放过，而且社长亦多次亲自校对了几次。编辑们告诉我："社长亲自动手认真校对的书，亦是不多见的。"由此我感到他们对咱们北京民宅文化的重视。

北京有这样的出版文化群体，我们的文化事业错不了。

谢谢，你们，学苑出版社的社长、编辑。

我没想到的是袁大威找的出版社是学苑出版社，张翔来了一聊，才知我与其老社长原来是小学同学——李维国兄。维国对我的图一直非常肯定，认为我做了一件功德无量之事。他在几个出版社都有朋友，但他不想让我的图沾上"走后门"之嫌，他说："好东西总会有亮点的。"今天，这些图没有"走后门"，也能展现在广大读者面前，这是北京民居文化不灭的闪光。

维国兄多次认真校对，把关。谢谢了维国兄。

借此还要感谢远在美国的赵晓梅老师，我用您赞助的钱买了DV机，才能在北京民宅拆迁大潮中，与推土机抢时间，记录、收集了必要的民居资料，有待我今日慢慢整理、出版，将北京民居丰富的美景还原给北京的人们。

还有我兄郑希志及马旭初、高天岭、冯公度之曾孙冯庆元、郭观云、田景等多位老人的回忆，让我在当时已经杂乱不堪的大宅院中，从他们的叙说中理出头绪，复原了那些大四合院的原貌。

白皓、王兰顺、高和、左玉罡、张艺群、马龙、赵惠茹、赵玉杰、徐晨等，有的帮我提供的好宅院、有特色的院落的地点和历史，有的帮我提供电脑光盘制作以及纸张、笔、夹子、大画板等用具，还有我需要的书籍画册，清末和民国地图及1943年的北京航拍图等资料，对我画图提供了非常有效的帮助。他们还一再表示："帮助你，就是为了保护北京四合院出点力。"谢谢他们！这本书的出版，我只是执笔，是保护北京民居文化的群体共同努力的结果。

谢谢，谢谢一切曾帮助过我们的人们。谢谢一切在我寻访四合院的过程中对我提供方便、帮我指路认门儿的人们。

郑希成
2008年12月26日晨3点